Introduction

...ep that head on a swivel! The editors of Portable
...ve investigated the seedy underbelly of society,
...ith the most outrageous, ambitious, far-fetched,
...etimes downright idiotic schemes in the world
... But criminals shouldn't get all that time in the
...t (especially since they hate it so much). Learn
...e advancement of forensics, how polygraphs tell
...one is lying, and notorious unsolved cases. From
...ious disappearances to bizarre burglary plots to ironic
...of fate, this book will have you eyeing your neighbor
...iously, wondering what types of skeletons they have in
...loset (hopefully, just the figurative kind).

...NING: This book is about the dark side of human
...e—the ugly side of society. Some of the subject matter
...rk, deviant, and disturbing. Lock your doors, shut those
...ls, and turn on all the lights...for a deep dive into the
...y world of *Strange Crime*.

STRANGE CRIME

EDITORS OF PORTABLE PRESS

**PORTABLE
PRESS**

SAN DIEGO, CALIFORNIA

Portable Press
An imprint of Printers Row Publishing Group
10350 Barnes Canyon Road, Suite 100, San Diego, CA 92121
www.portablepress.com • email: mail@portablepress.com

Copyright © 2018 Portable Press

All rights reserved. No part of this publication may be reproduced, distributed, or transmitted in any form or by any means, including photocopying, recording, or other electronic or mechanical methods, without the prior written permission of the publisher, except in the case of brief quotations embodied in critical reviews and certain other noncommercial uses permitted by copyright law.

Printers Row Publishing Group is a division of Readerlink Distribution Services, LLC. Portable Press is a registered trademark of Readerlink Distribution Services, LLC.

All notations of errors or omissions should be addressed to Portable Press, Editorial Department, at the above address.

Publisher: Peter Norton • Associate Publisher: Ana Parker
Publishing/Editorial Team: Vicki Jaeger, Tanja Fijalkowski, Lauren Taniguchi
Editorial Team: JoAnn Padgett, Melinda Allman, Dan Mansfield
Production Team: Jonathan Lopes, Rusty von Dyl
Contributing writer: Jay Newman
Interior design: Lidija Tomas
Illustrations: Sophie Hogarth, Rusty von Dyl
Cover design: Michael Sherman

Printed in the United States of America

Strange Crime
ISBN: 978-1-68412-277-6
Library of Congress Cataloging-in-Publication Control Number:
2017049227 (print)

ISBN: 978-1-68412-277-6

22 21 20 19 18   1 2 3 4 5

> "After all, crime is on
> form of human e

—John Hus

WAR
natu
is da
blin
sha

Better ke
Press ha
riddled
and som
of crime
spotligh
about t
if som
myste
twists
suspic
their

"POLLY WANT A LAWYER?"

Just because bird testimony may not be admissible in court doesn't mean it can't influence the outcome of a case.

PARROT: Lorenzo, a parrot owned by a Colombian drug cartel

BACKGROUND: In 2010 police raided a suspected cartel hideout in the city of Barranquilla, Colombia. Their suspicions were confirmed when Lorenzo recognized their police uniforms and squawked, "Run! Run! You're going to get caught!" "The parrot was sending out alerts," officer Hollman Oliveira told reporters. "You could say he was some sort of watch bird."

WHAT HAPPENED: Police arrested four men in the raid and seized a large quantity of drugs. They also took Lorenzo and two other lookout birds into custody see if they could be coaxed into revealing anything else about the gang. "Parrots like to talk, and we are good listeners," Oliveira said. Colombian police estimate that as many as 2,000 parrots have been trained to act as lookouts for drug cartels.

PARROT: Hercule, a parrot owned by Vijay and Neelam Sharma of India

BACKGROUND: In 2014 Neelam Sharma was murdered by robbers who burglarized her home. Police had little to go on and were unable to identify a suspect.

WHAT HAPPENED: Heera the parrot was home at the time of the attack and apparently witnessed the crime. He provided the first clue about a week after the murder. When Vijay's nephew, Ashutosh Goswami, visited the house, Heera became visibly agitated. "During discussions, too, whenever Ashutosh's name was mentioned, the parrot would start screeching," Sharma told *Time* magazine. "That raised my suspicion and I informed the police." They brought Goswami in for questioning, and he eventually confessed. Police also found the murder weapon and some of Neelam's jewelry in his possession.

PARROT: Max, an African gray parrot owned by Santa Rosa, California, resident Jane Gill in the early 1990s
BACKGROUND: Like Hercule, Max apparently witnessed his owner being murdered in her home. Two days passed before Gill's body was discovered; when it was, Max was found in his cage nearby, hungry and dehydrated. When his health returned he began screeching, "Richard, no, no, no!"
WHAT HAPPENED: Gill's friend and former housemate was a man named Richard. When other evidence pointed to Gill's business partner, Gary Rasp, the police arrested and charged him. At his murder trial, Rasp's attorneys tried to have the testimony of Max the parrot introduced as evidence, but the judge refused to allow it. When that trial ended in a mistrial in 1993, Rasp was tried a second time, and in March 1994 he was found guilty.

THE SWIFT HAND OF JUSTICE

Roll the blooper reel.

CRIME: In January 2004, an unknown man grabbed a bag out of a car stopped at a stoplight in Sydney, Australia.
INSTANT JUSTICE: The car belonged to Bradley McDonald, a local snake catcher. In the bag was the snake he had just caught—a four-foot-long, venomous, red-bellied black snake. "It might teach him a lesson," McDonald said.

CRIME: In July 1996, 37-year-old Willie King snatched a wallet from the coat of an old woman on a street in Greenwich Village, New York City.
INSTANT JUSTICE: The woman was 94-year-old Yolanda Gigante. Who's that? The mother of Vincent "the Chin" Gigante, reputed head of the Genovese crime family, one of the country's most powerful criminal organizations. King was caught a short time later, and as soon as he realized who he'd mugged, he agreed to plead guilty to grand larceny. Sentence: up to 3 years in prison. "My client admitted his guilt at the earliest opportunity, because he wants to put this incident behind him," King's lawyer told the judge. "He hopes the Gigante family will, too."

Fighting Fire with Fire

Better safe than sorry.

Carjacking is terrifying. You're just sitting in your car at a stoplight, when suddenly a thug runs up to your window with a gun and demands you get out and give him the car. There aren't a lot of ways to prevent such a sudden, and ultimately speedy, crime. But in South Africa, where carjacking is an epidemic, an inventor did figure out a way to punish carjackers before they get away with it: fire. Lots of fire. Charl Fourie introduced the Blaster to the South African car-peripherals market in 1998, at a price of 3,900 rand (about $655 back then). At the first sign of trouble, the driver activates the Blaster from the steering column. The Blaster squirts flammable liquid from a holding tank in the trunk out of two nozzles under the driver's-side door. The Blaster then emits an electric spark, which ignites the gas . . . and the carjacker.

A Throwback Case of Affluenza

Rich kids up to no good.

THE CRIME: In 1924 the body of a boy was found nude and drowned in a culvert in Wolf Lake, Indiana. He'd been struck on the head and then suffocated. Police identified the victim as Bobby Franks, the son of a Chicago millionaire. Nearby, cops also found an expensive pair of glasses, which they eventually traced to 19-year-old Nathan Leopold. Leopold had spent the day with Richard Loeb, a distant cousin of Bobby Franks. Under police questioning, both men broke down and confessed to killing Franks. Each blamed the other.

THE SUSPECTS: Leopold and Loeb were graduate students at the University of Chicago. Brilliant scholars who were pampered by their wealthy families, the teens came to believe that they were superior beings, or what the philosopher Friedrich Nietzsche called "supermen." To prove their status, they decided they would commit a perfect crime. They picked up Franks in their car, struck him on the head with a chisel, and suffocated him. After throwing his clothes in the brush and pouring acid on his corpse to thwart identification, the pair notified the Franks that their son had been kidnapped and asked for a $10,000

ransom. But before the supermen could get their money, Bobby's body was found—and so were Leopold's glasses.

THE TRIAL: Leopold and Loeb were represented by famous American trial lawyer Clarence Darrow. Expected to argue that the pair were innocent by reason of insanity, Darrow instead stunned the country when he made them plead guilty—to avoid a vengeful jury and give sentencing power to a thoughtful judge. Darrow also brought in psychiatric experts who testified to the immaturity and "emotionally diseased" state of his teenage defendants. Darrow reminded the court that it was capable of mercy—unlike his deranged clients.

THE VERDICT: Life plus 99 years

HISTORIC CONSEQUENCES: Clarence Darrow's closing argument took 12 hours and is still referred to in anti-death penalty arguments. The men that he'd saved became model prisoners, running a school to educate other prisoners. In 1936, Loeb was murdered by another inmate, and in 1958, Leopold was paroled. He moved to Puerto Rico, where he worked at a hospital and dreamed of making a great medical breakthrough so he'd be remembered as a hero instead of a killer—it didn't pan out, and he died in 1971.

The Stoneman

The true story behind one of India's best-known unsolved mysteries.

The case of the "Stoneman" spans two periods and two locations: The first, from 1985 to 1988 in Bombay; the second, from June to December 1989 in Calcutta. During this time, 25 people were killed—12 in the first three-year span, and 13 more over just six months in Calcutta. The method by which the Stoneman took his victims' lives was especially macabre, and earned him (or her) that odd nickname. In all of the cases, someone crept up to a destitute person sleeping outside alone on a street or in an alley, and dropped a large stone—weighing around 50 pounds—on the victim's head, crushing the person's skull and killing the victim instantly. Indian police aren't convinced that the two series of murders were carried out by the same person, saying instead that the Calcutta murders were probably carried out by a copycat killer. Since 1989, several similar cases have emerged, and authorities are unsure if this is the work of the same person or other copycat killers who are riding the notoriety of the Stoneman murders. There has never been a suspect in the Stoneman cases.

STRANGE CRIME

DUMB CROOKS

PAIN IN THE . . .

"A Boise man stole a dog at gunpoint, then tucked his gun in the waistline of the back of his pants and drove off with the dog. But the gun began bothering him while he was driving, so he reached back to reposition it and shot himself in the butt. Then, when he tried to remove the gun from his pants, he shot himself in the butt again. He was hospitalized in serious condition and the dog was returned to its home."

—*Boise Statesman-Journal*

THAT WAS UNWARRANTED

"A man who had committed crimes in Morgantown, West Virginia, was curious to know if the police suspected him. He approached two officers and asked if there were any arrest warrants out on him. There were."

—*Chicago Sun-Times*

BUT WHERE WERE THEIR HELMETS?

"Roger Yost, 40, and William Isberg, 40, were arrested in Fairbanks, Alaska, when they tried to heist a 500-pound safe from a Moose Lodge hall, forgetting that they had arrived at the lodge on bicycles."

—*Medford Mail Tribune*

The Mob Accountant

This guy knew that crime pays, because he kept the books.

The Rise: Born Maier Suchowljansky in 1902 in Grodno, Russia, Meyer Lansky came to New York with his family as a child. The studious Meyer was known as "a good Jewish boy" until he teamed up with Bugsy Siegel to form the Jewish "Bugs and Meyer Mob." The small-statured Lansky provided the planning and financial know-how, while Siegel and friends provided the muscle. In 1920, Prohibition was the law, so Lansky and Siegel joined forces with their old friend Lucky Luciano. Together they made a fortune selling liquor to speakeasies. In 1931, Lansky helped Luciano rise to power and create La Cosa Nostra.

The Reign: La Cosa Nostra grew so powerful that Lansky later described it as "bigger than US Steel." The Mob was pulling in millions, and the bosses were coming to Lansky for financial advice. Some historians believe that Lansky, nicknamed the "Mob Accountant," actually ran the Mafia through Luciano. Lansky stayed under law enforcement's radar. After Prohibition ended, Lansky opened illegal gambling casinos in New York, New Orleans, and Florida. They were so profitable that, when Lansky wanted to open some offshore casinos in the 1950s, Cuban dictator Fulgencio Batista welcomed him into Havana. Bugsy

Siegel's hotel-casino in Vegas had lost so much money that the Commission had him killed in 1947 (Lansky ordered the execution), but Lansky stayed in power because he made crime pay.

The Fall: Even Lansky couldn't win forever. In 1959, he lost $7 million in Mob money when Fidel Castro overthrew Batista and nationalized Cuba's casinos. In the 1970s, the feds went after him, so he fled to Israel. Two years later, he was deported back to the United States. On his return in 1973, Lansky faced income-tax evasion charges but was acquitted. He never spent a day in jail, but the FBI claimed that he had millions stashed away when he died of lung cancer in 1983. *Forbes* magazine believed it, too, listing him among their 400 wealthiest people in America in 1982.

LOUIS LOUIS

World's most counterfeited items: Louis Vuitton purses. The company estimates that only 1 percent of "Louis Vuitton" purses are authentic.

Mediocre Masterminds

Maybe you can knock 'em for tryin' after all.

FAIL AGAIN

In 2001 Shawn Myers drove his pickup truck *into* Lynn's Market in Wellsville, Pennsylvania. Backwards. He crashed through the window and tried to steal the ATM machine by dragging it with a chain attached to the truck. It didn't work. A few days later, he went back and crashed his truck through the plywood that was covering the broken window and tried to steal the ATM. Again, he failed. A few days after that, he drove through the front window of nearby Rutter's Farm Store. This time he actually made off with the ATM bouncing along behind the truck . . . until it hit a parked car and broke free. Several months later, Myers returned to Lynn's Market, drove through Lynn's window (again), chained up the ATM, and drove off. The ATM stayed with him; he got away and broke into the machine . . . but there was no money in it. Myers was arrested, ordered to pay thousands of dollars in restitution, and sentenced to six years in prison. He told the judge he tried to steal the ATMs because he needed money for court costs from previous trials.

THAT WAS JUST PRACTICE

Two men in Benicia, California, did almost everything right: Ski masks? Check. Semiautomatic handguns? Check. Burst into the bank and order everyone to lie down on the floor? Check. Get the money? Uh, there was no money. It was a credit union that didn't use cash. They ran away and were never caught.

Underwear That's Not So Fun to Wear

Sometimes, a headline tells you all you need to know. For example: "Man Who Crashed through Slidell Airport Gate Arrested in Underwear After Alleged Encounter with Snake." But the headline left out one important detail: voodoo! The suspect was 43-year-old Kevin Bolton of Hattiesburg, Mississippi. The incident took place in October 2017 in Louisiana. According to reports, Bolton drove his Chevy to the small airport and crashed through one gate, then entered through another gate and crashed into a telephone pole, which fell on his truck. He fled the scene and was found two hours later, lying in his underwear in the middle of a nearby road. He told officers that he was in town to see a "voodoo doctor," but at some point, a snake climbed into his pants, which caused the accident . . . and caused him to remove his pants.

According to police, "He may have been under the influence of a narcotic."

He who holds the ladder is as bad as the thief.
—**German proverb**

Can't Help Themselves

NICE TO MEAT YOU

Brice Edward Bennett Jr., 52, from York County, Pennsylvania, appealed a July 2013 conviction for shoplifting, claiming there was a "lack of evidence" in his original case. So the appeals court judge took a look at the evidence: 1) Several supermarket employees saw Bennett, with overloaded pockets, run out of the store; 2) A police officer testified that he "saw hot dogs fly out of Bennett's pocket as he tried to run away"; and 3) When the cop caught Bennett, there was "a pork loin and a shrimp wheel stuffed inside his jacket." The conviction stood.

ARMED BURGLARY

After a Frederick, Maryland, tattoo shop was burglarized, the shop's owner looked at the surveillance video and saw that the burglars had covered their faces. But one of them—Max Goransson—forgot to cover up his arms, one of which had a large tattoo that was recently inked at the shop he burgled.

A LITTLE HELP HERE

In 2014 police in the Netherlands received a call from a crying drunk man who said he was trapped inside a building. He told them (through sobs) that he'd broken a window and tried to steal several items, but then he couldn't find his way out. So the police came and freed—and then jailed—him.

THE DEATH OF VICKI MORGAN

Was Vicki Morgan murdered by her mentally disturbed housemate or by her powerful enemies in the Republican establishment?

VICTIM: Vicki Morgan, model and longtime mistress of Alfred Bloomingdale, one of the wealthiest men in America. (He was heir to the Bloomingdale's department store fortune, and a member of Ronald Reagan's Kitchen Cabinet.)

HOW SHE DIED: On July 7, 1983, Morgan was found in her apartment, beaten to death with a baseball bat. Her roommate, Marvin Pancoast, confessed.

BACKGROUND

- Morgan was Bloomingdale's mistress for 12 years. When Bloomingdale contracted terminal throat cancer and was hospitalized, his wife, Betsy, cut off Morgan's income—which was reportedly between $10,000 and $18,000 a month.

- In response, Morgan decided to go public. She first tried to publish her memoir, *Alfred's Mistress*. When that attempt fizzled—allegedly because of White House pressure—she filed a $10 million palimony suit against Bloomingdale in which she revealed all of Bloomingdale's indiscretions. She described him as "a drooling sadist" with a fondness for bondage and beatings. She also accused him of loose talk about "secret and delicate matters such as campaign contributions for Mr. Reagan."

- The case was thrown out, but the trial was an enormous embarrassment to the Bloomingdales and high-ranking Republican officials.

SUSPICIOUS FACTS

- Pancoast had a history of mental illness. He had previously confessed to crimes he hadn't committed, including the Tate-LaBianca murders committed by the Manson family.

KISSING AND TELLING

- Bloomingdale may have used Morgan to gather dirt on top-level Republican officials. Reportedly, Bloomingdale had his Hollywood house wired with state-of-the-art video cameras in every room and hidden behind false walls.
- Anyone who was important in the pre-administration and the administration of Ronald Reagan and who wanted divertissement called on Alfred, regardless of what his or her fetish might be. Bloomingdale allegedly got it all on tape.
- Morgan's apartment wasn't sealed by the LA Police Department until more than 24 hours after the murder. According to author Anne Louise Bardach, "People could just walk in and walk out . . . If there were any 'sex tapes' in the condo, then they could easily have disappeared during those 24 hours."
- The night before she was killed, according to her friend Gordon Basichis, "Vicki confided in me that she was afraid of being murdered. I have a feeling that someone with knowledge of the Bloomingdale 'tapes' had approached her, possibly through Pancoast, with a proposal for blackmail."

POSSIBLE CONCLUSIONS

- Pancoast killed her. After all, he confessed and was sentenced.
- Someone in power had Morgan killed. If the videotapes did exist, they would have been severely damaging to the Reagan administration.

Falsely Accused

You're just doing your thing, and then—bam!—someone accuses you of a crime you didn't commit.

THE ACCUSED: Francis Evelyn, 58, a custodian at Brooklyn's Public School 91 in New York City

BACKGROUND: Having spent nearly 20 years on the job, Evelyn was well respected at work and in his neighborhood.

STORY: In 2007 police officers arrived at PS 91, arrested Evelyn, cuffed him, and took him away for questioning. The police commissioner announced that Evelyn was accused of the "heinous rape of an eight-year-old student on multiple occasions." They said they had DNA evidence against him. Then the police took the unorthodox step of locking him up in Rikers Island Prison with actual murderers and rapists.

OUTCOME: Three days later, police finally interviewed the accuser. It turned out that she was known as a troubled child who had lied about being abused on previous occasions. Worse still, the girl described her attacker as a bald, white man, yet cops arrested Evelyn, who is black. The charges were dropped. But the story had already gained worldwide attention. "On the bus home," Evelyn said, "a woman was reading the paper with my picture on the cover. The headline said 'The Rapist.'" He couldn't walk down the street without people pointing at him or insulting him. Evelyn sued the City of New York for $10 million.

Defense lawyer Phillip Robertson, trying to make a dramatic point in front of the jury at his client's recent robbery trial in Dallas, pointed the pistol used in the crime at the jury box, causing two jurors to fling their arms in front of their faces and others to gasp.

Though Robertson was arguing that his client should be sentenced only to probation, the horrified jury gave him 13 years.

—"The Edge," in the *Oregonian*, September 10, 1997

The Elephant in the Room

THE PLAINTIFF: A Polish hunter named Waldemar

THE DEFENDANT: Jaworski Jagdreisen, a German travel agency that specializes in African hunting expeditions

THE LAWSUIT: Waldemar *really* wanted to shoot an elephant, so in 2010 he booked a vacation with Jaworski Jagdreisen, which sent him to a game reserve in Zimbabwe (one of the few countries where it's still legal to hunt elephants). Waldemar was told that if he found an elephant's excrement, he could pick up the animal's trail and shoot it. But he found neither excrement nor elephants, and went home empty-handed. After he complained, the agency gave him a free trip back to Zimbabwe, and this time, he shot and killed an elephant. Nevertheless, Waldemar sued the travel agency for $130,000 for failing to provide him with an elephant to kill on the first trip.

THE VERDICT: Case dismissed. The judge remarked, "The fact that elephants were not encountered during the hunt does not testify that elephants were not there."

FREAK-OUTS

After a neighbor's dog pooped
on his lawn, Walter Travis, 68,
shot the neighbor several
times (but not the dog).

. . . .

Danny Ginn stole a garbage
truck at gunpoint because the
truck's driver kept using his
driveway to turn around.

. . . .

Kevin French, 45, shot his
neighbor in the head with an
air rifle because he "mowed
his lawn too often."
(The neighbor recovered.)

Ding zui is a Chinese term for hiring
someone to stand trial and serve time
on someone else's behalf. The term
translates to "substitute criminal."

Think It Through

You think crime pays? Think again.

LOCKUP

The Crime: A Savannah, Georgia, man wanted to steal guns from the back of a squad car parked near a police station.
Gotcha! After he climbed in, he realized his goof: The back doors of police cars lock automatically when someone gets inside. Cops arrested the would-be thief a few minutes later.

TWINKLE TOES

The Crime: Cornered by police in Charles City, Virginia, a drug dealer carrying 12 bags of cocaine ran into a forest to escape. The trees were thick—he was certain the police would lose him.
Gotcha! He must have forgotten he was wearing light-up sneakers that flashed when he took a step. The cops followed the blinking lights through the forest—straight to him.

COVER ME!

The Crime: A person walking by a convenience store in Detroit Lakes, Minnesota, was stopped by a man asking a favor. The man informed the passerby that he planned to rob the store but needed a disguise. Then he gave the person a dollar to go inside and buy him a scarf to cover his face.
Gotcha! The bystander took the dollar, went inside the convenience store . . . and called the police.

Seeing Double

How much do you love your sibling?

TWINS: Bernic Lee and Breon Alston-Currie, 19

BACKGROUND: In May 2002, both brothers were being held at the Durham County jail in North Carolina. Bernic Lee was awaiting trial for murder, and Breon was being held on an unrelated robbery charge.

TWO-TIMING: On the day that Breon was scheduled for release, the jail's computer crashed. The guards, working from a handwritten list of inmates to be released, went to Bernic Lee's cell and asked if he was Breon. Bernic said yes. His face matched the photo on the release form (they're twins, remember) and he gave the right home address.

OUTCOME: Bernic spent about seven hours on the outside, then turned himself back in. He later pled guilty to second-degree murder and was sentenced to 9 to 12 years in prison. County officials never figured out whether Breon played any part in the snafu. "I have no information to believe that," says the jail's director, Lt. Col. George Naylor. "I have no information not to believe it, either."

TWINS: Carey and David Moore, 27

BACKGROUND: Both brothers were serving time in the Nebraska State Penitentiary in October 1984.

OUTCOME: One afternoon they met up in a conference room in the prison and switched clothes when nobody was

looking. Afterward Carey, posing as David, was released into the prison yard. David, posing as Carey, was escorted back to Carey's cell. The ruse was exposed when Carey reported for David's kitchen duty. The kitchen supervisor realized that "David" wasn't David and reported the incident to the guards.

WHAT HAPPENED: When confronted, the twins confessed. It's unlikely that they would have kept it up much longer— David was serving 4 to 6 years for burglary; Carey was awaiting execution on death row.

TWINS: Tony and Terry Litton, 19

BACKGROUND: Tony was serving a two-year sentence for burglary when Terry came to visit him in March 1990.

TWO-TIMING: Somehow, the brothers managed to strip down to their underwear and switch clothes in the middle of a bustling, guarded visitors room. When the visit was up, Terry went back to Tony's cell and Tony walked out of the prison with the rest of the visitors.

A word of advice to identical twins: If you're planning to trade places, don't have your names tattooed to the backs of your necks. Tony and Terry did; when an inmate noticed that Tony's now read "Terry," he alerted a guard.

OUTCOME: Tony was caught three days later and returned to jail to serve out his *full* sentence (no parole this time), plus extra time. Terry served some time of his own for helping him.

VIGILANTE JUSTICE

Crime: Roy A. Gendron broke into a home in Alabama.

Instant Justice: The homeowner's son, Richard Bussey, caught Gendron loading furniture and other items onto his truck. Bussey had a gun in his car, so he pulled it on Gendron. But he didn't have a telephone and didn't know what to do next, so he made the burglar mow the lawn—with a push mower—while he thought about it. He eventually took Gendron's driver's license, which the police used to track down and arrest the thief a short time later. Assistant DA Brian McVeigh told reporters that if he ever found himself in a similar situation, "I'll try to get some yard work out of the guy."

Crime: In 2003, 18-year-old Michael Watt walked into a health-food store, pulled out a knife, and demanded money.

Instant Justice: The sole employee, 48-year-old Lorraine Avery, refused. "I thought, 'He's not having our money, I've worked hard for it.'" She looked for something to hit the thief with but couldn't find anything. So, she grabbed an industrial-sized bottle of salad dressing, pointed it at him, and told him to get out. Watt wouldn't go—so she started squirting him with the dressing. "He kept coming at me with the knife," Avery told reporters, "and I kept squirting him." It worked! The would-be robber left the store, and police were able to track him down . . . by following the trail of salad dressing.

A Famous Phony

The story of one of history's boldest—and funniest—impostors.

BACKGROUND: In 1906 shoemaker and career criminal Wilhelm Voigt was released from a German prison after a 15-year sentence for robbery. His identity card and passport were confiscated, and he was broke. Then he remembered how he had learned to mimic the speech and mannerisms of Prussian officers whose boots he had mended when he was young. It gave him an idea.

MOMENT OF "TRUTH": He bought a secondhand army uniform and went to a local army barracks. When a corporal and five privates came marching by, he stepped in, started barking orders, and instantly became the leader of a tiny army. They marched down the road collecting five more men and a bus along the way. Once in Kopenick, Voigt marched his men into town hall. After pretending to inspect the accounts, he had the mayor arrested, and helped himself to 4,000 marks from the treasury. The mayor was sent in custody to military headquarters in Berlin, and "Captain" Voigt quietly disappeared.

UNMASKED: Nine days later, Voigt was captured and arrested. The story made headlines around the world and unintentionally brought world attention to the abuses of the German prison system. Some believe that Kaiser Wilhelm pardoned the lifelong crook—who had already spent 27 of his 57 years in prison for petty crimes—because he found the whole ordeal funny.

MONKEY SEE, MONKEY DO

*Sure, committing crimes looks glamorous
and fun on the screen, but try it in real life and
the result is often two thumbs down.*

MONKEY SEE: In the 1971 film *The Godfather,* Corleone family henchmen intimidate a Hollywood mogul by killing his prize racehorse and sticking the horse's head in his bed.

MONKEY DO: In 1997 two New York crooks decided to use a similar method to intimidate a witness scheduled to testify against them. On the morning of the trial, the witness found an unwelcome surprise on his doorstep. "We wanted to leave a cow's head," admitted one of the crooks, "because his wife is from India, and they consider cows sacred." Unable to find a cow's head in Brooklyn, they went to a butcher and got a goat's head. "We figured it was close enough." It wasn't. They both went to prison.

MONKEY SEE: In 1996, 17-year-old Steve Barone of Royal Palm Beach, Florida, was *really* into *Pulp Fiction, Reservoir Dogs,* and *Goodfellas.*

MONKEY DO: After he was caught trying to rob a gun store, Barone claimed that he'd been taken over by another personality—a combination of the "wise guys" from those three crime movies. The judge rejected the "*Pulp Fiction* defense," as the press called it, and sentenced "Mr. Vincent Vega Henry Hill White" to four years in prison.

The Night Stalkee, Part I

Over the course 14 months in 1984 and 1985, a maniacal serial killer terrorized Los Angeles, targeting his victims at random. The string of home invasions (the nature of which are too heinous to describe here) had left at least a dozen people dead. The police had few leads in the case, until a partial fingerprint on a stolen car led them to Richard Ramirez, a 25-year-old satanic drug addict who fit the description, and had been in trouble with the law before.

Ramirez's mug shot was plastered everywhere, and a massive manhunt ensued. However, Ramirez knew nothing about it. He'd spent that night on a bus ride home from Arizona. When he arrived at a Greyhound station in East Los Angeles on that hot August morning, he hopped off the bus and walked right past officers who were looking for someone getting *on* a bus. Ramirez, wearing a Jack Daniels T-shirt, walked into a corner store. An old woman started yelling, "El matón! El matón!" ("The killer! The killer!") Ramirez looked up at the woman, and then noticed his own face on the front page of the newspaper. The jig was up.

He ran out of the store, crossed the highway, jumped a fence, and started running through backyards, where, according to LA Police Commander William Booth, "at least one man struck him with barbecue utensils."

Ramirez escaped that predicament and instantly found himself in another when he jumped into a running Ford Mustang that belonged to 60-year-old Faustino Pinon's daughter. Faustino was underneath the car working on it. He shimmied out and was able to grab Ramirez before he could drive away. "I have a gun!" said Ramirez.

"I don't care what you have, you're not taking my daughter's car!" After a brief struggle, Ramirez ran across the street and tried to steal Angelina De La Torre's car. She screamed for her husband, who ran out, grabbed a metal pipe, and whacked Ramirez over the head with it. By this point, several other neighbors had joined in the fracas, and before Ramirez knew it, he was bleeding and being chased down Hubbard Street by several large men. They caught and beat the daylights out of the Night Stalker.

The strangest part of this story is yet to come.
Go to page 171 for part II.

"Obviously crime pays, or there'd be no crime."
—**G. Gordon Liddy**

HEY . . . I'M RIGHT HERE!

A FINE METH

"Yep, those are meth-making components," remarked Franklin County, Missouri, detective Jason Grellner while watching a video that Jennifer Harrington posted on her Facebook page clearly showing her and some friends manufacturing meth. The video led to several arrests for drug offenses.

NOT HER BEST SIDE

As part of their Facebook "Warrant Wednesday" program, Columbus, Ohio, police posted a mug shot of Monica Hargrove. Unhappy with how she looked in the photo, Hargrove called and said, "I want my picture down." The detective told her, "Come on in and we'll talk about it." So Hargrove did . . . and was immediately arrested on the outstanding warrant that put her on the department's Facebook page in the first place.

FROM WINNER TO LOSER

In 2014 after eluding North Carolina police for nine months on felony burglary charges, Bradley Hardison, entered a doughnut-eating contest. Good news: he wolfed down eight glazed doughnuts in two minutes for the win! Bad news: the contest was part of the "Elizabeth City Police Department's National Night Out Against Crime" event. When a newspaper printed Hardison's picture the next day, police had their man. "I did congratulate him," said the deputy who arrested Hardison. "Good for him. He can eat a lot of doughnuts."

Jack Ruby's Gun

Jack Ruby was a Dallas strip-club owner and small-time mobster who killed Lee Harvey Oswald, the alleged killer of President John F. Kennedy. Just why he did it remains a mystery. But on November 24, 1963, in the basement of the Dallas jail—which at the time was crowded with police officers, reporters, and cameramen—Ruby walked right up to Oswald and shot him once in the side. The gun he used was a .38-caliber Colt Cobra revolver that he bought at Ray's Hardware and Sporting Goods (on the advice of Dallas police detective Joe Cody).

The gun was returned to Ruby's family, where it promptly became tangled in a legal battle over Ruby's estate between the lawyer who was appointed executor and Ruby's brother, Earl. It wouldn't be resolved until 1991, when a judge found for Earl Ruby, who immediately put the gun up for auction and sold it to a collector named A. V. Pugliese. Price: $220,000. In 1992 a friend of Pugliese's brought it to Washington, DC, and offered to show it to Speaker of the House Thomas Foley. The gun was seized by police and almost destroyed, per DC's strict gun-control laws, but lawyers were able to get it back. On November 24, 1993, the 30th anniversary of the shooting, Pugliese had Earl Ruby fire 100 shots with the gun and offered the spent shells for sale. Price: $2,500 each. (They only sold a few.)

True Crime or Tall Tale?

The real scoop behind a popularly circulated crime story.

THE STORY: A traveler visiting New York City meets an attractive woman in a bar and takes her back to his hotel room. Next thing he knows, he's lying in a bathtub filled with ice and surgical tubing is coming out of two freshly stitched wounds on his lower chest. There's a note by the tub that says, "Call 911. We've removed your left kidney." The doctors in the emergency room tell him he's the victim of thieves who steal organs for transplants.

HOW IT SPREAD: French folklorist Veronique Campion-Vincent has traced the story to Honduras and Guatemala, where rumors began circulating in 1987 that babies were being kidnapped and murdered for their organs. The alleged culprits: wealthy Americans needing transplants. From there the story spread to South America, then all over the world. Wherever such stories surfaced—including the US—newspapers reported them as fact.

THE TRUTH: National and international agencies have investigated the claims, but haven't been able to substantiate even a single case of organ theft anywhere in the world. "These incredible stories ignored the complexity of organ transplant operations," Jan Brunvald writes in *The Baby Train and Other Lusty Urban Legends*, "which would preclude any such quick removal and long-distance shipment of body parts."

The city of Perm, Russia, spent a fortune on a crime-fighting robot designed to patrol streets and beam video to police stations, alerting officers to crimes in progress. After just three hours on the job, the six-foot tall, egg-shaped robot broke down. Reason: it was raining, which shorted out the robot's electrical system.

YOUNGEST AND OLDEST CONVICTED MURDERS

YOUNGEST

Twelve-year-old Curtis Jones was convicted in 1999.

OLDEST

Leonard Nathan Sherman of Daly City, California, was 85 in 1999 when he got life in prison for shooting his sister.

AMERICAN CANNIBAL

*Alferd Packer, the self-proclaimed "mountain man,"
did more than just explore.*

A DUBIOUS DISTINCTION

Born in Colorado in 1847, Packer drifted into the Utah
Territory, supporting himself as a small-time con artist. In
the fall of 1873, he persuaded 20 greenhorns to grubstake
an expedition to the headwaters of the Gunnison River in
Colorado Territory. He swore that the stream was full of gold
and promised to lead them to it if they financed the operation.

GOLD FEVER

With Packer leading, they plunged into the San Juan
Mountains and promptly got lost. The party was near
starvation when they stumbled into the winter quarters of
the friendly Ute tribe. The Ute nursed them back to health,
but the leader, Chief Ouray, advised them to turn back.
Winter snows had blocked all the trails. Ten of the party
listened and returned to Utah. The other 10, still believing
Packer's tales of gold-filled creeks, continued with him.

Days later, exhausted and out of food, they found refuge
in a deserted cabin. Most were now ready to give up and
go back to Salt Lake City. The exception was Alferd Packer.
When the others fell asleep, Packer shot four of them in the
head. The fifth woke and tried to defend himself, but Packer
killed him with the barrel of his rifle. He robbed them and
used them for food. He packed enough "human jerky" to

get back to the Los Pinos Agency. Upon arrival, he shocked everyone by asking for whiskey, instead of food. Suspicions grew when he flashed a big bankroll.

WELL, YOU SEE, OFFICER . . .

Packer's explanations were vague and contradictory. First, he claimed he was attacked by natives, then he claimed that some of his party had gone mad and attacked him. On April 4, 1874, two of Chief Ouray's braves found human remains. General Charles Adams locked him up and dispatched a lawman named Lauter to the cabin to investigate. While Lauter was away, Packer escaped. He returned to Utah and lived quietly for 10 years as "John Schwartze," until a member of the original party recognized him. Packer was arrested on March 12, 1884, and returned to Colorado for trial.

Packer claimed innocence, but as the evidence against him mounted, he confessed. He reveled in the attention his trial gave him and even lectured on the merits of human flesh. The judge was not impressed and reportedly said: "Alferd G. Packer, you no good sonofabitch . . . You're gonna hang by the neck until dead!"

SAVED BY A TECHNICALITY

However, the crime was committed in 1873, in the *territory* of Colorado. The trial began in 1884, in the new *state* of Colorado. The state constitution, adopted in 1876, did not address such a crime, so the charge was reduced to manslaughter. Packer was sentenced to prison. He was a model prisoner and was paroled after 16 years. In 1907, Alferd G. Packer died quietly in his sleep.

Canine Corpse Patrol

When the FBI can't find a body, they call in the big dogs.

Bomb-sniffing dogs can smell materials used to make explosives. Drug-sniffing dogs can sniff out marijuana stashed in a school locker. Human Remains Detection Canines, or HRD dogs, are trained to recognize . . . the smell of death. And they do it with amazing accuracy: a trained dog can detect the scent of a dead body on the ground, even if it was removed from the spot a *year* earlier.

HRD training starts with "fresh scent sources." (Yes, it's as icky as it sounds.) Dogs learn to sniff out hair, bone, teeth, tissue, blood, and other bodily fluids, but not from live humans—only from corpses. By the end of training, HRD dogs can find bodies both above and below the ground. They can even tell if a body has been dumped in a lake. How? By sniffing the water's surface for tiny gas bubbles seeping from a corpse rotting underwater.

The FBI usually calls in HRD dogs to find a specific missing person. If that person is a murder victim, finding the body is a crucial step in solving the crime. Thanks to HRD dogs, the FBI "nose" where to look!

THE FBI WHISTLE-BLOWER

In the 1990s, Frederic Whitehurst became the first agent to successfully blow a whistle on misconduct in the FBI. Whitehurst, who held a doctorate in chemistry from Duke University, was the senior explosives expert in the FBI's crime lab. When the FBI concluded that the suspects in the first World Trade Center bombing of 1993 had manufactured a urea nitrate explosive, Whitehurst saw irregularities in the report. He conducted his own investigation and concluded that there was no proof, and that urea could have come from 80 gallons of sewage scattered over the bomb wreckage. Contrary to Whitehurst's analysis, the FBI put an unqualified lab technician on the stand to testify that it was a urea bomb. Whitehurst performed a double-blind test to show a urea nitrate mixture made from fertilizer had properties identical to those of urine. When Whitehurst's analysis was submitted to the court, the lab technician who testified conceded that he could not tell the difference.

Though the suspects were convicted, the episode embarrassed the FBI, which relieved Whitehurst of his duties and assigned him to another section of the lab. He filed suit, charging violation of whistle-blower statutes; the suit was settled out of court for a reported $1.16 million. In 1997 Whitehurst achieved vindication when the inspector general of the US Department of Justice ordered a major revamp of the crime lab based on the 1993 case. As a result, the lab implemented 40 major reforms, including an accreditation process to prevent future lapses.

A Royal Toast

Back in the 1500s, when Henry VIII yanked England away from Catholicism because he wanted a divorce in order to marry a younger woman, the people who stayed with the Catholic Church were accused of being traitors. When James I inherited the throne in 1603, the persecution continued. Priests were expelled from the country, and Catholics who didn't attend Anglican services were fined. One fed-up Catholic, Robert Catesby, launched a plot to change all that. In 1604, he gathered a band of followers that included Guy Fawkes, a formidable soldier and explosives expert, and rented a cellar in the Parliament building. The idea was, while the king addressed the legislators, Fawkes would blow up the building. The others would kidnap James's young daughter Elizabeth and force her to rule as their puppet (and Catholic) queen.

THE PLOT THICKENS

By October 1605, Guy Fawkes had hidden 36 barrels of gunpowder in the cellar and the conspirators were all set to give the king an explosive surprise on November 5. But an anonymous letter alerted the House of Lords to stay away from Parliament that day, so instead of blowing up the building on November 5, Fawkes was captured and tortured until he finally admitted to the plot. Catesby and his men were hunted down, and those who weren't immediately killed were drawn and quartered.

King James made November 5 a holiday because uncovering the plot saved his life, so everyone was supposed to be happy. Today, the English still celebrate Guy Fawkes Night with bonfires and fireworks, but history remembers it as one of the world's most famous fizzled terror plots.

> "If women didn't like criminals, there would be no crime."
>
> —Ice-T

The Real Soprano on *The Sopranos*

STAR: Tony Sirico, who played Paulie "Walnuts" Gualtieri on *The Sopranos* (1999–2007)

BEHIND BARS: Sirico is probably the only *Sopranos* star whose real-life rap sheet is as long as that of the mobster character he played. Arrested 28 times for robbery and other crimes as a young man, Sirico was serving time in New York's Sing Sing prison in the early 1970s when an ex-con acting troupe called the Theater of the Forgotten staged a play there. "I was truly captured by the magic of the performance," Sirico told an interviewer in 2003. "It was the major step in me getting my life straight." After his release, Sirico called a friend, actor Richard Castellano (who played mobster Peter Clemenza in the 1972 film *The Godfather*), and asked for help breaking into acting. Castellano helped him land a part in the 1974 mob film *Crazy Joe*. "That film got me a Screen Actors Guild card, which gave me a life," Sirico said. "Instead of a life sentence."

EXTRA: Sirico says he got the best advice of his career at his very first acting class. "I was this 30-year-old ex-con villain sitting in a class filled with fresh-faced, serious drama students. [The instructor] leaned over to me after I did a scene and whispered, 'Tony, leave the gun home' . . . He meant for me to also leave my former life behind, to be an actor."

CSI: Contaminating (the) Scene Investigator

Police in southern Germany feared that a female serial killer was on the loose. After comparing evidence gathered over a period of 15 years, they noticed the same woman's DNA was present at 40 crime scenes, linking her to dozens of robberies and three murders.

It wasn't until 2009 that police made a major breakthrough in the case: the matching DNA samples didn't come from the evidence, they came from the cotton swabs that had been used to collect it. They concluded that a batch of cotton had been accidentally contaminated by a female worker at the factory many years earlier. The crimes remain unsolved.

DID YOU KNOW?

Frank Sinatra was arrested twice for the same crime. In 1938 he was first arrested in Hackensack and charged with seduction. When it was discovered that the lady in question was married, the charges were dropped. A month later the police arrested Sinatra again for the same encounter, only this time his crime was adultery. These charges were eventually dismissed, too.

The Baader-Meinhof Gang

The 1960s were famous for student protest marches
and lifestyles of sex, drugs, and rock and roll. In
1968, in West Germany, student Gudrun Ensslin
and her boyfriend Andreas Baader added violence
to the mix. In their anger at what they saw as the
sins of capitalism, they set fire to two department
stores. Baader went to jail, but escaped with the help
of an antiestablishment journalist, Ulrike Meinhof.
In 1970, Baader, Ensslin, and Meinhof, along with
their young, middle-class followers, launched a
"revolution." They called themselves the Red Army
Faction (RAF), though to most people they were
simply the Baader-Meinhof Gang.

THE CAUSE OF IT ALL

Professing support for the Palestinian cause and
for bringing an end to the Vietnam War, the RAF
robbed banks, kidnapped people, bombed military
buildings, and murdered anyone who got in their
way. They even blew up the offices of a newspaper
that gave them bad press. By 1976, Meinhof had
hanged herself in prison, and Baader and Ensslin
were both behind bars. But that only spurred more
violence as the rest of the gang desperately tried to
free their leaders.

In 1976, the battle went international as the "German Autumn." In September, the RAF kidnapped Hanns-Martin Schlever, a powerful businessman with a Nazi past, and demanded their leaders' release in exchange for Schlever's life. On October 13, their Palestinian allies hijacked a German Lufthansa 757, threatening to blow up the plane and passengers unless the RAF's demands were met. After a grim five-day standoff, a unit of German commandos managed to kill the hijackers and liberate the passengers.

FROM BAADER TO WORSE

When Baader and Ensslin learned that the hijacking had failed, they took their lives in a suicide pact— one by gunshot, the other by hanging (though the government's role in their deaths remains controversial). The RAF pulled off more bombings and assassinations, but its power diminished and support from students faded. In 1998, the RAF formally dissolved with this message: "The revolution says: I was, I am, I will be again."

The Cleveland Police Scandal

THE PERPS: Forty-four cops in Cleveland, Ohio

THE STORY: On January 21, 1998, the FBI completed a two-year investigation into organized crime in Cleveland by staging the biggest sting operation in their history to date, and most of the people arrested were cops. What agents had discovered during the initial stages of the investigation was a network of police officers in several different agencies who had been taking payoffs to protect—and take part in—major drug-smuggling operations. The leader of the ring: corrections officer (and mobster wannabe) Michael "Guido" Joye, who once told an undercover agent, "These guys I have working for me, we're a specialty, like a goon squad."

OUTCOME: The operation resulted in the felony convictions and prison sentences of 30 Cleveland-area cops, including Joye.

EXTRA: During the course of the operation, the FBI staged a fake "Mafia" induction ceremony, during which Officer Joye had to kneel on the floor in front of a table covered with a white cloth and candles to be "sworn in" as a "made man." A cop who later testified against Joye said, "He came out white as a ghost. He said he was in the Mafia now. He totally believed it."

Life Imitates Art

THE THOMAS CROWN AFFAIR AFFAIR

With similarities to the 1999 remake of *The Thomas Crown Affair*, a bank robber staged a daring heist in October 2008. Like in the film, he used human decoys to steal cash from a Bank of America in Monroe, Washington. Prior to the robbery, he placed an ad on Craigslist for road maintenance workers telling them to show up outside of the bank at 11 a.m. for a well-paid gig. Many recruits arrived wearing yellow vests, blue shirts, and safety goggles. The robber slipped in among them wearing the same clothing. He then snuck up on a guard removing money from an armored truck, hosed him down with pepper spray, grabbed a bag of cash, and made a run for it. Even crazier: The crook escaped by floating down the Skykomish River in an inner tube. Authorities later found his "getaway vehicle" on a riverbank, but the robber was long gone.

THE TOWNIES

In the 2010 film *The Town*, a group of thieves rob a Boston bank while wearing some creepy nun masks. The following spring, two crooks did the same thing in Illinois. The duo burst into a TCF Bank branch just before closing time wearing masks like those in the film. After jumping over counters and forcing staff members to enter the vault, they stuffed a bunch of cash into a gym bag and quickly made their escape in a getaway car.

USING THE FORCE

In 2010 a man dressed as a Sith lord strolled into a Chase branch on Long Island, New York. After pointing a gun at a clerk, he left with a few stacks of cash. He was last spotted fleeing on foot through the bank's parking lot. As security camera footage later revealed, the robber's costume didn't match up with the suit Darth Vader wears in the films. He made do with a blue cape instead of a black one . . . and a pair of camouflage pants.

BEASTLY MISTAKE

"After Cody Johnston, 22, of Bozeman, Montana, was fined $195 for a traffic violation, a court computer error turned it into a conviction for deviate sexual conduct. That's the way it appeared in a crime report in the High Country *Independent Press,* where Johnston's parents read it. When he told them it wasn't true, his wife and his sister accused him of being in denial and urged him to seek counseling. Even though the *Independent Press* printed a correction, Johnston filed a libel suit against the paper and the court system, noting, "I've heard every sheep joke you can imagine."

—**Weird News**

PLAYING TO STEREOTYPES

Michael Zaydel, a 21-year-old man from Redford Township, Michigan, was wanted by police for several outstanding warrants. In a private message on the department's Facebook page, he wrote: "If you're [sic] next post gets a thousand shares I'll turn myself in along with a dozen doughnuts. And that's a promise." The cops decided to take that bet. They posted a screenshot of Zaydel's offer, along with this message: "Donuts!!!! He promised us donuts! You know how much we love Donuts!"

It didn't take long for the post to amass—and then surpass—1,000 shares. True to his word, Zaydel showed up at the police station with a box of doughnuts. Although much appreciated, the sweet treats didn't get him any leniency, and he spent the next 39 days in jail.

'TIL LIFE DO YOU PART

San Diego Superior Court judge Patricia Cookson officiated the wedding of Danne Desbrow and Destiny Winters. What's weird about that? Desbrow had shackles around his ankles—because a few minutes earlier, Judge Cookson had sentenced him to life in prison for first-degree murder. (She did have the good sense to have the victim's family escorted out of the courtroom first.) Desbrow and Winters were high school sweethearts but lost contact for nearly 20 years until Desbrow went on trial in 2013 for a 2003 murder. He claimed it was self-defense, but the jury found him guilty. During the two-month trial, the lovebirds rekindled their romance; Desbrow proposed, and Winters said yes. And they asked Judge Cookson to officiate—no matter the trial's outcome. The judge agreed and even baked a cake especially for the occasion. But instead of going on a honeymoon, Desbrow went to prison, and Winters went home.

The Oldest Trick in the Book

Well known as the bane of email users everywhere, the old "Nigerian trick" has actually been scamming people long before the Internet age.

PSST!

You know the con: Someone is in trouble, usually in Nigeria, hence the name, but other countries are also used. The person, allegedly a wealthy refugee, is blindly contacting someone outside the country asking for help. The subject line of his email usually reads something like "Urgent Business Transaction." The writer is very polite, but he sounds desperate. He has a lot of money, though it's tied up in a bank.

The authorities are after him—sometimes because of a political uprising in his home country; other times because of the actions of a dictator—so he must be discreet. If you will help, through a donation, you will receive a large sum of money for your trouble as soon as he's free. Send a few thousand dollars, and you'll be rewarded with much more.

HEY, SUCKER!

For many, the Nigerian scam sounds too good to pass up. Some people lose a few hundred dollars, but some fall hard. Victims have been lured to Nigeria or elsewhere to collect their imaginary winnings and have wound up in lots of trouble. The US State Department has issued warnings about people who travel to meet the people behind the emails and

end up "beaten, subjected to threats and extortion, and in some cases murdered."

WHO DEALS WITH IT?

If you report a Nigerian scam to the government, you'll be referred to the Secret Service. Established in 1865 to deal with counterfeiting, the Secret Service protects a lot of America's financial interests, in addition to protecting the president. A local Secret Service office will handle the case, but these crimes are notoriously difficult to solve. First, the authorities have to find the perpetrator and then transport him to the victim's country for prosecution.

Nigeria established the Economic and Financial Crimes Commission (EFCC) in 2003 to combat the problem and to improve the country's image in the global community. In 2006, the EFCC announced that it would start punishing Internet service providers in Nigeria if they helped the scammers complete their cons. The penalty for not taking proper security measures: up to 20 years in prison. Still, some scammers find a way to circumspect the laws. Con artists have been able to target people who have contacted the EFCC to report being scammed. Posing as EFCC representatives, they get personal information out of past victims and use that to access bank accounts.

Nigerians would love to put this scandal and its name behind them. Until then, beware the email that begs for help and promises huge rewards in return.

No Body, No Crime

Officer, arrest that robot.

Coke-Stealing Contraption. A French teen known by his YouTube handle "ioduremetallique" achieved Internet fame with a $1,200 robotic arm built for one purpose: to steal $1 cans of coke. A hooked appendage with a mechanical pincer, operated by a video-game controller, can penetrate even the most unwilling vending machine and raid its sweet treasures. It's nothing less than the best French invention since the guillotine. But there's no such thing as a perfect crime. The arm's first public theft: a Coke Zero.

Cyberbot Crime. Remote control isn't new, but virtual-reality robot avatars are. According to the BBC, robots controlled remotely over the Internet are becoming increasingly common, raising troubling criminal concerns. Burglars in Botswana could send a bank-robbing bot to Boise with virtually no risk to themselves.

Cross the Border-Bots. Narco-trafficking has been on the rise for decades, so it's no surprise drug lords are increasingly investing in robotic technology. In 2007 three Colombian men were convicted of using an unmanned robotic submarine to transport millions of dollars of cocaine across international waters. The academic journal *IEEE* warns of gun-packing, drug-selling robots roaming our streets someday. But if cocaine-vending machines ever do come to pass, police can just use that French YouTuber's robot arm to steal the stuff back and keep the streets safe.

Was It ... Murder?

A mysterious death reveals a deep, dark secret.

LAST NIGHT

In 2003 a 75-year-old socialite named Jean Ann Cone drove home from a fund-raising event, tailed by a friend who wanted to make sure she got home safely. When the two women arrived at the Cone residence, her friend watched as Cone pulled into her garage, then drove home. It was the last time anyone saw Mrs. Cone alive.

NOBODY HOME

Cone's daughter went to her mother's house after she failed to show up for appointments. In the garage, she saw Cone's car parked in a puddle of green antifreeze. Slumped in the driver's seat was Jean Ann Cone.

WEIGHING THE EVIDENCE

Cone was on medication, and the autopsy revealed that her blood-alcohol level at the time of her death was 0.18 percent. The police ruled Cone's death accidental.

THE PLOT THICKENS

When Mr. Cone returned home and heard of his wife's death, he was inconsolable. But just 13 days later, friends read a puzzling wedding announcement in the newspaper. Douglas Cone had remarried—and hadn't told his three children. Their son asked police to reopen the investigation.

MYSTERY MAN

First, they investigated Cone's new wife. Her name was Hillary Carlson, and she was already married. The Carlsons and the Cones traveled in the same exclusive social circles. Both families had given lots of money to the prestigious Berkeley Preparatory School. Cone didn't travel in diplomatic circles like Carlson—he was in road construction. Had Jean Ann Cone and Hillary Carlson compared notes, they might have noticed something unusual: Jean Ann's husband was away on business during the week and home on weekends, while Hillary's husband was away on weekends but home during the week. Douglas Cone and Donald Carlson were never in the same place at the same time.

THE JIG IS UP

Douglas Cone had to reveal his secret: For more than 20 years, he had been living a double life. On weekends, he lived with his wife Jean Ann, but during the week he posed as Donald Carlson, living with his mistress, Hillary Carlson, and their two children. Douglas Cone's "business trips" were simply a ruse so he could spend the week with Hillary.

REST IN PEACE

The police now believe that Jean Ann Cone's death was an accident. "The family was only suspicious because Douglas Cone remarried too quickly," says Tampa Police Sergeant Jim Simonson. "Turns out that can be easily explained; it's not like he met the woman two weeks before."

LAWYERS ON LAWYERS

Quotes from the world's most famous lawyers.

"I get paid for seeing that my clients have every break the law allows. I have knowingly defended a number of guilty men. But the guilty never escape unscathed. My fees are sufficient punishment for anyone."
—**F. Lee Bailey**

"An incompetent lawyer can delay a trial for months or years. A competent lawyer can delay one even longer."
—**Evelle Younger**

"I've never met a litigator who didn't think he was winning . . . right up until the moment the guillotine dropped."
—**William F. Baxter**

"We lawyers shake papers at each other the way primitive tribes shake spears."
—**John Jay Osborn Jr.**

"I don't want to know what the law is, I want to know who the judge is."
—**Roy Cohn**

Phoning It In

*Some criminals actually go someplace to commit
their crimes and get caught. These guys figured
they could just phone it in. They were right.*

NO SUCH THING AS A FREE RIDE

"In August of 1996, 19-year-old Donterio Beasley was stranded
in Little Rock, Arkansas, and called police to request a ride
downtown. When informed that it was against police policy,
he hung up, waited a few minutes, and called back. This time
he reported a suspicious-looking person loitering near a phone
booth . . . and then he gave a complete description of himself.
He thought he'd get a free ride downtown to the station, where
he'd be questioned and released. Instead he got a free ride
downtown and was charged with calling in a false alarm."

—*Dallas Morning News*

A BOMB FOR THE BOMBED

"Thirty-nine-year-old Ronnie Wade Cater of Hampton, Virginia,
was arrested in 1997 after phoning in a bomb threat. Cater
was at a bar, drunk, and wanted to drive home without being
nabbed for DUI. So he phoned in his bomb threat, saying
there was a bomb at another local bar, hoping to divert police
attention. The call was traced and he was arrested."

—*News of the Weird*

THE WORLD'S SECOND-DUMBEST OUTLAW

"Blackjack" Tom Ketchum (1862?–1901)

BACKGROUND: Ketchum was an ordinary cowboy before turning to crime. He returned from a cattle drive one day and learned that his girlfriend had eloped with another man. The rejection pushed him over the edge.

CLAIM TO FAME: He ran with members of Wyoming's notorious Hole-in-the-Wall gang, but botched so many stick-ups that getting away with a few dollars was the best he usually managed. He had a strange reaction to failure, as Jay Robert Nash explains in *American Eccentrics:* whenever a caper of his went wrong, he would methodically beat himself on the head with the butt of his six-shooter.

In 1898 Ketchum and his boys robbed a train in New Mexico of about $500. Not exactly a king's ransom, but it was enough to keep Ketchum coming back for more. Ketchum went after the same train, at exactly the same remote spot, a total of four times. On the fourth, lawmen were waiting for him. There was a shootout, and Ketchum was wounded and captured. So why was Ketchum only the second-stupidest outlaw? Because his brother, Sam, was even dumber. While Black Jack was in prison, Sam masterminded yet another identical robbery of the same train. He got himself killed in the attempt.

Crimes from the Big Leagues

NAKED HUNGER

In 2006 Detroit Lions defensive-line coach Joe Cullen was ordering food at a Detroit-area Wendy's drive-through. Police later pulled him over after receiving a call from Wendy's—because Cullen was nude. A week later, Cullen was pulled over again by Detroit police. This time he was clothed, but he was drunk. For the naked incident, he paid a $500 fine, for the drunk driving he paid a $300 fine, and for both he paid a $20,000 misconduct fine to the NFL.

HE CAUGHT A BULLET

Plaxico Burress was a wide receiver for the New York Giants who caught the game-winning pass in the 2008 Super Bowl. Later that year, Burress went to the New York City nightclub LQ. He brought along a large Glock handgun, which he hid by tucking it into the waistband of his jeans rather than using a holster. At one point, the gun started to slip down his leg, and when Burress went to reach for it, he accidentally pulled the trigger and shot himself in the right thigh. Burress sought medical treatment and then turned himself in to the NYPD. Not only had he injured himself, he'd committed a crime—the gun was unlicensed. Burress had a license to carry a concealed handgun, but only in Florida, and it had expired. He pleaded guilty to weapons charges and was sentenced to two years in prison.

Nobody Helped

It's called the Genovese syndrome; the phenomenon
of a crime being witnessed by numerous people
who don't try to stop it or call for help.

Kitty Genovese got home from work very late. In Queens, New York, on March 13, 1964, when the 28-year-old, 105-pound Genovese parked her car at 3 a.m., there was someone waiting for her. As Kitty began to walk toward her home, the man waylaid and stabbed her.

A CRY FOR HELP

She shrieked in terror, "Oh, my God, he stabbed me! Please help me!" Genovese's neighbors in the snug apartment complex, many of whom knew her, turned on their lights and opened their apartment windows. One male neighbor shouted from his window, "Leave that girl alone!" Kitty's attacker left. She began staggering to her apartment, bleeding from several stab wounds, while her neighbors shut their windows and turned off their lights. Kitty no doubt thought the worst was over. But her attacker returned and stabbed her again. "I'm dying!" she screamed. Her neighbors threw open their windows again, but nobody came out to help. Kitty's attacker fled.

Kitty crawled into the vestibule of an apartment house and lay there bleeding for several minutes. Once again her assailant returned. He assaulted her, and took the $49 from her wallet before stabbing her one last, fatal time. It was not

until 3:50 a.m., a full 50 minutes after the attack began, that a neighbor called police. Two minutes later, police arrived to find Kitty's body.

NOT MY PROBLEM

Police questioned Genovese's neighbors and discovered that at least 38 people had witnessed the killer attacking Genovese, yet no one had tried to intervene. Only one had called the police—after Kitty was already dead. The neighbors offered numerous excuses for their behavior. They hadn't wanted to get involved, they said. They could see that others were witnessing the crime; surely *those* people were calling the police. There was no law forcing witnesses to call for help.

SOME CONSOLATION

The murderer was caught less than a week later. He readily admitted to killing Kitty Genovese, as well as two other local women. In June 1964, 29-year-old Winston Moseley was found guilty.

But Kitty Genovese has not been forgotten. The case has lived on in plays and TV dramas—it even spawned a whole new branch of psychology. When experts refer to the Genovese syndrome, they're theorizing that the neighbors' failure to act was due to "diffusion of responsibility"—there were so many people watching the crime that no one person felt they had any personal responsibility, believing someone else would do something. The case is still taught in every Psych 101 class in the country.

My Precious President

Turkey's president, Recep Tayyip Erdogan, elected in 2014, has been widely mocked for not being able to take mockery. Several people—including journalists—have been fired, jailed, or even beaten for "insulting the president," which is actually a crime in that country. Bilgin Çiftçi, a doctor in Turkey's public health service, discovered that the hard way after he posted a Facebook meme comparing President Erdogan to Gollum, the skulking creature from *The Lord of the Rings* films. Or did he?

When Erdogan saw the meme—three side-by-side pictures of himself and Gollum with similar facial expressions—he had Çiftçi fired from his job and put on trial for "publicly denigrating a state official." The doctor was facing two years in prison if found guilty.

When the case made international headlines, it caught the attention of *Rings* writer/director Peter Jackson. In a statement (with the other two screenwriters), Jackson came to the defendant's defense by pointing out that the character has a split personality, one of which is the "evil, conniving, malicious" Gollum, and the other is the "joyful, sweet Sméagol." "If the images are in fact the ones forming the basis of this Turkish lawsuit," said Jackson, "we can state categorically: none of them feature the character known as Gollum . . . who should never be confused with Sméagol."

THE VERDICT: The doctor was acquitted.

The Summerdale Scandal

The Perps: Eight Chicago police officers

The Story: In July 1959, 23-year-old Richie Morrison was arrested while burglarizing a Chicago business. He wasn't too worried about it at first, but when the help he seemed to expect didn't arrive, he started talking. And what a story: the "Babbling Burglar," as he became known across the nation, told investigators that over the previous 15 months he had carried out a string of burglaries . . . with the help of eight Chicago cops. They all worked the night shift at the city's 40th, or "Summerdale," police district. They had helped plan the robberies, Morrison said, and had even used their squad cars to take away the loot.

Outcome: The eight officers were arrested, and all of them were eventually convicted on various felony charges. Two paid fines, and the other six served time in prison. Unlike some other police scandals, Summerdale actually resulted in significant changes to the department, most importantly the establishment of the Chicago Police Board—a five-member civilian panel that oversees many aspects of police administration, including the handling of cases of misconduct. The board still exists today.

Hooligans with a Heart

*Just because you lead a life of crime
doesn't mean you can't be well-mannered.*

PLEASE AND THANK YOU

In January 2004, a man went into a Wells Fargo branch in Phoenix, Arizona, waited his turn in line, and walked up to the counter. "This is a robbery," he told the teller. "I need $1,500 in fifties, please." He made no threats and had no weapon. The teller gave him what she had, and he strolled out the door. "It was like Emily Post does a bank robbery," said Officer Rick Tamburo.

CHECKING OUT

Nazareno Rodriguez and Sebastian Gallardo, two prisoners in Argentina who had been accused of robbery, were able to unscrew their jail cell door and make a middle-of-the-night escape. Police were surprised when they later found a note in the empty cell. "We love our freedom and can't live locked in," it read. "We're sorry for any inconvenience we might have caused you." "They were so cheeky," a police officer said. "We couldn't believe they left a note. But we'll find them!"

BAG MAN

A thief stole more than $207,000 from a London ATM machine . . . and seven days later returned $187,000 of it. Barclays bank employees found it in a garbage bag just inside their door. A bank spokesperson told the *Sun,* "We do offer cashback facilities, but we didn't expect anything quite like this."

> "Make crime pay. Become a lawyer."
> —**Will Rogers**

Dam Nation

One of the most intriguing environmental legal battles took place from 1997 to 1998 between the Spring Pond beavers of Marne, Michigan, and the Michigan Department of Environmental Quality (DEQ). The beavers, doing what beavers do best, dared to construct a dam on Marne resident Stephen Tvedten's property.

CHARGE: Illegal dam building

The trouble began when Ryan DeVries, one of Tvedten's neighbors, complained to the Michigan DEQ about flooding on his property caused by a dam located on Tvedten's property. The DEQ responded to DeVries instead of Tvedten, accusing DeVries of participating in unauthorized activity, specifically the construction of two illegal wood debris dams across an outlet stream of Spring Pond. Such illegal activities carried a fine of $10,000 per day. The DEQ ordered DeVries to cease and desist construction on the dams and to remove all wood and brush in time for a site inspection by DEQ agents.

THE REBUTTAL

DeVries forwarded the letter from the DEQ to Tvedten, because it was Tvedten's dam, not his. When Tvedten received the DEQ letter from DeVries, he responded to the DEQ on the Spring Pond beavers' behalf. Tvedten asked all

the right questions:

- Was the DEQ discriminating against the Spring Pond beavers, or were all beavers required to file a permit before beginning dam construction?

- To prove that there had been no discrimination, Tvedten asked for copies of dam permits filed by other beavers.

- He informed the DEQ that if they were serious about dam removal, they had better tell the proper parties— the beavers.

- Mr. Tvedten was especially concerned that the state preserved the beavers' civil rights. Was the state going to arrest the beavers? Would the beavers be read their rights? Would the state provide legal representation? He concluded, "In my humble opinion, the Spring Pond beavers have a right to build their . . . unauthorized dams as long as the sky is blue, the grass is green, and water flows downstream." The Michigan DEQ inspected the site and dropped the investigation after the dam was removed and the beavers moved on.

EPILOGUE

It is rumored that the beavers have returned to Spring Pond, the original scene of the crime, for an encore performance. The saga continues.

WILD WILD WEST

The story behind one of the West's most infamous outlaws.

Billy the Kid—christened Patrick Henry McCarty in New York City—was practically a kid, (just 21) when he died. It's said that he was a "nice boy" and a good dancer. Unfortunately, he fell under the influence of a young man known only as "Sombrero Jack," which led to Billy's first crime, at age 16—stealing clothes from a Chinese laundry in Silver City, New Mexico.

He worked as a cowhand for the next two years, until the day when he shot his first victim, a blacksmith who had called him a "pimp." There was no turning back. Going by "Billy the Kid," "William H. Bonney," and a few other aliases, Billy spent the rest of his short life stealing horses, rustling cattle, robbing stagecoaches, and killing the occasional lawman here and there.

In 1880, acting on a tip, Sheriff Pat Garrett found Billy and arrested him and some of his gang. The Kid was convicted for the murder of Sheriff William Brady some three years before. He was scheduled to be hanged, but escaped—killing two deputies in the process.

Garrett tracked Billy down a few months later and, before the Kid had a chance to go for his gun, shot him right through the heart. Two states—New Mexico and Texas—claim to be the final resting place of Billy the Kid.

Public Enemy No. 1

THE RISE: Al Capone's parents emigrated from Naples to Brooklyn, where the gangster-to-be was born in 1899. Al was a B student until he quit school in sixth grade. He grew up in a rough neighborhood and joined two kid's gangs: the Brooklyn Rippers and the Forty Thieves. He worked various low-paying jobs, but found he made better money working for gangsters. He went to work for gangster Frankie Yale at the Brooklyn Inn, where he insulted a patron. Her companion attacked Capone with either a knife or razor, which is how Capone got the wounds that gave him the nickname "Scarface." By 1918, Capone had killed two men and fled to Chicago, where he started working for mobster Johnny Torrio.

THE REIGN: One of Capone's first jobs was to kill Torrio's boss. He was careful to arrange an alibi for the murder, a precaution he kept during his career. He quickly became Torrio's second in command, and Torrio, as the new boss, assigned Capone to manage bootlegging, prostitution, and gambling operations in Chicago and its suburbs.

In 1925 a rival tried to assassinate Torrio, who fled Chicago, leaving the "business" to Capone. Capone lived large and made headlines like a movie star. He controlled Chicago's politicians and police. He launched ruthless wars on rival bootleggers.

On February 14, 1929, Capone's men and their machine guns mowed down seven rival gangsters in what came to be known as the St. Valentine's Day Massacre.

THE FALL: The massacre brought Capone national attention as "Public Enemy No. 1," but the authorities had trouble pinning the crime on the man who always had an alibi (and who owned the Chicago police force). Finally, an IRS investigator accidentally found incriminating receipts that landed Capone in an Atlanta federal prison for tax evasion. Capone ran his organization from prison until 1934, when he was transferred to Alcatraz to cut him off from his gang and the outside world. By 1938, he was serving his sentence in the prison hospital suffering from dementia brought on by syphilis. After his release in 1939, he retired to his estate in Palm Island, Florida. He died of natural causes in 1947.

Not Your Average Nuclear Family

This bedtime story is sure to keep you up at night.

Between 1979 and 1983, five young men between the ages of 14 and 25 were kidnapped, drugged, tortured, and murdered in and around the South Australian city of Adelaide. In 1984 Bevan Spencer von Einem, an Adelaide accountant, was convicted of committing one of the murders and is currently serving a life sentence. Although police believe von Einem took part in *all* of the murders, they lacked sufficient evidence to prove it. And anonymous witnesses—anonymous because they'd been threatened— informed police that while von Einem was guilty, he wasn't alone: he was only one member of a shadowy group of prominent Adelaide citizens, including lawyers and doctors, who used their bountiful resources to prey on young men. Other members of this group, called "the Family" in the press, are believed to have taken part in all five murders—and possibly others—with von Einem. Von Einem never revealed who his accomplices were, though he hinted at a group being responsible, and that he was unable to provide further information out of fear. A $1 million reward still stands for information leading to further convictions. The cold case was reopened in October 2008, but despite reports of new evidence, no further arrests have been made, and the case remains open.

Stop, Drop, and Roll

Here's a criminal plot that backfired . . . literally.

Herbert Ridge built a gas-siphoning contraption with an electric pump. One afternoon in October 2012, he was stealing gas from a parked car in East Mesa, Arizona, when the pump sparked and ignited the gasoline, which caught Ridge's T-shirt on fire. He started rolling around in the street, much to the bemusement of kids walking home from school. Then he jumped in his pickup truck and sped away. Only problem: He was still on fire. And so was his truck. Ridge jumped out of the truck and ran away. His flaming pickup, however, kept on going until it smashed into a house and set the building on fire. Neighbors put out the house fire and apprehended Ridge, who was taken to the hospital, and then to jail.

The Leech of Your Worries

In 2001 two men broke into the home of 71-year-old Fay Olsen on the Australian island of Tasmania, tied her to a chair, "poked her with sticks," and robbed her of $550 ($504 US). Police found no evidence at the scene except for a leech—fully engorged with blood from a recent meal—on the floor. Officers checked the woman and themselves for signs that the leech had been attached to one of them, and determined that it must have fallen off one of the robbers. DNA samples were taken from the blood in the leech. Seven years passed. In 2008 a 56-year-old Tasmanian man was arrested on drug charges and a routine DNA sample was taken from him and cross-checked against a database. It matched the DNA taken from the leech. Peter Alec Cannon eventually confessed to the seven-year-old crime and was sentenced to two years in prison. (His accomplice was never apprehended.) Tasmanian police said that, to their knowledge, it was the first time DNA from a leech had assisted in solving a crime anywhere in the world.

Forensic Science— 1800s Edition

Though forensics is a relatively new official science, it's been centuries in the making.

1813: Mathiew Orfila publishes the first treatise that systematically catalogs poisons and their effects. For this, he gets the title of "Father of Modern Toxicology," although there probably wasn't an official ceremony. Orfila was also one of the first to develop forensic blood tests and to examine blood and semen with a microscope for forensic purposes.

1835: Scotland Yard investigator Henry Goddard determines that a butler had staged an attempted robbery when he traces a bullet back to a bullet mold owned by the butler. This is the first example of bullet matching, as well as one of the first actual recorded cases of "the butler did it."

1863: Is that blood or a spot of ketchup? A German scientist named Schönbein creates the first presumptive test for blood when he discovers that hemoglobin will oxidize hydrogen peroxide. Mixing peroxide and ketchup will simply give you inedible ketchup, although it's unclear if Schönbein made this observation.

1880: Trouble in Tokyo! There's been a burglary, and an innocent man has been blamed for the heist! In steps Scottish physician and missionary Henry Faulds, who uses fingerprints not only to clear the accused, but also to help bring the actual criminal to justice. Faulds writes about using fingerprints for crime-solving in the science journal *Nature,* and then spends the next couple of decades in a nasty little letter-writing spat with one Sir William Herschel, about which of the two of them thought up the idea first. (Herschel—not to be confused with the other Sir William Herschel, the guy who discovered Uranus—concedes the point, finally, in 1917.)

1892: Sir Francis Galton of Great Britain publishes *Fingerprints,* the first book to codify fingerprint patterns and show how to use them in solving crimes. Meanwhile, in Argentina, police investigator Juan Vucetich develops a fingerprinting classification system based on Galton's work and uses it to accuse a mother of murdering her two sons and then slitting her own throat to make it look like the work of someone else. Seems she left bloody fingerprints on a doorpost. That'll teach her.

THE MURDEROUS EYES OF LOGTOWN

Today, Logtown is an overgrown ghost town near Jacksonville, Oregon. Back in 1861 it was a thriving mining town. But then tragedy struck. Mary Hinkle and her two daughters, aged 6 and 16, were killed in a fire. Right away, the locals suspected that this was more than an accident— it was a triple murder. The motive: a horde of gold that, rumor had it, was hidden somewhere in Hinkle's cabin.

During the investigation, a young photographer told police that the last thing a person sees before death leaves an image on their retinas. With photography in its infancy, the idea wasn't so uncanny. So the photographer set up his gear and took photos of the dead woman's eyes. When the plates were processed . . . there was no image of a killer. (No one was ever formally charged for the crime.)

That young man, by the way, was a Swiss emigrant named Peter Britt, who would go on to become one of Oregon's most celebrated citizens. He not only started the grape industry in the Rogue Valley, but he was also the first person to photograph what is now Crater Lake National Park. Today, the Britt Music Festival carries on his name. (Irony alert: no cameras allowed in the venue.)

Facebook Felons

DEAD WRONG

FRIEND: Mark Musarella, 46, of Staten Island, New York

STORY: Musarella was an emergency medical technician with the Richmond University Medical Center. When he was called to an apartment where a 26-year-old woman had been murdered, he took a photo of the dead body with his cell phone . . . and posted the photo to his Facebook page.

BUSTED! One of Musarella's friends saw the photo and called the hospital where he worked. He was immediately fired, then arrested. Musarella—a former highly decorated NYPD detective—also lost his EMT license.

FACEBOOK CROOK

FRIEND: Paul Franco, 38, of Queens, New York

STORY: In February 2010, Franco hacked the Facebook account of his ex-girlfriend, Jessica Zamora-Anderson. Then he changed her password and held the account hostage, demanding hundreds of dollars for its return. Zamora-Anderson had met Franco 16 months earlier . . . on Facebook. They started dating, and she eventually found out that he wasn't a teacher, but continued dating him because he claimed he had a tape of them having sex and said he'd put it on the Internet if she left him.

BUSTED! Franco was arrested, and Zamora-Anderson got her Facebook account back. (It turns out Franco didn't have a sex tape.)

So Sue Me Then

THE PLAINTIFFS: The Cherry Sisters, an Iowa singing group
THE DEFENDANT: The *Des Moines Register*
THE LAWSUIT: A landmark libel case. At the turn of the century, the *Register* ran a scathing review of the Cherry Sisters' act. Their reporter wrote that "their long, skinny arms, equipped with talons at the extremities . . . waved frantically at the suffering audience. The mouths of their rancid features opened like caverns, and sounds like the wailing of damned souls issued therefrom." Outraged and humiliated, the singers sued for libel.
THE VERDICT: The judge asked the sisters to perform their act for him in court . . . and then ruled in favor of the newspaper.

THE PLAINTIFF: Robert Kropinski, a 36-year-old Philadelphia real-estate manager
THE DEFENDANT: The Transcendental Meditation Society and the guru Maharishi Mahesh Yogi
THE LAWSUIT: Kropinski worked with TM groups for 11 years, but he finally sued them because "he was never able to achieve the 'perfect state of life' they promised, and suffered psychological disorders as a result. One broken agreement: he had been told he would be taught to 'fly' through self-levitation, but he learned only to 'hop with the legs folded in the lotus position.'"
THE VERDICT: A US district court jury in Washington, DC, awarded him nearly $138,000 in damages.

The Disappearance of Judge Crater

Who: Judge Joseph Crater

Claim to Fame: Newly appointed justice of the New York Supreme Court and a potential appointee to the US Supreme Court

Disappearance: Crater and his wife were vacationing in Maine on August 3, 1930, when he received a phone call from New York City. Clearly disturbed, he announced to her that he had to go "straighten those fellows out." Then he left. Nine days later, his wife notified the police, and a massive manhunt began.

What Happened: Police searched Crater's apartment and found nothing suspicious. But as the investigation continued, police—and the public—were astonished to see Crater's carefully constructed facade unravel. It turned out that he'd kept a number of mistresses and had been seen on the town with showgirls. More surprising was his involvement in graft, fraud, and political payoffs. It also seemed as though he'd be implicated in the Ewald scandal, which involved paying for a city appointment. There was even evidence that Crater had paid for his own appointment to the bench. Some were sure he was murdered by gangster associates. Others—noting that the judge had removed files containing potentially incriminating evidence from his office just before he disappeared—speculated that political cronies had killed him to shut him up. Maybe the judge had committed suicide rather than watch his career crumble because of scandal. Whatever happened, it was assumed Crater was dead.

Postmortem: Crater's wife suffered a nervous breakdown and didn't return to their New York apartment until January 1931. There, she found an envelope in the top drawer of her dresser. It contained $6,690 in cash, the judge's will, written five years before (leaving his entire estate to her), and a three-page penciled note that listed everyone who owed the judge money. It closed with the words, "Am very weary. Love, Joe." The police had searched the apartment thoroughly, and had kept a 24-hour guard on it since the disappearance—so no one could imagine how or when the envelope had gotten there. Another possibility: Crater had intentionally disappeared. In July 1937, Crater was declared legally dead, and his wife collected on his life insurance. By then, New York's police commissioner believed that "Crater's disappearance was premeditated."

During the Middle Ages, murdering a traveling musician was not considered a serious crime.

Irony in the Court

- A 1986 court case did not go well for the Otis Elevator Company. It might have had something to do with the fact that the jury—on their way to hear the case—got stuck for 20 minutes in an Otis elevator.

- A similar thing happened to the Pacific Gas & Electric Company in 2000. While on trial for "failure to trim vegetation around power lines," a branch fell off a tree and knocked out power to the courthouse.

- In 1992 the US Postal Service was defending itself against an unemployment discrimination lawsuit. In order to proceed, the defense had to mail a list of expert witnesses from Washington, DC, to Dayton, Ohio. The list was sent via the USPS's Overnight Express Mail delivery service, but did not arrive in Dayton for ten days.

- A production company won a $1.8 million judgment against a former employee accused of stealing the concept for a television game show. Name of the stolen show: *Anything for Money*.

CANADIAN ON THE ROCK

The prisoner who spent the most time in the notorious prison on Alcatraz Island in the San Francisco Bay was a Canadian. Alvin "Old Creepy" Karpis was born in Montreal in 1908. By his 10th birthday, he'd fallen in with a bad crowd that corrupted his morals. First arrested for burglary in 1926, Old Creepy got hired into an entry-level position in the murderous Barker Gang and quickly worked his way up the ladder to an upper management position, increasing gang profits by innovating a successful strategy of kidnapping industrialists for ransom. Victims included William Hamm Jr. of the Hamm's Brewing Company (netting $100,000, the equivalent of $1.5 million today) and Edward Bremer, president of a Minnesota bank ($200,000 or $3 million today). As proof of his commitment to the organization, Karpis had his fingerprints surgically removed so he couldn't be traced easily.

United States bureaucrats caught him anyway and arrested him in 1936, sending him briefly to Leavenworth prison in Kansas, and finally to Alcatraz. When Alcatraz closed in 1962, Karpis was transferred to McNeil Island Penitentiary in Washington, where he taught a young Charles Manson (whom Karpis called "lazy and shiftless") how to play guitar. In 1969 he was deported to Canada. He died in 1979.

The Rampart Scandal

THE PERPS: Dozens of Los Angeles police officers

THE STORY: Rafael Perez was an officer with the LAPD's Rampart Division. He was also a member of Community Resources Against Street Hoodlums, or CRASH—an elite LAPD anti-gang unit. In 1998, Perez was arrested for stealing six pounds of cocaine from an evidence room. He was offered a five-year sentence and immunity . . . in exchange for testimony against fellow officers. Perez agreed, and gave more than 4,000 pages of testimony implicating dozens of his fellow CRASH officers in drug deals, murder, robbery (even a bank robbery), perjury, falsification of police reports, extortion, and more.

OUTCOME: Of the 70 officers Perez implicated, seven resigned, twelve were suspended, and five were fired. Only seven were tried on criminal charges, and just three of those were convicted—and their convictions were later overturned. But the city of Los Angeles ended up paying over $125 million to settle more than 140 civil suits against the city of Los Angeles. In 2000 the CRASH unit was closed down for good.

EXTRA: The investigation found that at least three CRASH officers were on the payroll of hip-hop mogul Marion "Suge" Knight, and his label, Death Row Records. In 2007 Perez and two other Rampart officers were named in a wrongful death lawsuit, alleging that they had carried out the drive-by murder of rapper Notorious B.I.G. That lawsuit was dismissed in 2010. (The murder of Notorious B.I.G. remains unsolved.)

IS THAT SPAGHETTI SAUCE ON YOUR SHIRT?

In the world of organized crime, you can't trust no one.

BACKGROUND: Joe "the Boss" Masseria was an old-line Sicilian mob boss whose ultimate goal was to become head of the Mafia in New York. Not sharing Masseria's dream, though, were younger "family" members Lucky Luciano and Vito Genovese. They wanted him out of the picture, as did powerful mobsters Lepke Buchalter and Owney Madden. When another rival mafioso, Salvatore Maranzano, began to encroach on Masseria's businesses, Joe the Boss fought back. That was the beginning of a power struggle that came to be known as the Castellammarese War, during which more than 60 men (on both sides) were killed. Luciano and Genovese secretly contacted Maranzano and offered him a deal: If he'd end the bloodshed, they'd whack Masseria. Maranzano agreed.

THE PLACE: On April 15, 1931, Luciano invited Joe the Boss to the Nuova Villa Tammaro restaurant, a cheap "spaghetti house" in Coney Island. They ate, played some cards, and then Luciano went to the bathroom.

THE HIT: While Luciano was in the bathroom, two unknown men strolled into the restaurant, fired 20 shots at Masseria, and strolled out again. Luciano took over Masseria's crime family. The Nuova Villa Tammaro's owner, an Italian immigrant named Gerardo Scarpato, shut down the restaurant and moved back to Italy. Six months later he returned to New York and was murdered. No one was ever convicted.

Benched!

Judge not, lest ye be judged.

THE HONORABLE A. HITLER PRESIDING

Douglas County judge Richard Jones was suspended by the Nebraska Supreme Court after an investigation into 17 complaints concerning his conduct. Judge Jones had taken to signing court documents with names like A. Hitler and Snow White, and setting bail amounts in imaginary currencies. He was also accused of urinating on courthouse carpets, making an anonymous death threat against another judge (he says it was a "prank that went wrong"), and throwing firecrackers into the same judge's office. Judge Jones contested a number of the charges but admitted he threw the firecrackers. "I was venting," he explained.

WHERE'S YOUR LAWYER?

Dogged by a state investigation into claims that he was abusive to defendants, Judge Fred Heene announced that he would not seek reelection. An example of Judge Heene's conduct: A woman convicted of a traffic violation asked for more time to complete her community service because she'd been bedridden—on doctor's orders—during the final weeks of her pregnancy. The judge denied her request and sentenced her to 44 days in jail. When she protested that she had a seven-day-old baby at home, the judge replied, "Ma'am, you should have thought about that a long time ago."

THE BLACK PANTIES BANDIT STRIKES AGAIN

There are some odd and outlandish thieves out there.
Like the ones dressed up . . .

. . . **AS PRIESTS:** Police in Serbia said three men disguised as Orthodox Christian priests, complete with fake beards and ankle-length cossacks, entered a bank, gave the traditional "Christ is born" greeting, then pulled shotguns out of their robes. They stole more than $300,000.

. . . **AS COPS:** On the night of March 18, 1990, two men disguised as cops knocked on the door of the prestigious Isabella Stewart Gardner Museum in Boston. The security guards on duty let them in and were immediately overpowered by the thieves. They made off with several paintings—a Vermeer, a Manet, and three Rembrandts, among other masterpieces—worth about $300 million. It still ranks as the largest art theft in US history and has never been solved.

. . . **AS A PAIR OF UNDERWEAR:** Police in Canada announced in 2004 that they had finally caught the "Black Panties Bandit," who had robbed at least five convenience stores while wearing a black pair of women's underwear over his face as a disguise.

Police Blotter: Cheeseburger Edition

On February 21, 2012, a man attempted to trick the employees of a Denny's restaurant in Madison, Wisconsin. This is the actual police report describing the incident.

INCIDENT: Disturbance

DATE: 02/21/2012 - 4:32 p.m.

ARRESTED: James B. Summers, age 52, Madison. Mr. Summers was arrested for Fraud, Disorderly Conduct, Possession of Drug Paraphernalia, and Possession of an Electric Weapon.

VICTIM: Female, age 38, Madison

DETAILS: He never announced he was one of the pros from Dover, but the briefcase-toting gentleman wearing a maroon tie and long black trench coat was quite clear: he had been sent by corporate. He claimed he was the new general manager, that he had worked for the restaurant chain for 30 years, and that he was starting his new job—right now. She was in the process of counting the day's receipts at the Denny's on Thierer Road. She had heard nothing from corporate about a new general manager.

He said it was final and he was going to commence his duties. It was at this point that the manager began making calls up the chain. She was able to reach the man in charge

of all hiring at her location. By this time the new "GM" had left the office, but not the restaurant, and she had shut the office door in order to carry out this important, private conversation.

While on the phone, she waved off kitchen staff as they rapped on her door, trying to get her attention. She was not to be interrupted while talking with corporate. What the staff wanted her to know was that the new "GM" was cooking a cheeseburger and fries for himself and had gotten himself a soda. He was in the midst of dining when she let him know that the gig was up: she had talked with corporate, and he was no new hire. The manager called 911. When the responding officer arrived, he saw the suspect walking away from the restaurant. Upon contact, he told the officer there was a misunderstanding, that he was the new GM, but there must have been a paperwork goof-up.

The manager prevailed and the man was arrested. The officer found, beneath the man's trench coat and suit jacket, that he was packing a stun gun on his belt. The officer asked if the suspect had a concealed carry permit. The man replied, "It's in the pipeline." He was cooperative with the officer, but as he was being led from the restaurant, he yelled out to those eating: "This is why you don't dine and dash, kiddies."

DUMB CROOKS OF THE OLD WEST

In the town of Coffeyville, Kansas, in 1890, Bob, Emmett, and Gratton Dalton, along with two other men, formed a gang of outlaws. They wanted a big payoff and the fame that goes with it—and that could only come from a legendary bank heist. They planned it all out . . . all wrong:

1. The Daltons aimed to rob two banks at once: Two men would rob the First National Bank, while the other three hit Condon & Co. across the street. They thought they'd get double the loot, but they only doubled their chances of getting caught.

2. Instead of traveling to another town where no one knew them, they chose Coffeyville—where everyone knew them.

3. The street in front of the banks was being repaired the day of the heist. They could have postponed it, but went ahead anyway. They had to hitch their horses a block away, making a getaway that much more difficult.

4. Smart: they wore disguises. Dumb:
   the disguises were wispy stage mustaches
   and goatees.

The townsfolk saw the Dalton boys coming and armed themselves. They did get $20,000 from First National, but came up empty at the other bank. When they emerged, an angry mob was waiting for them in the street. A hail of bullets followed, killing every member except Emmett Dalton, who went to prison. He emerged from the penitentiary to discover that the Dalton Gang's story had been immortalized, but not as legendary outlaws . . . only as hapless screw-ups.

Felonious Fact

In the early 1990s, Pablo Escobar became the richest (known) criminal in the world. He was making nearly $1 million per day providing the United States with 80% of its cocaine.

BIG FAKERS

ARM WRESTLER. In 2007 a professional arm wrestler named Arsen Liliev tried to qualify for a lower (and easier) weight class at a European tournament by sending a look-alike to the weigh-in. Liliev was caught when officials noticed that his look-alike didn't look anything like him.

1950S SINGING GROUP. In July 2007, Florida passed a law that made it a crime to be a fake band. Singing groups from the 1950s and 1960s were touring the casino- and elderly-heavy state, but people who paid to see "The Drifters" were really watching a band with one or two replacement members and a bunch of hired singers. The legislation was introduced by Jon "Bowzer" Bauman, of the group Sha Na Na (which made a career of singing other people's hits).

NUN. Mollie Brusstar, a secretary at the Catholic Diocese of Arlington, Virginia, put fake names on her employer's payroll and issued checks to herself. Then she used the money to fly to another state (Utah), where she charged dental work and cosmetic surgery to the diocese. Why would doctors allow Brusstar to charge their services to the church? She was dressed as a nun.

Dismembered Hand Grenade

In October 2017, a 26-year-old Portland, Oregon, man named Jason Schaefer caught the attention of police after purchasing bomb-making materials. When a federal officer confronted him at a probation meeting, Schaefer ran to his SUV and drove home, only to find more feds waiting for him, so he fled again, this time with several squad cars in pursuit. When they finally caught up with Schaefer and surrounded his vehicle, he held up a lighter and a small bomb, and declared, "We're all f***ing dying today!" Then he detonated the device, which caused (according to the police affidavit) a federal officer to be struck by glass "and by the flesh from Schaefer's mangled left hand." So, in addition to the explosives and evading police charges, Schaefer was also hit with an assault charge.

COP TALK

A "yard bird" is suspect who's caught while hiding in bushes.

DOIN' TIME . . . AND A LOT OF IT

The stories behind some of the longest-recorded prison sentences ever served in modern history.

PAUL GEIDEL

The Crime: On July 26, 1911, Geidel, 17, broke into the hotel room of 73-year-old William H. Jackson. Geidel, who had been living on his own since the age of 14, had worked in the hotel as a bellhop, but had recently been fired. Rumor had it that Jackson, a retired Wall Street broker, kept a lot of cash in his room. Geidel jumped the older man while he slept, and suffocated him—possibly unintentionally—with a chloroform-soaked rag. It turned out the rumor was wrong: Geidel fled with just $7. He was arrested 15 hours later.

The Time: Geidel received a prison sentence of 20 years to life. In 1974, after almost 69 years in prison, Geidel was finally granted parole. Only problem: he didn't want to go. He was eventually convinced to leave in 1980, at age 86. It remains the longest time served in US prison history.

WILLIAM HEIRENS

The Crime: In 1945 two women were murdered in Chicago. At the scene of the second crime, the killer wrote a message on a wall in lipstick: "For heaven's sake, catch me before I kill more. I cannot control myself," leading

the press to dub him the "Lipstick Killer." Then, in 1946, a six-year-old Chicago girl was killed and dismembered. Heirens, just 17, was arrested, and confessed to the crimes.

The Time: Heirens was sentenced to three consecutive life terms. He died on March 5, 2012, at the age of 83, in the 65th year of his sentence. (During his time in prison, Heirens became the first Illinois prison inmate to earn a four-year college degree.)

JOHN STRAFFEN

The Crime: Over the course of three weeks in July and August 1951, the 21-year-old Straffen strangled two girls, aged six and nine, in Bath, England. He had been in and out of trouble (and in and out of institutions for the "mentally defective") since he was ten, but was nonetheless allowed to move about on his own at the time he killed the girls. Straffen was deemed unfit for trial and sent to a high-security asylum for a term to be determined by psychiatrists. In 1952 Straffen escaped the asylum by climbing a fence. His escape was noted almost immediately, and he was recaptured within four hours—but in those four hours he managed to strangle a third girl to death, this one just five years old.

The Time: Straffen was tried, convicted, and sentenced to death. A British official recommended to Queen Elizabeth II that she give Straffen, who was clearly mentally ill, a reprieve from the death penalty. The queen agreed, and Straffen's sentence became life with no chance of parole. He died on November 19, 2007, at the age of 77. He had served 55 years in prison.

SOLD!

We all gotta make a living . . .

COLLECTIBLE: Fingernails and a cut-up Christmas card from a convicted murderer

STORY: Southern California isn't all palm trees and sunshine. It was also the stomping grounds for 10 percent of the world's known serial killers during the 20th century. Among them were Lawrence Bittaker and Roy Norris, who met in prison in San Luis Obispo in the 1970s and, after their release, bought a windowless van they nicknamed "Murder Mack". During the summer of 1979, they cruised beaches, photographing and picking up girls. They raped and murdered at least five. Norris eventually testified against Bittaker for a sentence of 45-years-to-life—Bittaker got the death penalty.

In the 1970s, collectors had begun seeking out "murderabilia," souvenirs from heinous crimes and killers. Bittaker sold his prison-issued socks, but Norris hoped to really cash in. While imprisoned, he clipped his fingernails and taped them to a piece of a cut-up Christmas card. He authenticated the card with a long, handwritten note, his signature, and his fingerprint. It's unclear who or how many people the card belonged to over the years, but it turned up on eBay in 1999.

SELLING PRICE: The item got just one bid . . . for $9.99.

CAPTIAL(IZING) CRIME

Turning a profit on other peoples' crimes.

Background: In 1974 a man named Ronald DeFeo murdered his parents and four siblings as they slept in their home in Amityville, New York. He was convicted of the crimes and sentenced to six consecutive life sentences in prison. The "murder house" was later sold for a song to a struggling couple named George and Kathy Lutz, who moved in a week before Christmas in 1975. Twenty-eight days later, they moved out, claiming the house was haunted and that the evil spirits that had driven them away also probably caused DeFeo to murder his entire family. Their story inspired the best-selling 1977 book *The Amityville Horror,* and then the hit film that premiered in 1979.

Exposed: In 1979 Ronald DeFeo's defense attorney, William Weber, filed a lawsuit against the Lutzes, accusing them of fraud and breach of contract, claiming that they reneged on an agreement to collaborate with Weber on the book. So where did the haunted house story come from? In an interview with the Associated Press, Weber admitted that he and the Lutzes had "concocted the horror story scam over many bottles of wine."

The Bigfoot of Crime

He hijacked an airplane, stole a small fortune, then parachuted out of sight . . . and straight into legend.

DAREDEVIL

In 1971 a man wearing a plain dark suit, white shirt, black tie, and sunglasses approached the Northwest Orient Airlines ticket counter in Portland, Oregon. He paid $20 in cash for a one-way ticket to Seattle on flight 305. Once the 727 was airborne, the man summoned the flight attendant, introduced himself as "Dan Cooper," and handed her a note. It said he had a bomb and would blow up the plane if they didn't meet his demands. He wanted two parachutes and $200,000 in $20 bills. When the plane landed, Cooper kept the pilot and crew hostage, but let the passengers off in exchange for the ransom. Then, he ordered the pilot to take off for Mexico with these instructions: keep the landing gear down, and the flight speed under 170 mph. Twenty-five miles northeast of Portland, Cooper strapped on a parachute, tied the money to his waist, and jumped out of the plane. He was never seen again.

VANISHED

In the ensuing investigation, the FBI questioned a man named Daniel B. Cooper. Although never a serious suspect, the FBI reported that they'd interrogated "D. B. Cooper." Those initials became forever linked with the skyjacker.

The FBI manhunt that followed was unprecedented in scope and intensity. Every inch of ground in the vicinity of the purported landing site was searched for eighteen days. It was a humbling moment when, after weeks of tracking down leads, the FBI admitted that they hadn't found anything. A complete dead end. One frustrated FBI agent referred to Cooper as the "Bigfoot of Crime" because there was no proof of his existence anywhere. If Cooper survived, he'd pulled off the crime of the century.

THE LEGEND

The hijacking caught the public's imagination. Media reports raved about the audacity of the crime and the calm, competent way Cooper carried it out. According to the flight attendants, Cooper was polite throughout the ordeal, even requesting that meals be delivered to the crew while they were in Seattle, waiting for the ransom money to be delivered. He became a folk hero, a modern-day Jesse James. Many books, mostly by former FBI agents, provided theories about what happened to him. He was living the high life on a beach in Mexico. He'd slipped back into his former life somewhere in the States, undetected and unnoticed. On February 13, 1980, a family picnicking on the Columbia River, 30 miles west of Cooper's landing area, found three bundles of disintegrating $20 bills ($5,800 total). The serial numbers were traced to the ransom. The rest of the cash—and the man behind the legend—was never found.

FALSE ALARM

GIMME A NINE . . . GIMME A ONE . . .

In 1999 a 911 dispatcher in Arkansas received a call, but there was nobody on the line—all she could hear was a football game. She hung up and called the number back, but nobody answered. A short time later it happened again, and again, nobody on the line. A few minutes later it happened again . . . and again . . . and again. Dispatchers were called 35 times before police finally traced the call . . . to a football fan who had his cell phone set to speed-dial 911. It was in his pocket and had dialed every time he stood up to cheer.

PIZZA 'N' NUTS

In 2005, 86-year-old Dorothy Densmore of Charlotte, North Carolina, called 911 and complained that a nearby pizza shop refused to deliver pizza to her. The dispatcher advised Densmore that calling 911 for non-emergencies was a crime and hung up. Densmore called back, and kept calling back. She called more than 20 times. An officer was sent out to her home to arrest her . . . but not before being kicked, punched, and bitten on the hand by Densmore. (She had also complained to the dispatcher that someone in the pizza parlor called her a "crazy old coot.")

Not Too Bright

HE BLEW IT

"A Warrensburg man burned himself and is facing criminal charges after he used a lighter to check on his efforts to steal gasoline from a dump truck, causing a fire that destroyed a forklift. Glen Germain, 19, suffered minor burns in the blaze when he lit a lighter to see how full the gas can he was filling had become, sheriff's investigators said. The lighter ignited gas on his hands and in the can; the gas can fire then spread to the forklift, destroying the vehicle. Germain admitted he was responsible for the fire, telling investigators he was trying to see the progress of the siphoning process."

—*Post Star*

QUICKIES

- A couple rushing to make a high school graduation ceremony led police on a high-speed chase that ended when they sped through a train crossing and crashed into a nearby home (no one was hurt). The wrecked car was going to be a surprise present for the graduate.

- A five-time burglar from Detroit found himself back in the can, charged with yet another burglary. How'd they catch him? He had played with some Silly Putty in the home he'd just robbed and left his fingerprints.

The Unsolved Case of the Rainbow Maniac

*The story of one of Brazil's most
notorious unsolved serial killings.*

Thirteen gay men between the ages of 20 and 50 were murdered in Paturis Park in the Brazilian city of Carapicuíba (near São Paulo) between July 2007 and August 2008. Twelve were shot; one was beaten to death. In the neighboring community of Osasco, three other gay men were murdered, and police believe they may all be the victims of the same killer. The killer was dubbed the "Rainbow Maniac" in reference to the rainbow symbol of gay pride, because all the victims are believed to have been gay. Four months after the thirteenth murder, police announced they had arrested Jairo Francisco Franco, a retired São Paulo police officer, after a witness told them he'd seen Franco commit one of the murders on August 19, 2008. Another witness told police that Franco regularly visited the park, seeking gay men. Shortly after Franco's arrest, police inspector Paulo Fortunato told reporters, "We are convinced he is the 'Rainbow Maniac' we have been looking for." However, Franco went to trial in August 2011, and was found not guilty by a jury in a 4–2 decision. Undercover agents now patrol the park at night, and the identity of the Rainbow Maniac remains unknown.

A Case for DNA

*Ever wonder when and how DNA
became a part of forensic science?*

In 1986 Barry Scheck and Peter Neufeld were sent a case
file regarding a man in a New York prison. Scheck and
Neufeld had attended law school in the late 1960s and were
steeped in the social justice movements that defined the
era. As young lawyers in the 1970s, they'd cut their teeth
as public defenders in the South Bronx, where they had
worked on the most desperate cases—similar to the one
they'd just been handed.

Marion Coakley, 30, had been convicted of a violent
robbery, kidnapping, and rape that had taken place in a
Bronx hotel in 1983. The victim had described her
attacker as a dark-skinned black man with a Jamaican
accent and a short Afro. She later picked Coakley—a
light-skinned black man with no Jamaican accent
and no Afro—out of a lineup. Seventeen people,
including a priest, said they were with Coakley at a
church meeting miles from the scene of the crime at
the time it occurred. He was convicted anyway.

A NEW TECHNOLOGY

Scheck and Neufeld agreed to look into the file. A blood
expert they worked with, Robert Shaler, told them this was
a good case to test out an emerging technology called "DNA

testing." That DNA could be used to identify individuals had been discovered only a few years earlier, and it had never been used in a criminal case in the United States. It was being used for the first time in a case in England.

THE VERDICT

Scheck and Neufeld tried to use DNA testing to get Coakley's conviction overturned. It didn't work: not enough DNA could be extracted from the evidence to identify the attacker. Fortunately, they were still able to get Coakley's conviction overturned by proving his innocence via other evidence, including a bloody palm print on the rearview mirror of the victim's car. Coakley was released after serving two years. Though the use of the technology hadn't been successful, Scheck and Neufeld knew that it was a game changer. For the next couple of years, both law enforcement and science worked to figure out how DNA testing was going to fit into the world of forensics. Fingerprinting took decades to be integrated into forensic science. If DNA testing was going be accepted, it would have to be understandable to investigators, judges, and juries. Scheck and Neufeld became closely involved with this process. They are credited with integrating DNA testing as a standard part of forensics—quickly and thoroughly. In 1992 Scheck and Neufeld went on to found the Innocence Project—an organization that provides legal representation for wrongfully convicted people.

MORE LAWYERS ON LAWYERS

Quotes from the world's most famous lawyers.

"The ideal client is the very wealthy man in very great trouble."

—John Sterling

"I'm not an ambulance chaser. I'm usually there before the ambulance."

—Melvin Belli

"This is New York, and there's no law against being annoying."

—William Kunstler

"The court of last resort is no longer the Supreme Court. It's *Nightline*."

—Alan Dershowitz

"The 'adversary system' is based on the notion that if one side overstates his idea of the truth and the other side overstates his idea of the truth, then the truth will come out . . . Why can't we all just tell the truth?"

—David Zapp

"I bring out the worst in my enemies and that's how I get them to defeat themselves."

—Roy Cohn

MONEY TO BURN

Destroying currency is a crime. Destroying £1 million (approximately 1.35 million US dollars) in the name of art is a strange crime. Why would someone burn that much cash? Don't ask Bill Drummond or Jimmy Cauty, two former pop stars turned performance artists who pulled the stunt in 1994. They're still not sure. The duo, known as the K Foundation, decided to burn their profits from their defunct music career in the name of art. A year later, they released a film called *Watch the K Foundation Burn a Million Quid*. It consisted of 67 minutes of the artists tossing £50 notes into a fire. After each screening, there would be a Q&A session . . . in which Drummond and Cauty would ask the audience questions. The tour received mixed reviews. Apparently, wantonly destroying cash angers a lot of people. Despite recording their strange crime, the men were never charged. And they still can't sum up their exact motivation. "I wish I could explain why I did it so people would understand," lamented Drummond. "It's a hard one to explain to your kids, and it doesn't get any easier."

You Are Feeling Verrry Generous

Police in the eastern European nation of Moldova reported in 2005 that they were on the lookout for a robber who hypnotized bank clerks. The hypno-thief was identified as 49-year-old Vladimir Kozak, a trained hypnotist from Russia. Police said Kozak would start a conversation with a teller, make eye contact, and put the teller into a hypnotic trance. He would then have the teller hand over all the money in the till. Kozak's total haul: nearly $40,000 (one clerk in the city of Chisinau reportedly handed over more than $12,000). Police put wanted posters with Kozak's face around the nation . . . but warned bank clerks not to make eye contact with it.

WANNABE DEXTER

According to amateur filmmaker Mark Twitchell's Facebook profile, "Mark has way too much in common with Dexter Morgan." Who's Dexter Morgan? He's the fictional lead character on the television show *Dexter*, about a crime-scene investigator (Michael C. Hall) who moonlights as a vigilante who traps and murders rapists and serial killers.

In November 2008, Twitchell, of Edmonton, Alberta, turned one of *Dexter*'s plots into a real-life nightmare. After he answered an online personal ad, pretending to be a young woman, Twitchell lured 38-year-old Johnny Altinger to his house. Except Altinger wasn't a serial killer; he was just a man looking for a date. His body was never found, but police identified enough evidence in Twitchell's garage—including a script to a "show" that detailed his evil plot—to charge him with first-degree murder. Twitchell was sentenced to life in prison.

WESTFIELD'S MURDER MYSTERY

A cold case that grabbed national attention . . . twice.

When the Westfield New Jersey Police Department received a call to check out the List family's Victorian mansion on Hillside Avenue, they figured it would be a routine call. The Lists were supposedly away visiting a sick relative, but neighbors and friends had grown concerned. For a month, there'd been no communication from anyone in the family. Even though all the lights were on, there were no obvious signs of people in the house.

But when the police entered the residence through an unlocked window, they were in for a bizarre discovery. Inside the cold mansion, loud organ music played over an intercom system. Officers went into the mansion's vast ballroom, where they discovered four bodies. The victims were Helen List and her three teenaged children, Patty, John Jr., and Fredrick. Upstairs, Helen's mother-in-law, Alma List, was found dead in her attic apartment. But the man of the house was nowhere to be found.

VANISHED!

Though police and FBI immediately set up an intensive search for John List, one week after the bodies were discovered the authorities admitted that the trail was cold. Having told everyone that the family was leaving town, List delayed the discovery of the bodies for 28 days. Though

police didn't then know it, List had moved to Denver, Colorado, and established a new identity with a phony Social Security number and the alias Robert P. Clark.

DOWN A COLD TRAIL

In 1989, 18 years later, *America's Most Wanted* decided to run an episode that featured the List case. The problem was figuring out what he might look like 20 years later. They turned to forensic sculptor Frank Bender, asking him to make an "age-progression bust" of 64-year-old John List. When the bust was televised on *America's Most Wanted,* friends of a man called Bob Clark were astounded to see how much he resembled the murderer from New Jersey. The show brought in a tip that Bob Clark had moved from Colorado to Virginia.

THE NATION WATCHES

List was extradited to New Jersey for trial. A jury found List guilty and he was sentenced to life in prison.

THE TIFFANY SOLUTION

In a mysterious act of suspected arson, the List home burned down nine months after the murders. The fire that demolished the house also destroyed the ballroom's Tiffany stained-glass ceiling—a signed original that was worth at least $100,000 in 1971. Ironically, had List understood its value, he could have sold the magnificent ceiling, kept his house, and solved his financial problems with cash left over to put in the bank.

Head Case

Talk about a close call.

After a domestic-violence conviction in April 2009, Donald Sexton was ordered to stay away from his wife, Tammy, for six months. But a week into the restraining order, he went to her rural Mississippi home in the middle of the night, intending to murder her. As Tammy Sexton lay in bed, Donald shot her in the head, and then went outside and shot himself. He died instantly; Tammy Sexton, however, did not. When police arrived, she was conscious and had a rag around her head and was drinking a cup of tea. A medical examination at the University of Alabama revealed that the .38-caliber bullet had somehow entered Tammy's forehead and exited through the back of her head, passing through the lobes of her brain without leaving any damage whatsoever. The sheriff investigating the case, Mike Bryd, expressed his own amazement at the unlikeliness of such an occurrence. "You just don't hear of something like this. Somebody gets shot in the head and they're dead."

Criminal Headlines

Calling the grammar cops: it's these headline writers who should have been brought up on charges.

Juvenile Court to Try Shooting Defendant

MAN ROBS, THEN KILLS HIMSELF

NJ Judge to Rule on Nude Beach

Mayor Says DC Is Safe Except for Murders

Man, Shot Twice in Head, Gets Mad
Deadline Passes for Striking Police

COCKROACH SLAIN, HUSBAND BADLY HURT

MAN SHOOTS NEIGHBOR WITH MACHETE

32 Ignorant Enough to Serve on North Jury

Hostage Taker Kills Self; Police Shoot Each Other

POTENTIAL WITNESS TO MURDER DRUNK

Prosecutor Releases Probe into Undersheriff

BOMB HIT BY LIBRARY

ROBBER HOLDS UP ALBERT'S HOSIERY

Multiple Personality Rapist Sentenced to Two Life Terms

STOLEN PAINTING FOUND BY TREE

MAN STRUCK BY LIGHTNING FACES BATTERY CHARGES

Man Found Dead in Cemetery

BAR TRYING TO HELP ALCOHOLIC LAWYERS

Defendant's Speech Ends in Long Sentence

42 Percent of All Murdered Women Are Killed by the Same Man

Silent Teamster Gets Cruel Punishment: Lawyer

CRACK FOUND IN MAN'S BUTTOCKS

Two Convicts Evade Noose, Jury Hung

"It's interesting that these themes of crime
and political corruption are always relevant."
—**Martin Scorsese**

Dumb Crime

COULDN'T BUY A CLUE

A man walked into a gas station with a knife and demanded that the attendant give him all the money in the cash register. The attendant replied that he had to buy something before she could open the register. The confused robber told her that he had no money, so he couldn't buy anything. The clever attendant told him that she was very sorry, but there was nothing she could do— she had to follow the rules. And the would-be crook left . . . empty-handed.

LOVESICK LOSER

While robbing a bank, the thief fell head-over-heels in love with the teller he was robbing. He got away, but he was so smitten that he actually called her, *at the bank* . . . to ask for a date! She talked to him—but not to make a date. She kept him on the line long enough for the police to trace the call.

HELLO, MY NAME IS . . .

In Long Beach, California, several employees of a large aerospace company got the bright idea to rob a bank on their lunch hour. They had it all planned out—except for one thing: they forgot to remove their company ID tags while they were robbing the bank.

HEY, THAT'S A FAKE . . .

. . . BIG SPENDER. One night in 2007, Damon Armagost visited Deja Vu, a "gentlemen's club" in Nashville, Tennessee, where he lavishly tipped the dancers. The manager grew suspicious and called police, who discovered the money was fake—Armagost had downloaded an image of a $100 bill and printed out a stack on his home printer.

. . . TSAR. Russian tsar Ivan the Terrible died in 1584 (historians believe he was the victim of poisoning). His youngest son, Dmitriy Ivanovich, disappeared. Three men came forward in 1605, all claiming to be Dmitriy and also claiming a right to the throne. Grigory Otrepyev was determined to be the real one, and ruled as tsar from July 1605 until he was murdered in May 1606—not because he was a fraud (which wasn't discovered until much later) but because he was believed to be the son of Ivan the Terrible.

. . . BASEBALL PLAYER. In 2006 a Florida chiropractor named Rhonda Schroeder began dating New York Mets pitcher Pedro Martinez. They met through a patient of Schroeder's named Shirley Gordon. When Martinez kept encouraging his new girlfriend to give Gordon gifts of hundreds of thousands of dollars, Schroeder realized that her boyfriend probably wasn't the real Pedro Martinez and called the cops. He wasn't. And Gordon was already wanted by police on identity-theft charges.

Why the Juice Wasn't Loose

In 1995 NFL Hall-of-Famer O. J. Simpson was found not guilty of murdering his ex-wife, Nicole Brown Simpson, and her friend Ronald Goldman. Simpson may have been acquitted, but the court of public opinion found him guilty. Simpson's career as an actor and pitchman was over. In a 1997 civil suit brought by Goldman's family, Simpson was found liable in the deaths and ordered to pay Goldman's family $33.5 million.

Initially, Simpson managed to avoid paying because California law protected his NFL pension. But the Goldmans didn't back down, and in 1999, Simpson auctioned off his Heisman Trophy and other memorabilia to pay the Goldmans $500,000. To avoid paying more (and to escape a back-taxes bill in excess of $1 million), Simpson moved to Florida to protect his estate.

In December 2001, FBI agents searched his Florida home after receiving a tip that he was involved in a drug-trafficking ring. Authorities didn't find any narcotics on the premises, but they did discover that O. J. was pirating cable, leading to tens of thousands of dollars in fines and legal fees.

A year later, Simpson was caught speeding a 30-foot powerboat through a wildlife-protection zone and got hit

with another fine. But despite his various run-ins with the law, he was still a free man.

Then, on the night of September 13, 2007, Simpson and a group of men burst into Bruce Fromong's room at the Palace Station Hotel and Casino in Las Vegas. Simpson was convinced that Fromong, a sports memorabilia dealer, had stolen some of his NFL mementos. Simpson and the group fled the scene after nabbing several items. The following day, he told a *Los Angeles Times* reporter that he wasn't a suspect. "I'm O. J. Simpson. How am I going to think that I'm going to rob somebody and get away with it?" He also contrarily quipped, "I thought what happens in Las Vegas stays in Las Vegas."

Unfortunately for Simpson, one of his accomplices brought a tape recorder along to the crime. The former NFL star was arrested a few days later on charges that included robbery and conspiracy. Simpson was found guilty on all charges and was sentenced to prison in December 2008. The presiding judge offered him little leniency and demanded that eight of the ten counts run concurrently for a maximum sentence of 33 years. Simpson served 9 years in prison and was released in late 2017.

The villain in *Scream* was based on a Florida serial killer known as "the Gainesville Ripper."

The Gorilla Killer

*The unknown origins of this killer's nickname
have led to some wild stories. No gorillas were
harmed in the writing of this article.*

Between February 1926 and June 1927, Earle Leonard
Nelson murdered 22 women, all boardinghouse landladies,
in various locations across the United States and Canada.
He was convicted of two of the murders and executed by
hanging in Winnipeg, Manitoba, in 1928. The exact story
of how he got his nickname appears to have been lost, and
several versions are passed around today. One suggests that
he got the name because of the strength he exhibited in
carrying out his crimes: Nelson strangled all his victims
with his bare hands. (Side note: gorillas are not known to
practice strangulation.) Another story says that he had a
severely receding forehead, large protruding lips, and very
large hands, the combination of which made him look like
a gorilla. And the oddest version: Investigators interviewed
Nelson's aunt during his killing spree, and she told them
that as a young boy, Nelson had been struck by a trolley
and sent into a coma for several days. After he woke up, he
suffered periods of mania, during which he would curl up
his legs and walk around on his hands, making him look,
she said, like a gorilla.

Weird Crime News

In April 2005, 18-year-old Nicholas Buckalew of Morrisville, Vermont, decided that he wanted to make a creative and unusual "bong" (large marijuana pipe). Late one night, Buckalew went to a cemetery, broke into an aboveground tomb, and took the skull from an interred body, along with the eyeglasses and bow tie that were with it. Police said he told friends he was going to bleach the skull and make a pipe out of it. In 2006 Buckalew pleaded guilty to "intentionally removing a tombstone and intentionally carrying away the remains of a human body." He was sentenced to one to seven years in prison.

A BOY'S BEST FRIEND IS HIS MOTHER

ON THE SCREEN: In Robert Bloch's 1959 novel *Psycho* (and in the 1960 Alfred Hitchcock film that starred Anthony Perkins), innkeeper Norman Bates impersonates his dead mother and blames "her" for the crimes he commits.

IN REAL LIFE: In 2003 Thomas Parkin of New York City pretended to be his deceased mother so he could collect her Social Security and benefits. He even wore a wig, sunglasses, and painted nails when he went to the DMV to renew "her" license. In 2009 when police arrested Parkin, he said, "I held my mother when she was dying and breathed in her last breath, so I am my mother."

THE REAL
SCRUFF McGRUFF

Slogan: "Take a Bite out of Crime"

Story: In 1980 the nonprofit National Crime Prevention Council hired ad agency Saatchi & Saatchi to create a kid-friendly mascot and slogan. Copywriter John Keil considered a lion who "roars at crime" and an elephant who "stomps out crime" but finally opted for a dog who "takes a bite out of crime." Inspired by TV's *Columbo*, artists drew the dog as a grizzled gumshoe in a trench coat. The character appeared in public service announcements (Keil provided the voice), urging kids to report *any* crime they witnessed, from bullying to drug dealing. The dog wasn't named until a 1982 contest—a New Orleans police officer suggested McGruff the Crime Dog (runner-up: Sherlock Bones). The NCPC says that 75 percent of American children today recognize and trust McGruff . . . and know the slogan.

Judges Gone Wild

What do you get when you combine a robe,
a gavel, and delusions of grandeur?

JUDGE BREWSKI

While presiding over deliberations in a drunk-driving case, Lakewood, Washington, municipal court judge Ralph H. Baldwin disappeared into his chambers and returned a short time later with a 12-pack of beer. Then he invited the attorneys, jurors, and court staff to "stay for a cool one," but admonished them not to tell anyone. "I'll deny it if you repeat it," he said.

Afterward, he brazenly carried an open container of beer to his car, telling onlookers, "I might as well drink and drive. I do it all the time anyway." Judge Baldwin later admitted that he made the statement but claimed he was joking and that the beer can was empty. "When I thought about it later, I thought, 'Oh, my God, you fool!' " he explained.

BRIBES AND MISDEMEANORS

While running for reelection in 2008, Philadelphia traffic court judge William F. Singletary—also a church deacon—attended a "Blessing of the Bikes" motorcycle club gathering in a Philadelphia park. "If you all can give

me $20," he said over the PA system, "you're going to need me in traffic court, am I right about that? . . . Now you all want me to get there." Video footage of the deacon's attempted bribe soon found its way to YouTube—and then to the authorities. Singletary was charged with four counts of misconduct and found guilty of all four, enough to cost him his judgeship.

WORSHIP ME!

Elizabeth Halverson—a Clark County, Nevada, district court judge—took the bench in January 2007. In her first few months on the job, the state's Judicial Discipline Commission received more than a dozen complaints about her behavior. They alleged that Halverson abused court staff with racial and religious slurs, sexually harassed a bailiff and made him feel like a "houseboy" by assigning him menial personal chores, hired a computer technician to hack into courthouse email accounts, made false statements to the media about three other judges she believed were conspiring against her, fell asleep on the bench during two criminal trials, and ordered a clerk to swear in her husband so that she could question him under oath about whether he'd completed his chores at home. "Do you want to worship me from near or afar?" she reportedly asked one court employee. Six months into her judgeship, Halverson was suspended and charged with 14 counts of judicial misconduct. In 2008 she was removed from the bench for life.

The Deadly Year of the Wayne

For some unknown reason, there were a lot of violent criminals with the middle name "Wayne" in the news during 1996.

Conan Wayne Hale:
Confessed to his priest that he killed three people.

. . . .

Michael Wayne Thompson:
Murderer who escaped from prison and was the subject of a multistate manhunt. (He was captured in Indiana.)

. . . .

Danny Wayne Owens:
Murdered his neighbor in Alabama.

. . . .

Ellis Wayne Felker:
Executed for the 1981 murder of a college student.

. . . .

Larry Wayne Cole:
Died while running from the law on rape charges.

The Toilet Seat Whistle-Blower

A. Ernest Fitzgerald, a top civilian air-force auditor in the US Department of Defense, testified before Congress in 1968 that $2 billion in cost overruns had occurred in the military's Lockheed C-5A cargo plane program. He'd been reporting this to his superiors for two years, but they took no action and pressured him not to testify. When he did testify, they retaliated by stripping him of his civil service tenure, saying it had been awarded to him erroneously due to a computer error. His department was restructured to eliminate his position, and he was demoted to minor investigations, including cost overruns at a bowling alley in Thailand.

Fitzgerald, a US Navy veteran, fought back by filing suit and, after a four-year battle, was finally reinstated to his original position. He continued to report cost overruns and fraud. The Reagan administration threatened employees with loss of their jobs and security clearances unless they signed a gag order. Fitzgerald refused and beat back the order, which was withdrawn. His greatest fame as a whistle-blower came in the 1980s when he revealed that the Air Force was being billed $200 for hammers, $7,622 for coffee pots, and $640 for toilet seats. He wrote *The High Priests of Waste* (1972) and *The Pentagonists: An Insider's View of Waste, Mismanagement and Fraud in Defense Spending* (1989) before retiring from the Department of Defense in 2006.

GRANDMA METH-HEAD

A case for a case-by-case basis based judgment.

Many states restrict or ban the sale of cold medicines that contain the ingredient pseudoephedrine because it can be used to make crystal methamphetamine. In Indiana, you can buy only a certain amount of pseudoephedrine-based medicines in a seven-day period. But 70-year-old Sally Harpold didn't know that. In 2009 she bought a box of Zyrtec for her husband (who had allergies), and a few days later she bought her adult daughter some Mucinex-D for a cold. Harpold was arrested for intent to manufacture crystal meth. The charges were later dropped.

When Celebrities Attack

Famous people can be criminals, too.

CELEBRITY: Naomi Campbell

INCIDENT: On her way to the Toronto movie set of *Prisoner of Love* in 1998, the supermodel was delayed by Canadian customs officials. Finally arriving at her hotel, the diva blamed her assistant Georgina Galanis for the wait, grabbed her by the throat, and slammed her against a wall. Still furious, Campbell reached for a telephone and hit Galanis twice in the head with the handset, then threatened to throw her from a moving car on a busy highway. A Toronto criminal court ordered Campbell to take anger-management classes. Did she learn anything in class? Apparently not—according to news reports, she attacked another assistant in 2001.

CELEBRITY: Marilyn Manson

INCIDENT: The gender-bending rock star made headlines in September 2003 when a Minnesota jury found him not guilty of battery or any of the other charges against him (causing emotional distress, mental anguish, and

humiliation). The charges were the result of a stunt during a 2000 concert. Security guard David Diaz was working the front of the stage when Manson suddenly grabbed him and began rubbing his pelvis against Diaz's head. In July 2001, while performing in Michigan, Manson pulled the same stunt on security guard Joshua Keasler. That time he had to pay a $4,000 fine.

CELEBRITY: Russell Crowe

INCIDENT: In 1999, while spending some time on his 560-acre ranch in Australia, Crowe and his brother Terry went out for a drink and wound up in a brawl. Crowe spied radio DJ Andrew White at a local bar, approached him, and said, "I've listened to your program, and it's crap." White quickly replied, "So are most of your movies," prompting Crowe to turn to the DJ's wife and exclaim, "I'm going to belt the crap out of your husband!" The gladiator then went after White and several other bar-goers. Security cameras captured him in three separate fights kicking, punching, and biting like a wild man; during the melee Crowe even took a swing at his brother before biting a bouncer in the neck and fleeing the bar.

NOTE: Crowe once attacked the director of the British Academy of Film and Television Arts awards show for editing a four-line poem out of Crowe's Best Actor acceptance speech. Witnesses said Crowe's own security had to remove him, kicking and cursing.

Armed and Dumberous

The most disturbing and menacing thing about these crooks is their collective IQ . . . or lack thereof.

Police described the failed Smart Mart heist in Greentown, Indiana, as a "string of blunders." Blunder number 1: When the four robbers, all men in their 20s, forced the clerk and three customers into a back room, they failed to check the customers for cell phones. One of the customers called the cops, who showed up sooner than the robbers expected. Blunder number 2: One of the crooks dropped his credit card at the scene, which eventually led detectives to the criminal masterminds' headquarters (a trailer). Blunder number 3: The trailer had a surveillance system that had recorded the criminals "preparing for and returning from the heist." The police had more evidence than they needed to charge the robbers with several felonies.

Not So High Horse

A life-size fiberglass horse was the perfect topper for Bruce and Ellen Weatherton's new shop in Central Point, Oregon, called the Horse Blanket Saddles and Tack. Today, that horse is a well- known landmark. But back in 1983 when they first opened the store and put the horse on the roof, some pranksters decided it needed to come down. One day, at 2:30 a.m., Bruce received a call from a deputy: "Come get your horse. He's in the middle of the street." What really boiled Bruce's blood was the fact that the horse thieves used a hacksaw to cut the horse off at the ankles. "All four nuts were loose," he told the *Medford Mail Tribune,* "all they had to do was undo the nuts." So Weatherton brought the horse to the vet . . . er, a repair shop, and paid nearly as much to get it fixed as it cost in the first place.

Not long after it went back up, "I'll be damned if the kids didn't go back again!" That time, they actually broke the poor horse's legs . . . leading to even more costly repairs. The Weathertons weren't giving up, though. The only way to save the horse: chop down the walnut tree the pranksters were using to get to the roof. Problem solved, right? Wrong. The perpetrators simply climbed up an elm tree next to an adjacent building. So the elm was cut down, too. And the horse has stayed safe ever since.

The Lindbergh Baby: Part I

*Here's the story of one of the most widely
publicized kidnappings of the 20th century.*

On May 20, 1927, Charles Lindbergh completed a nonstop
flight of 33 1/2 hours from New York to Paris in the *Spirit of St.
Louis*. Lindbergh became a hero. He married New Jersey heiress
Anne Morrow and they had a son, Charles A. Lindbergh Junior
(nicknamed "the Eaglet").

On March 1, 1932, they stayed an extra few days in their
Hopewell estate—accessible only by a private airfield or winding
dirt road. The nurse tucked Little Lindy into bed in his second-floor
nursery at 8:00. At 10:00, the nurse checked on the baby, but he
was gone. After a search, Lindbergh called police to report that his
son had been kidnapped.

When the police arrived, they found a chisel and a handmade
extension ladder outside. There were footprints on the ground.
In the nursery, Lindbergh discovered an envelope with a note.
The misspelled note read: "Have 50,000$ redy . . . After 2–4 days
we will inform you were to deliver the Mony. We warn you for
making anyding public or for notify the polise the child is in gute
care." The note's signature—two interlocking, red circles with
three holes punched in the design—would be an indication of
correspondence from the kidnapper.

News of the crime went public. Reporters and gawkers were
immediately trampling the Lindbergh estate, destroying potential
evidence. Police had not taken casts of the footprints, and the
throngs ruined the chance to cast them.

One of the many citizens offering help to the Lindberghs was Dr. John "Jafsie" Condon, a retired principal living in the Bronx. He declared himself willing to negotiate with the kidnapper. Amazingly, Jafsie received a letter accepting his mediation offer—marked with the kidnapper's signature. Lindbergh authorized the inexperienced (and some said suspicious) Jafsie to negotiate on his behalf. Condon received more letters from the kidnapper—who also sent the Eaglet's pajamas. Following the kidnapper's orders, Jafsie went to a Bronx cemetery on April 2, 1932, and delivered $50,000 in gold certificates to a man with a foreign accent—nicknamed "Cemetery John."

In return, Jafsie received another letter that claimed Charlie was alive on a boat called the *Nellie*. A search ensued, but the *Nellie* was never found. On May 12, a truck driver went into the woods to relieve himself, and discovered the remains of a toddler. It was the Eaglet. The coroner deduced that it had been lying in the woods since the time of the kidnapping.

In 1934, police got a lead. A gas-station customer paid with a gold certificate that the attendant thought might be counterfeit. He wrote down the customer's license plate number and called police. The cops checked the serial number on the certificate—it was part of the Lindbergh ransom. This led authorities to Bruno Hauptmann, a carpenter from Germany. Hauptmann was an illegal immigrant whose description matched Cemetery John's. When police arrested him, they found more than $11,000 in ransom money.

Turn to page 276 for more on the trial.

Unauthorized Vehicles Only

It's about the ride, not the destination.

BED RIDDEN

Police in Ferrol, Spain, charged Antonio Navarro with driving while intoxicated on a highway. He was only going 12 mph, and he wasn't driving a car. Navarro is a quadriplegic, and police busted him driving his motorized bed on the freeway. Where did he need to go in such a hurry? Navarro was on his way to a local brothel.

STOOL SAMPLE

Police in Newark, Ohio, arrested 28-year-old Kile Wygle for drunk driving in 2009. But Wygle wasn't driving a car—he was driving a motorized bar stool, which he had built himself. Wygle was the one who called police. He was drunk. He lost control, fell off, and called 911 for medical assistance. Instead of paramedics, police arrived.

GETTING TANKED

At about 4:00 one morning in 2009, an 18-year-old British army soldier stationed in northern Germany decided to steal one of his squadron's tanks. He broke into the eight-ton Scimitar tank and made it about a third of a mile before the vehicle ran off the road and got stuck. So he returned to base and stole another tank. This time, British military police followed him. They blocked the soldier's path, forcing him to swerve and crash into a tree.

CROOKS LOVE OZZY

*How the Prince of Darkness unwittingly
led criminals to justice.*

THE RUSE: In November 2007, hundreds of people around
Fargo, North Dakota, received letters containing invitations
to a party. The invitations were printed on purple
stationery, had images of spiderwebs and skulls on them,
and were from an outfit called "PDL Productions."

THE HOOK: They weren't your average party invitations.
They were for a party at a Fargo nightclub . . . with British
rock legend Ozzy Osbourne. Osbourne was performing at
the Fargodome later that night, so the invitees were also
promised backstage passes to the show.

GOTCHA! Forty-four invitees showed up at the club . . .
and were arrested on the spot. It was all part of a sting
set up by Fargo Sheriff Paul D. Laney (that's what "PDL"
stood for), who had the specially made invitations sent to
hundreds of people who had outstanding arrest warrants.
When Osbourne heard about the stunt, he was not amused.
"This sheriff should be ashamed of himself for using my
celebrity to arrest these criminals," he said in a statement.
Laney said he "meant no disrespect toward Mr. Osbourne"
and added that several of his deputies had gone to his show
after the busts.

A Gentleman and a Scholar . . . and Assailant

DEATH BY DUEL

In 1859 Senator David Broderick of California, a power broker in the Democratic Party's antislavery faction, was challenged to a duel by political enemy and proslavery activist David Terry, California's chief justice. They dueled at Lake Merced, south of San Francisco. Broderick had the first shot, but when his gun misfired, Terry calmly put a bullet through Broderick's chest. Broderick now has the unique distinction of being the only US senator to be killed in a duel while in office. Terry was tried for murder and acquitted. In 1889 the elderly Terry was gunned down by the Supreme Court justice Stephen Fields's bodyguard after Terry confronted Field in a train station restaurant and slapped him.

STRANGE CRIME

SCORE ONE FOR THE SENATOR

In 1917 a war protester named Alexander Bannwart and two other men confronted Massachusetts senator Henry Cabot Lodge in his office. They wanted to urge Senator Lodge to vote no on the upcoming resolution to enter World War I. The words "coward" and "liar" were spoken. Then, the 67-year-old senator rose up and decked the 36-year-old pacifist . . . and laid him out cold. The protester was arrested, but Lodge said he was too busy to press charges. Two days later, Lodge voted with the majority of his fellow senators to go to war. Bannwart later caught the patriotic fever gripping the nation and, after announcing that he'd changed his mind, he enlisted in the army.

> "Life is indeed precious, and I believe the death penalty helps to affirm this fact."
> —Ed Koch,
> (former New York City mayor)

The Sniper in the Tower

He looked like a regular, clean-cut guy. Born in Lake Worth, Florida, in 1941 to a well-off family, Charles Whitman went to Catholic schools, excelled at piano playing, and became an Eagle Scout at age 12. But all was not perfect within the family home. His father, called C. A., abused his wife and wasn't much nicer to his kids. Even when Charles was 18, his father continued to beat him for what he saw as transgressions.

GOOD CONDUCT

He enlisted in the US Marines in 1959. He proved himself a model marine who excelled at following orders and earned a good-conduct medal, a sharpshooter's badge, and the praise of observers who noted that he was an expert at long-distance shooting, particularly when his targets were moving.

A TASTE OF FREEDOM

Whitman enrolled at the University of Texas at Austin to study engineering. But he struggled with his studies. He met his wife Kathleen there and the two married, but that didn't settle him down. He bounced in and out of the university over the next few years; at one point, he was ordered back to military service due to poor college grades.

In 1963 Whitman was court-martialed after threatening another soldier to whom he'd loaned money. He was sentenced to 30 days behind bars and 90 days of hard labor,

and stripped of his rank as well; he was a lowly private again. Miserable, he turned to his hated father to pull some strings to reduce his enlistment period. His father succeeded, and Charles was discharged in December 1964.

TAKE TWO VALIUM AND CALL ME IN THE MORNING

Charles returned to Austin. He was depressed and anxious about his inability to live up to his own standards. He visited the university's health center in March and reported to the attending doctor: He felt like a failure and despised his father. He also mentioned fantasizing about "going up on the tower with a deer rifle and shooting people." The doctor didn't take him seriously, and prescribed Valium to calm his nerves.

THE SCENE OF THE CRIME

Whitman first visited the tower on July 22, 1966, to stake it out. Shortly before noon on August 1, Whitman arrived on campus and talked his way into the tower. On the 28th-floor observation deck, he took his place and picked up a scoped rifle. Within about 90 minutes, he'd killed 14 people and injured 31 more. Almost two hours after he'd entered the tower, police officers finally made their way to the deck and shot him dead. In a note he left behind, he said he killed his mother and wife too (which turned out to be true), and that he was prepared to die. The tower was closed for 25 years after the shooting, but reopened in 1999.

MARIJUANA MISHAPS

The law about this is crystal clear. It says . . . we forget.

MUST-STASH

In February 2011, Joel Dobrin, 32, of San Diego, California, was driving down a road in Sherman County, Oregon. Some marijuana and hashish rode shotgun on the front seat of his pickup truck. He was pulled over by a sheriff's deputy. As the officer approached, Dobrin grabbed a sock that was lying on the floor of the truck and stashed his drugs inside it. But his dog, a pit bull, grabbed the sock and started playing tug-of-war with it, and the sock flew out the open window of the truck. The sheriff simply retrieved the sock and found the drugs. "I wish everyone traveled with their own personal drug dog," a sheriff's spokesman told reporters.

ABOVE THE LAW

Robert Watson was driving down an East Haven, Connecticut, road late one night in April 2011. Watson came across a police sobriety checkpoint, police found marijuana in his car. Watson was arrested for possession of marijuana. A blood test found that he also had small amounts of cocaine in his system. Unfortunately, Watson was a member of the Rhode Island House of Representatives—and had a record of stridently opposing marijuana legalization, and of voting for stiff penalties for drug offenses.

The Spy Who Wasn't

Mata Hari went down in history as the exotic dancer who loosened many lips in the service of the Germans during World War I. Far from it.

Mata Hari was born in 1876. She met husband-to-be Rudolph MacLeod through a personals ad and soon after joined him at his post in faraway Java. A few years later, she fled to Paris to begin her exotic dancing career. Parisian audiences flocked to her titillating performances. She was even booked into a few Italian opera houses.

By 1915 Hari's career was fading fast. She was doing less dancing on stage and more horizontal boogie with men in her bedroom. Recently unearthed French files reveal dozens of Mata Hari's clients, including German military attaché Major Arnold Kalle.

That affair was probably the one that killed her. In 1917 Mata Hari was arrested by the French and accused of spying for the Germans. They produced decoded messages outlining a German plan to hire her as a spy. But not only were the French unable to produce any evidence of secrets she'd handed over, high-ranking French officers testified that she had tried several times to give information on German activities to the French.

She was convicted of spying and executed 1917. Rumor was that she opened her blouse to distract the squad from firing. In truth, she went bravely with her blouse buttoned up.

"That Sucker's Coming Off!"

On a sweltering summer afternoon in 2017, a burglary suspect (unnamed in press reports) was jumping from rooftop to rooftop in a La Puente, California, neighborhood. The chase ended when the cops had the suspect trapped on the roof of a one-story home. Unsure of the man's mental state, they didn't want to risk a forceful takedown, afraid he might jump off the one-story house. So they called in a crisis management team, and a tense standoff ensued. No matter what the team tried, the man refused to budge. Five hours passed.

That's when Willard Burgess decided he'd had enough. The 83-year-old resident of the house told officers, "That sucker's coming off!" He went to his neighbor's, grabbed a ladder, and before police could stop him, he climbed up on the roof. Burgess yelled at the burglar and told him to get down. The burglar refused, so Burgess pushed him off. Deputies took him into custody, and then to the hospital.

SPEEDY JUSTICE

DEFENDANT: John Cracken, a Texas personal-injury lawyer

THE CRIME: Flaunting his wealth in public

BACKGROUND: In 1991 Cracken represented a disabled widow in a lawsuit against her husband's employer, the Rock-Tenn Company. Rock-Tenn was a recycling company, and the man was killed in a baling machine. Cracken sued for $25 million, but Rock-Tenn's case was so weak that there was talk that the jury might award as much as $60 million. Shortly before deliberations were to begin, however, some of the jurors happened to spot Cracken in the courthouse parking garage, driving a brand-new red Porsche 911.

THE SENTENCE: The jury awarded Cracken's client only $5 million. Why so little? One juror explained, "There was no way I'm going to buy that lawyer another fancy car."

FAMOUS TRIALS: THE CADAVER SYNOD

Here's the story of a trial that's stranger than anything you'll ever see on Court TV or Judge Judy.

HERE COMES GUIDO

In 891 Pope Stephen V turned to Duke Guido III of Spoleto for protection, because the Catholic Church was losing power as the Roman Empire disintegrated. To cement the relationship, Stephen adopted him as his son and crowned him Holy Roman Emperor.

AND POPE FORMOSUS

Pope Stephen V died a few months later and a new pope, Formosus I, was elected to head the Church. Guido was suspicious of the new pope's loyalty. He insisted that Formosus name Guido's son Lambert heir apparent. When Guido died in 894, Formosus backed out of the deal. Rather than crown Lambert emperor, he called on King Arnulf of East Francia to liberate Rome from Guido's family.

AND ARNULF

A year later Arnulf conquered Rome . . . and Formosus made him emperor. This relationship didn't last long either: within a few months, Arnulf had suffered paralysis and returned to Germany; a few months after *that,* Pope Formosus died.

AND LAMBERT AGAIN

Lambert, who had retreated back to Spoleto, used the crisis to rally his troops and march on Rome. He reconquered the

city in 897. The new pope, Stephen VI, quickly switched sides and crowned Lambert emperor.

THE TRIAL

What followed was one of the most peculiar episodes in the history of the Catholic Church. Eager to prove his loyalty to the Spoletos, Pope Stephen convened the "cadaver synod," in which he literally had Pope Formosus's nine-month-old, rotting corpse put on trial for perjury, "coveting the papacy," and other crimes. On Stephen's orders the cadaver was disinterred, dressed in papal robes, and propped up on a throne for the trial. Since the body was in no condition to answer the charges made against it, a deacon was appointed to answer questions on its behalf.

Not surprisingly, the cadaver was found guilty on all counts. As punishment, all of Formosus's papal acts were declared null and void. The corpse itself was also desecrated: the three fingers on the right hand used to confer blessings were hacked off, and the body was stripped naked and dumped in a cemetery for foreigners. Shortly afterwards, it was tossed in the Tiber River, where a hermit fished it out and gave it a proper burial.

WHAT GOES AROUND

While the synod was still in session, an earthquake struck Rome and destroyed the papal basilica. Taking this as a sign of God's anger with the upstart pope, and encouraged by rumors that Formosus's corpse had begun performing miracles, Formosus's supporters arrested Stephen and threw him into the papal prison, where he was later strangled.

The Hatfields vs. the McCoys

The Contestants: The Hatfields, headed by Anderson "Devil Anse" Hatfield, lived on the West Virginia side of the stream. The McCoys, whose patriarch was Randolph "Ole Ran'l" McCoy, lived on the Kentucky side.

How the Feud Started: During the Civil War, the Hatfields sided with the Confederacy, and the McCoys sided with the Union. In 1880 relations worsened when McCoy's daughter became pregnant by Devil Anse's son Johnse and went across the river to live—unmarried—with the Hatfields.

In 1882 Randolph's son Tolbert stabbed Devil Anse's brother Ellison in a brawl; when Ellison died a few days later, the Hatfields retaliated by tying three of the McCoy brothers to some bushes and executing them. The McCoys struck back one night in 1888. A group of Hatfields surrounded Ole Ran'l McCoy's house (he was away) and ordered the occupants to come out and surrender. When no one did, they set the house on fire. Ole Ran'l's daughter and son ran out; both were gunned down.

This last attack was so brutal that officials in both Kentucky and West Virginia finally felt compelled to intervene. One Hatfield who participated in the raid was convicted and hanged for the crime. Several others were sentenced to long prison terms. With most violent offenders behind bars and the rest of the clan members weary of years of killing, the feud petered out.

Dull and Delinquent

More proof that crime doesn't pay.

SIGN OF THE TIMES

Residents of a Portland, Oregon, neighborhood were concerned about an alleged "drug house." They had tried numerous times to get the police to investigate it, but to no avail. Then, in late 2011, someone in the area saw a flier, removed it from a pole, and brought it to the cops. That was all they needed to secure a warrant. When officers raided the house, they discovered marijuana, heroin, a sawed-off shotgun, thousands of dollars in cash, and the materials for a meth lab. What did the flier say? "Heroin for Sale"—and listed the address.

A CINDERELLA STORY

A thief in Severina, Brazil, stole a woman's purse and ran away. During his sprint, he put the purse strap in his mouth and dialed his cell phone (to order a pizza?). But the purse fell to the ground, and when he scooped it up, he left behind something else: his dentures. A witness found them and turned them over to the police. A brief investigation led officers to the home of Milton Cesar de Jesus, 34, who tried to keep his mouth closed. He was ordered to try on the dentures. They fit perfectly, and de Jesus was arrested.

THE BAD DR. KING

William Henry King grew up poor in mid-1800s Ontario, but became a doctor after his marriage to Sarah Lawson in 1855—her wealthy father picked up his medical school bill. The future seemed wide open for the newlyweds . . . until King let his true nature show after the birth of his first child.

Their daughter was born handicapped, and died after a month. Sarah suspected King of killing the baby outright, and fled to her parents' house. He managed to win her back. King built a successful medical practice . . . and started an affair with a woman named Melinda Vandervoort. William told Melinda that Sarah was ill and would soon die. Sure enough, Sarah came down with a sudden case of "cholera." King treated her with a powdered white medicine. Within a month, Sarah Lawson was dead.

Sarah's father organized an investigation into her death, and King panicked. He fled with Vandervoort to a farm in New York, but authorities tracked them down.

The murder trial was a sensation. A professor from Toronto testified that he had discovered 11 grams of arsenic in Sarah's stomach, and a jury convicted King of murder.

In Ontario's last public hanging, the doctor was trotted out in front of 10,000 spectators. Before his noose was tightened, King confessed to the crowd. He went to his grave believing that God had forgiven him for his crime.

Strange Crime?

Of all of history's unsolved mysteries, perhaps none is stranger than the fateful voyage of the Mary Celeste.

SAILING INTO THE UNKNOWN

On November 5, 1872, a ship named the *Mary Celeste* set sail from New York bound for Genoa, Italy, under the command of Captain Benjamin Briggs. On board were a crew of seven, along with the captain's wife and their two-year-old daughter. A month later, on the morning of December 4, the *Mary Celeste* sailed out of the fog off the coast of Spain and was spotted by the crew of the British ship *Dei Gratia*. The *Mary Celeste*'s sails were raised and the hull and masts appeared in good order. The crew of the *Dei Gratia* hailed the ship, but received no answer, so they boarded her, ready to extend their greetings. What they found was mystifying: the ship was completely deserted.

ANYBODY HOME?

The ship's cargo—1,700 barrels of alcohol—was untouched. The money box was full. There was plenty of food and water. In fact, some reports tell of finding a meal on the table, as if dinner had just been served. Toys were found on the captain's bed, as if his little daughter had just played with them. Everyone's clothes were still on board. The only things missing were nautical charts and maps, a lifeboat . . . and all the people. Where did everybody go?

WHAT HAPPENED?

The mystervious disappearance of the *Mary Celeste*'s crew had people all over the world wondering.

- Some believed the crew mutinied, murdered the captain and his family, then took the ship. But if that were true, why did they abandon it?
- Perhaps pirates attacked the ship and killed everyone aboard. But then why was nothing stolen?
- The most outrageous explanation offered was that the ship had been attacked by a giant squid. But a squid wouldn't have been interested in the ship's papers. And a squid wouldn't need a lifeboat.

A POSSIBLE EXPLANATION

The mystery of the *Mary Celeste* has puzzled people for over a century. In all that time, say experts, only one reasonable explanation has been proposed. According to this theory, four things happened, in succession:

1. The captain died of natural causes while the ship was caught in bad weather.

2. A crew member misread the depth of the water in the hold, and everyone thought the ship was sinking.

3. They panicked and abandoned ship in such a hurry that they took no food or water.

4. Everyone in the lifeboat eventually starved or drowned.

Is that what happened? Could be . . . but no one will ever know.

Family Films

THE LEGEND: There's a secret underground network of people who produce, collect, and enjoy "snuff films"—films that depict actual murders.

HOW IT SPREAD: In 1969 Charles Manson and his "family" were terrorizing Los Angeles with bloody murders and other violent crimes. At one point, they stole an NBC news truck and were known to be in possession of a few Super-8 cameras. In the 1971 documentary *The Family*, filmmaker Ed Sanders claims that Manson's followers used the equipment to make "brutality films" of their victims. Rumors of various serial killers recording their crimes, as well as police discovering these tapes, have surfaced.

THE TRUTH: No law-enforcement agency in the United States, Europe, or Asia has ever actually discovered a genuine snuff film. Very convincing fakes have been reported and turned over to authorities (in 1991 actor Charlie Sheen saw a Japanese movie called *Flower of Flesh and Blood* that was so convincing that he thought it was real and gave it to the FBI). But a real one has yet to surface. As for the Manson tapes, those are a legend, too. The Super-8 cameras and the NBC equipment was later recovered; there were no films of murders.

The Kinky Killer Colonel

In 2007 Colonel David Williams was a loving husband and respected member of the Canadian Armed Forces. Williams's interests in jogging and photography, however, fed a hidden perversion. During runs, Williams spied on neighbors. Over time, his behavior escalated. He broke into neighbors' homes and photographed himself wearing girls' underwear. Williams built a large collection of women's underwear, and a collection of photos of himself wearing the underwear.

In 2009 his behavior became more violent. He broke into a woman's home near his cottage in Tweed, knocking her out with a flashlight. He assaulted her and took photos of her and of himself with her underwear.

By 2009 his violent behavior became more extreme. He broke into the house of a woman who worked at his base and murdered her. When the body was found, Williams sent her father a letter of condolence.

In 2010 Williams kidnapped a young woman on a highway and killed her. Then, he dumped her body in the woods. The next day he piloted a troop flight to California.

Officers had a copy of the tire print left behind near the victim's house. When Williams pulled through a checkpoint, one diligent officer noticed that his tires matched the photo of the tire print. He was brought in for questioning, and after 10 hours, Williams confessed. After he signed a confession, he wrote his wife a note of apology. Williams was given two life sentences for murder, plus 120 years.

KILLER NURSE

The best nurses display compassion and empathy when dealing with patients. Jane Toppan, a nurse in New England in the late 19th century, decidedly did not fall into this category.

The coldhearted caretaker admitted to killing 31 patients in her care over the course of several decades. Some suspect the actual victim count was even higher. Toppan's murderous methods involved poisoning—specifically by using atropine (a drug derived from deadly nightshade) and morphine—and her victims ranged from those in hospitals to elderly patients who hired her as an in-home private nurse. Her undoing came after four members of the Davis family died within weeks of each other in 1901, all after having been treated by Toppan. The husband of one of these victims, Mary Gibbs, insisted on an autopsy, which revealed deadly levels of morphine and atropine in her system.

During Toppan's trial—which unearthed the fact that her father and sister had spent time in insane asylums—she didn't help her case; she reportedly claimed, "That is my ambition, to have killed more people—more helpless people—than any man or woman who has ever lived." Unsurprisingly, she was found to be insane and spent the rest of her life in the Taunton Insane Hospital, where she passed away at age 84.

Know Your Technology

"Bud" and "Jan" wanted a Cadillac sold by an Independence, Missouri, dealership. They just weren't keen on paying for it. Since stealing one was the only way, they nabbed a sweet model, equipped with the OnStar navigation system. Not only could OnStar tell them how to get places, it could also let the dealership know where the stolen vehicle was being taken. But Bud and Jan (who by all indications had done their research on the make and model of car with which they were absconding) were prepared; shortly after they stole the car, they ripped out the car's antenna—thereby silencing the onboard tracking system.

Or so they thought. What they had actually done was rip out the antenna for the Caddie's XM satellite radio service. While the Caddie could no longer get dozens of channels of CD-quality musical entertainment beamed to it from the cold, hard vacuum of space, it *could* still rat on Bud and Jan. Which is what it did and which is how police tracked down Bud and Jan later that same day. David Clutts, executive manager of the dealership from which the Caddie was stolen, summed up Bud and Jan's problem to the local newspaper: "They're like most people who commit stupid crimes. They didn't know what they were doing."

THE SARAJEVO PISTOL

On June 28, 1914, Gavrilo Princip shot and killed the heir to the Austro-Hungarian throne, Archduke Franz Ferdinand, and his wife, Sophie, in Sarajevo, Bosnia. The assassinations caused a chain reaction of events which, within five weeks, led to the start of World War I. The gun was a Browning semiautomatic pistol, model M1910, serial #19074.

Princip, just 19, was a member of the Serbian nationalist group called the Black Hand. He fired seven shots into the royal couple's car from five feet away, then attempted to shoot himself, but was stopped by passersby and quickly arrested. Princip died in prison of tuberculosis in 1918 (part of why he took the mission). After his trial, the pistol was presented to Father Anton Puntigam, the Jesuit priest who had given the archduke and duchess their last rites. He hoped to place it in a museum, but when he died in 1926 the gun was lost . . . for almost 80 years.

In 2004 a Jesuit community house in Austria made a startling announcement: They had found the gun (verified by its serial number). They donated it to the Vienna Museum of Military History in time for the 90th anniversary of the assassination that started a war that would eventually kill 8.5 million people. Also in the museum are the car in which the couple were riding, the bloodied pillow cover on which the archduke rested his head while dying, and petals from a rose that was attached to Sophie's belt.

LIZZIE AND O. J.

Though they took place nearly 100 years apart,
the murder trials of O. J. Simpson and Lizzie Borden
have some eerie similarities.

- Both defendants were well-respected members of society.

- Neither Borden nor Simpson had a criminal record, and the grisly nature of the murders shocked the nation.

- In both cases, the defendants were kept incarcerated throughout the trial because, in Borden's case, the judge said she was "probably guilty," and in Simpson's case, because "there is sufficient cause to believe this defendant guilty."

- Both sets of victims were a man and a woman, who were savagely murdered with a sharp object that was never found.

- Although both defendants later claimed that the real murderers were vagrants, the grisly nature of the killings led investigators to conclude that the heinous acts were personal.

- Neither defendant had a good alibi, and there were no witnesses to the murders.

- Both defendants were wealthy enough to hire the best and most expensive defense teams available.

- A guilty conviction was avoided in both cases, not by proving the defendants' innocence, but by poking holes in the prosecutors' cases and establishing reasonable doubt.

- Both defense teams shifted the blame from the murderers to the police forces, who they claimed were trying to frame the accused. (And neither police force helped their case by sloppily botching each respective crime scene.)

- Both juries reached their not-guilty verdicts in a very short time: one hour for Borden, and four hours for Simpson.

- Both cases spawned a famous rhyme:

  > *Lizzie Borden took an axe*
  > *And gave her mother forty whacks*
  > *When she saw what she had done*
  > *She gave her father forty-one.*

- And of course, "If it don't fit / you must acquit!"

- Both cases remain unsolved to this day.

In 2013, the Netherlands shut down 19 of the country's prisons. Reason? Lack of prisoners to fill them.

The Murder of Harvey Milk

Harvey Milk was the first openly gay person elected to the San Francisco Board of Supervisors. He was instrumental in the passage of San Francisco's first civil rights ordinance for gay citiens, and was politically buddy-buddy with the mayor, George Moscone. Their nemesis was Dan White, a conservative ex-cop and the only member of the board who voted against the civil-rights ordinance.

White had been so incensed by the passage of the ordinance that he resigned from the board. When he tried to get himself reinstated, he met a brick wall. On November 27, 1978, inside city hall, Dan White shot and killed both Harvey Milk and Mayor George Moscone.

Everyone expected a first-degree murder conviction. When the verdict came down as manslaughter (part of Dan White's defense centered around his instability due to eating too much junk food), it was followed by gay riots. The riots were answered by the San Francisco Police Department with an unprovoked attack on the city's gay neighborhood, the Castro district. Dozens of people were injured, and a bar, the Elephant Walk, was nearly destroyed. The "Twinkie Defense" became common parlance for someone who suffered from a diminished mental capacity due to the consumption of too much sugar.

Dan White was paroled in 1985 and committed suicide shortly afterward.

Video Games vs. Reality

Video games can be fun, but for some gamers,
the fun gets a little out of hand.

A LACK OF ELF CONTROL

In 2005 Robert Boyd entered a lingerie store and asked
for a discount on some women's underwear. When the
clerk refused, he pulled out a knife and robbed the place.
Boyd was later caught. At his trial, he blamed his crime on
Shadowrun, an online role-playing game that takes place
in a "magical future." In that world, Boyd explained, he is
an elf criminal named Buho—and it was Buho who was
"in control" during the crime. The prosecutor called Boyd's
story a "big lie," saying that he has an underwear fetish and
invented Buho as an excuse. The jury agreed, and sentenced
Boyd/Buho to two years in prison.

YOU CAN RUN, BUT YOU CAN'T HIDE

In 2009 Alfred Hightower thought he was home free. The
fugitive—wanted in Indiana on drug-dealing charges—
had fled to Canada three years earlier. But Hightower's
other hobby, *World of Warcraft*, allowed authorities track
him down online. They subpoenaed *Warcraft*'s publisher,
Blizzard Entertainment, for Hightower's IP address,
screen name, account history, and billing address. Shortly
thereafter, he was arrested and extradited back to the
United States. Game over!

STOP, ROBOT! THIEF!

DRONE DETECTIVE. Unmanned aerial vehicle (UAVs) manufacturers are peddling their wares to law enforcement agencies—and, boy, are they interested. Privacy and death-by-falling-robot concerns aside, drones promise clear crime-stopping benefits: improved surveillance, 24/7 aerial search efforts, and rapid crime-scene evidence transportation.

POSITRONIC PATROLMAN. Silicon Valley's latest obsession? A robot security guard named K5. This glorified Roomba patrols a tech campus perimeter in unpredictable patterns, whistling like a beat cop and wirelessly monitoring social media for "threats." That doesn't stop burglars, though, so K5 also records everything it sees in 360-degree, thermal imaging, night-vision high-definition. It also contacts police about suspicious behavior.

BUM BOT. If K5 is Paul Blart, then Bum Bot is Batman: a vigilante, covered in black, and extremely creepy. It uses prerecorded warnings ("You're trespassing!") and a high-pressure water cannon to disperse homeless vagrants from the area around the bar. Its inventor, Rufus Terrill, built this hulking monolith because he was tired of his old method of terrifying the dispossessed: threatening them with an assault rifle. Terrill claims that Bum Bot has reduced local crime by 50 percent.

Bank Robbin' Hood

In 1924 Charles Arthur Floyd was 20 years old, married, and working hard picking cotton in Atkins, Oklahoma. He became friends with John Hildebrand, a thief who taught Floyd the lucrative business of robbing gas stations and small stores. One of Floyd's theft victims described him to police as "a pretty boy with apple cheeks," which landed him the nickname "Pretty Boy." Floyd was arrested in 1925 and sent to prison, where he learned a lot more about the crime trade.

Pretty Boy's Gang. Paroled in 1929, Floyd went to Kansas City, where he soon became head of America's most successful gang of bank robbers. With the Great Depression came even more success: Floyd became a criminal philanthropist, tearing up mortgages so that people wouldn't lose their homes, or throwing wads of money to people from the window of one of his many getaway cars. According to some historians, he sent this message to the government: "If you ain't gonna do nothing to help the little guy, 'Pretty Boy' Floyd will!"

I'll Get You, My Pretty! Floyd had killed more than one police officer during his crime sprees, so not everyone considered him a hero. In 1933, when four officers were killed in what became known as the Kansas City Massacre, J. Edgar Hoover made Pretty Boy Floyd a prime suspect,

even though historians don't agree on the truth of the FBI charge—Floyd was more into making money than murder, and used his gun only in self-defense. This had been a shoot-out with no bank money involved. The FBI caught up with Floyd in 1934 and chased him through Ohio for two days before finding and killing him. Floyd's body was returned to Oklahoma. Thousands of people attended his funeral, making it the largest in Oklahoma history.

A KILLER MISTAKE

When US Representative Michele Bachmann kicked off her presidential campaign in 2011, she did so from Waterloo, Iowa. "John Wayne was from Waterloo," she boasted in her speech, "That's the kind of spirit that I have, too!" One problem: It was John Wayne Gacy who was from Waterloo—a serial killer who murdered 33 people. John Wayne the movie star was from another town on the other side of Iowa.

An "E" for Effort

SAAB STORY

Joshua E. Reed of Rutland, New York, was arrested on
theft charges in 2006, and as a condition of his bail, had
to report to the local sheriff's office once a day. One day in
November, he suddenly realized he didn't have a ride to the
sheriff's office and he was going to be late for his meeting
. . . so he *stole* a car. Rutland police spotted the green 1994
Saab, pulled Reed over, and arrested him. "He has a once-
daily reporting requirement and, as ridiculous as it sounds,
he was concerned about reporting on time," Reed's lawyer
said. "He just wasn't thinking." Reed was thrown back in
jail and now faces up to 12 years in prison.

WHEN THE DUMB TURN PRO

A 20-year-old man in a Springfield, Massachusetts,
courtroom was refused his request to be released without bail
after the judge looked at the identification form the man had
filled out. Under occupation he had written "drug dealer."

CLAUS, SANTA (D–NORTH POLE)

In 2004, 22-year-old Chad Staton was arrested after he
attempted to register more than 100 false names into the
Defiance County, Ohio, voter rolls. Some of the names he
used on the forms: Mary Poppins, Jeffrey Dahmer, and
Janet Jackson.

GIVIN' HIM THE FINGERS

*Mary Bach met a frightful end, but still was able
to point out her killer after death. Her famous
fingers are now on display in a museum.*

WHERE: Wood County Historical Center and Museum,
Bowling Green, Ohio

WHY: Carl and Mary Bach emigrated from Germany in the
mid-1800s and settled in northwest Ohio. They had a volatile
relationship and fought a lot, so Carl ended up sleeping in the
barn. In late 1881, as winter approached, Carl wanted to move
back into the house, but Mary refused him. So, he armed
himself with a corn knife, broke into the house, and killed
her. When she'd reached up to shield herself from his attack,
he cut off three of her fingers. Carl turned himself in the next
day, and prosecutors used the fingers as evidence in the trial.
Carl was convicted and hanged shortly thereafter.

The fingers used to convict him were preserved and
remained on display at the Wood County courthouse until the
early 1980s, when they were transferred to the Wood County
Historical Center and Museum. Today, they're featured in an
exhibit that also includes the corn knife used in the murder,
Carl's pipe, a German-language Bible, the noose used in the
hanging, and a ticket to the public execution. Morbid? Maybe,
but also extremely popular. According to one museum official,
"Those fingers built this museum."

Code Name: The Milk Man

Slangin' the white stuff like it's 1799.

In 2009, some "consumers" in Maryland ordered milk online from an Amish farm in Pennsylvania. The owner of the Amish farm, Daniel Allgyer, delivered the milk to the people in Maryland.

GOTCHA! Busted, Amish milk farmer! Those guys in Maryland weren't milk drinkers—they were FDA agents, and they'd been investigating Allgyer's farm for more than a year. Why? Because he was selling raw, unpasteurized milk, which the FDA says "should not be consumed under any circumstances," as it can contain dangerous bacteria—and he was transporting it across state lines, which made it "illegal interstate commerce." Result: In April 2010, US marshals and FDA inspectors staged a surprise early morning raid on Allgyer's farm, during which they took pictures and notes. The next day, Allgyer got a letter from the FDA telling him to stop selling raw milk. He didn't. The FDA filed suit against him.

Zero Tolerance for Zero Tolerance

We had to fire the guy who wrote this article because he came to work in a suit and tie on casual Friday. Hey, how can we keep someone who won't follow the rules?

CRIME: In 2002 seven fourth-grade boys at Colorado's Dry Creek Elementary School were playing "Army" in gym class, but because toy guns were not permitted at the school, they pointed their fingers at each other and said, "Bang!"

PUNISHMENT: All seven students were suspended for violating the school's weapons policy, which included "facsimile" guns.

CRIME: In 2013 Josh Welch, a second-grade student from Baltimore, Maryland, bit his Pop-Tart into the shape of a mountain. A teacher walking past his lunch table thought it was a gun and "freaked out." Josh insisted that it was a mountain (he'd drawn one earlier in art class and was trying to re-create it in his Pop-Tart), but the teacher didn't believe him.

PUNISHMENT: Josh was suspended for two days. His dad sued the school district to keep the blemish off his son's record. "I mean, it's a pastry," he said.

CRIME: In 2013 Kiera Wilmot, 16, a Florida high school student, was working on her science fair project before class one morning when she combined a few pieces

of aluminum foil and some toilet cleaner in a bottle of water. The reaction set off a loud "pop" not dissimilar to a firecracker. There was no damage and no one was injured, but several students and teachers heard the "explosion."

PUNISHMENT: Kiera was arrested and charged with domestic terrorism for "detonating a bomb on school property." She was also suspended for 10 days and then reassigned to a charter school. But Kiera, a bookish cello player who said she wants to build robots when she grows up, insisted that she was just doing an experiment. An online "Justice for Kiera" petition sprang up, calling on authorities to drop all charges, and it generated nearly 200,000 signatures.

HAPPY ENDING: The criminal charges were later dropped, and that's not all that happened. News of the suspension reached Homer Hickam, who trains astronauts for NASA. Turns out that when Hickam was a high school student in the 1980s, he and his friends launched some homemade rockets, one of which started a small forest fire. Hickam's high school principal and physics teacher both intervened with the police on his behalf, and he was cleared of the charges, free to pursue a life in science. So when Hickam heard about Kiera, he presented her (and her twin sister Kayla) with a scholarship to attend Space Camp. "I'm really excited about going," Kiera told reporters. "Especially the zero-gravity tank, I've always wanted to do that."

Suin' for a Tattooin'

THE PLAINTIFFS: David Jonathan Winkelman and his stepson, Richard Goddard

THE DEFENDANT: KORB, an Indiana hard-rock radio station

THE LAWSUIT: In 2000 DJ Ben Stone announced on the air that any listener who had the station's call letters tattooed on their forehead would receive $150,000. Winkelman and Goddard decided to take them up on the offer. But first they went to the station and asked if the deal was legitimate. They were told it was, so they went to a tattoo parlor and got their foreheads inked with the station's slogan: "93 Rock, the Quad City Rocker." When the two men went to the station to claim their prize, Stone photographed them and then informed them it was just a practical joke. Winkelman and Goddard received no money, but their pictures were displayed on the station's website. Winkelman lost his job, and neither man could find work because of the big tattoos on their foreheads. Winkelman and Goddard sued, claiming that the radio station set out to "publicly scorn and ridicule them for their greed and lack of common good sense."

THE VERDICT: Goddard's case was dismissed when he didn't show up at court. Winkelman later dropped his suit. The station changed its format to easy listening.

The Godmothers

Queenpins can be just as ruthless as kingpins.

SHE'LL NEVER CHANGE HER SPOTS. In 2000 police arrested Erminia Giuliano, a mob leader in Camorra, Naples. Police claim she had ruthlessly and casually ordered numerous executions, and was ranked one of Italy's 30 most dangerous criminals. When arrested, she made a special request of the police—she wanted to go to the hairdresser and wear a leopard-skin outfit to prison.

MOB BOSS MADAM. Erminia Guiliano's rival in Naples was Maria Licciardi, who took over her family after her husband's arrest. She built the family's business by forging alliances with other Camorra clans and by adding prostitution to heroin trade and extortion. The alliances eventually crumbled, and between 1997 and 1998 she dragged her family through gang wars that killed more than 100 people. She was arrested in 2001.

BAD HAIR DAY. In 2002 there was an argument in a Naples hair salon between Clarissa Cava and Alba Graziano. The Cavas and the Grazianos were rivals for 30 years. Several days later, Graziano and her two daughters, aged 21 and 22, drove up to the car occupied by the 21-year-old Cava, her two aunts, and her sister—and machine-gunned them to death. The Grazianos were later heard laughing and toasting the killings on police surveillance tapes.

STRANGE CRIME

FISHY FELONY

In April 2006, someone reported to Kentucky Fish and Wildlife officers that they'd found something odd at Lake Barkley in Kentucky: A basket containing five live bass, tied to a dock just below the waterline. That aroused the suspicion of the officers, who knew that a fishing tournament was scheduled at the lake that weekend. So they marked the fishes' fins and watched the site. Sure enough, on Saturday morning a boat pulled up, retrieved the stashed fish, and left. The boat belonged to two Kentuckians—Dwayne Nesmith, 43, and Brian Thomas, 31—who were registered in the tournament.

The officers posed as staff and were at the weigh-in when Nesmith and Thomas dropped off the marked fish. They didn't win anything (they were just ounces shy of earning prize money), so when the officers identified themselves, the two could only be charged with misdemeanors. But an investigation revealed that Nesmith and Thomas had entered other tournaments as well—and had been uncannily lucky in them, netting thousands of dollars in prizes and even winning a $30,000 boat. The fishy fishing buddies were arrested and charged with 10 felony counts of theft.

Hotel Hell

MEET MR. MUDGETT

Mudgett (or Henry Holmes, his alias at the time) operated in Chicago at the time of the 1892 Columbian Exposition. Mudgett killed women in a baroque chamber of horrors he had secretly built into his mansion/hotel on 63rd Street. He lured them there by offering them jobs.

IF IT'S TUESDAY, IT MUST BE BETSY

Over the course of two years, Mudgett had something on the order of a hundred secretaries, a fact you'd think someone would notice—but apparently no one did. However, this was 1892, and the sort of woman who had to work out of the home was also the sort of women who was less likely to be missed. Mudgett also went out of his way to "employ" new arrivals to town, who had the added benefit of no one to look out for them.

A MAN OF MANY INTERESTS

Mudgett was not just a crazed whacko who liked killing people. He was a crazed whacko who liked killing people and taking their money. Before he offed his victims, he would gain their trust and then convince them to give him their life savings. His rationale, perhaps, was that once he was done with them, they wouldn't need it anyway.

GORY DETAILS

Mudgett was seriously screwed up. Abusive parents, early episodes of animal mutilation—all the classic signs of

total bonkerness. Mudgett used his medical expertise to perform horrifying "experiments" on his victims. After he had his fun, Mudgett disposed of the evidence in a special cremation oven in the basement—or if he chose to sell the bones to a local medical school, as he did from time to time, there was always the lime pit.

WHAT TIME IS CHECKOUT?

No one knows how many people Mudgett killed; estimates go up into the hundreds. Beyond the "secretaries," Mudgett also offed guests at his "hotel." His cover was the Columbian Exposition, a huge World's Fair taking place a few blocks away; it attracted a vast number of people from faraway places. They wouldn't be missed, at least not by anyone local who might put two and two together.

MR. MUDGETT'S BUDGET

Mudgett's downfall came in the form of Benjamin Pitezel, whom a penny-pinching Mudgett decided to kill for insurance purposes. Wouldn't you know, the insurance company had suspicions, as did Pitezel's wife. Mudgett's response was to murder three of Pitezel's kids before the cops got him in Boston. At that point, they worked backward, found Mudgett's hotel (now a smoking ruin—another insurance scam), and evidence of his terrifying serial murders. Mudgett was tried, convicted, and hanged. Mudgett's last words were that he had really only killed two women.

The Night Stalkee, Part II

(Continued from page 31.)

Around 8:30 on a sweltering Saturday morning in 1985, LA County sheriff's deputy Andy Ramirez arrived at what looked like a typical street fight. Six men had another man pinned down on the sidewalk, who was begging, "Let me go! Let me go!" The deputy took custody of the injured suspect and asked his name. "Ricardo Ramirez," he answered, but Deputy Ramirez didn't realize that this was *the* Night Stalker. Then an angry mob of dozens of people approached. They knew who he was. "Shoot him! Shoot him!" they chanted.

"You could see the anger," Deputy Ramirez later recalled. "They were getting closer and closer." The cop put the killer in handcuffs and into the back of his squad car. Only later did it dawn on him that he had the Night Stalker in custody. When Officer Jim Kaiser from the LAPD arrived, Ramirez (the cop) quickly put Ramirez (the killer) in Kaiser's car and told him to get him out of there before a riot ensued.

The ride to the station is one that Kaiser will never forget. "He had cold, black eyes," he recalled. When they arrived at the precinct, the Night Stalker threw up green vomit—Linda Blair in *The Exorcist* style—all over the parking lot. "He was the ultimate manifestation of absolute evil," said Kaiser.

Richard Ramirez was convicted of 13 murders and sentenced to death, but before he could be executed, he died of cancer in 2013.

DON'T LEAVE A PAPER TRAIL

"Sam" and "Paul" knew this about cash registers: Just as cracking a walnut's hard outer shell yields the nutty goodness inside, so will the cash register issue forth green wads of cash and metal disks of change. This money goodness is why the industrious duo kicked in the door of that Austin, Minnesota, restaurant, wrenched the shop's cash register from its moorings, and fled the scene just as they were spotted by a passing cabdriver, who called the cops to report their adventure.

What Sam and Paul apparently didn't realize is that money is not all that a cash register stores. Some models (including the model they stole) also store long rolls of paper used to print out receipts for the customers. How long are these rolls of paper? Well, their lengths do vary, but in this particular case, it was just long enough that police called to the scene of the crime noticed that it had slipped out from the register, and followed its trail into the nearby bushes—whereupon they found Sam, Paul, and the cash register, all in very close proximity to each other. Sam and Paul were arrested, of course. Hopefully they'll get a receipt with their charges.

KILLER QUOTES

Be warned: these are as disturbing as they are fascinating.
(Number of murders in parentheses.)

"If you shoot someone in the head with a .45 every time, it becomes like your fingerprint, see? But if you strangle one, stab another, and one you cut up, and one you don't, then the police don't know what to do. They think you're four different people. What they really want, what makes their job so much easier, is pattern. What they call a *modus operandi*. That's Latin."
—**Henry Lee Lucas (convicted of 3, confessed to 3,000)**

"The fantasy that accompanies and generates the anticipation that precedes the crime is always more stimulating than the immediate aftermath of the crime itself."
—**Ted Bundy (36+)**

"If I knew the true, real reasons why all this started, before it ever did, I wouldn't probably have done any of it."
—**Jeffrey Dahmer (7)**

"Have you ever seen the coyote in the desert? Watching, tuned in, completely aware, he hears every sound, smells every smell, sees everything that moves. He's in a state of total paranoia, and total paranoia is total awareness."
—**Charles Manson (9)**

"We've all got the power in our hands to kill, but most people are afraid to use it. The ones who aren't afraid control life itself."
—**Richard Ramirez, the Night Stalker (16+)**

Role Models Are People Too

Role Models: Art McKoy and Abdul Rahim, heads of a Cleveland, Ohio, anti-crime organization

Setting an Example: In 1998 they were sentenced to prison for spending $617,597 that the City of Cleveland accidentally deposited in the bank account of their organization. According to news reports, the money landed in their account "when a city data operator punched in the wrong wire-transfer number while intending to pay a utility bill."

Role Model: Susan John, chairperson of the Rochester, New York's Committee on Alcohol and Drug Abuse

Setting an Example: In March 1997, she pleaded guilty for "driving while impaired"—in other words, drunk driving. Her public statement: "This will give me additional insights into the problem of drinking and driving, and I believe will allow me to do my job even more effectively." Sure.

Keep Your Eyes on the Prize, Not the Pies

"A 280-lb. thief broke into a Romanian bakery and stole $250, but couldn't resist the sweet temptation. He got stuck trying to exit through a window—after stuffing himself full of pies. The 29-year-old man was still stuck there in the morning when the shop owner, Vasile Mandache, arrived for work. He said, 'I saw all the pie wrappers on the floor, and then saw a pair of stubby, fat legs hanging out the window. I just had to call my friends to come and have a look before we called the police, it was so funny.'"

—*Short News*

CLERGY GONE WILD

EM-BEELZEBUB-MENT

Parishioners at St. Vincent Ferrer Church in Florida were shocked when auditors reported that $8.7 million was missing from the church's account. They were even more shocked to learn that Fathers John Skehan and Francis Guinan were skimming donations to buy gambling trips, rare coins, a condo, and a pub in Ireland. Skehan was sentenced to 14 months in prison; Guinan got four years. Judge Krista Marx called their crimes "unmitigated greed and unmitigated gall."

THE PARTYIN' RABBI

Rabbi Baruch Chalomish told police he'd rented an apartment in Manchester, England, so he could "relax and have a party." However, his parties caught the attention of the cops, who raided the apartment and arrested Chalomish for dealing cocaine and hiring prostitutes. At his trial, Chalomish told the jury he was a just a wealthy guy who liked to assist people less fortunate than

himself, and he only used cocaine when he couldn't sleep. (He later admitted to spending $1,600 a week on the drug.) The rabbi was cleared of distribution charges but found guilty of possession.

REVEREND JOHN

Reverend John Kameron Erbele of Burnsville, Minnesota, "looks nothing like a traditional pastor," wrote the *Missoula Independent*. Erbele's flock adored him, which is why they were crushed when he was one of 16 men lured to a hotel room to pay for sex in a 2009 police sting. Erbele pleaded guilty and was sentenced to probation and "John School," an educational program for men who solicit prostitutes.

In 2008, a beach was stolen in Jamaica. Over 500 truckloads of pristine white sand was carted off. The thieves remain at large.

The Bandit Queen

The wanted poster read "Cattle and Horse Thief," listed her aliases as "unknown," and identified her crime as heading a band of rustlers in Oklahoma.

THE MAKINGS OF AN OUTLAW

Belle Starr's father, John, ran an inn. Her mother, Eliza, was related to the infamous Hatfield family of Hatfields and McCoys fame. Starr was born Myra "Belle" Shirley in Carthage, Missouri, in 1848. The Shirleys were Confederate sympathizers, and one of their sons was killed during the Civil War. Belle aided the Confederacy during the war, too— the teenager spied on Union troops. It was during this time that she made her first illicit connections: she met outlaw Cole Younger, his brothers, and Jesse and Frank James.

BECOMING THE BANDIT QUEEN

The Shirley family moved to Texas, where Belle married farmer Jim Reed. The couple had two children: Pearl (possibly fathered by Cole Younger) and Ed. There wasn't much money in farming, so Jim Reed began working with the Youngers, the James brothers, and a cattle- and horse-thieving Cherokee clan called the Starrs. Over the next three years, Jim Reed robbed stagecoaches, killed at least one person, and went on the run with his family. The police suspected Belle was in on the crimes—she started

gambling in saloons, wearing a Stetson, and carrying pistols. But there was never any direct evidence that she helped her husband. When Jim was killed by a sheriff's deputy, Belle sent the kids to live with relatives and took his place in the Starr clan.

NEW HUSBAND, OLD PROBLEMS

In 1880, Belle married Sam Starr, and by most accounts, she became the brains behind the family's criminal horse thievery and cattle rustling. Both Belle and Sam were soon caught and charged with horse theft, cattle rustling, and various other crimes. Finally, they ended up before Texas's notorious "Hanging Judge" Isaac Parker, who sentenced them to one year in prison.

BLAST FROM THE SADDLE

The time in jail didn't halt Belle's criminal activities. She continued to be part of the Starr family business even after Sam was killed in a gunfight in 1886. Her next husband and her teenage son were also both indicted for stealing horses during the 1880s. Finally, in February 1889, her outlaw life caught up with her. When Belle was riding home from a shopping trip, a shotgun blast from the woods threw Belle from her saddle. Her spooked horse raced back to the Starr house, alerting Belle's daughter Pearl, who went looking for her mother. But it was too late. Belle Starr was dead just two days before her 41st birthday. Her killer was never caught.

Written in the Pen

Machiavellian ideas have landed people in power or in prison . . . including Machiavelli himself.

Niccolò Machiavelli lived during a time of great plotting and political upheaval in Italy. Initially, he aligned himself with a government that expelled the ruthless and powerful Medici family, which had ruled Florence for 60 years. But when that government fell apart and the Medicis came back with a vengeance, Machiavelli was tossed into prison and tortured. Behind bars, he wrote *The Prince*, a philosophical treatise on politics that said leaders should rule by force instead of by law. In *The Prince*, Machiavelli wrote, "Anyone compelled to choose will find greater security in being feared than in being loved." It was from this book that the term "Machiavellian" came into use to describe a ruthless, deceitful, and cunning leader. Reportedly, Soviet dictator Joseph Stalin was a fan of *The Prince* and kept a copy next to his bed.

Escaping the Rock

*A daring escape from one of the world's
most notorious prisons.*

LIFE ON THE ISLAND

Alcatraz is a 12-acre sandstone island in San Francisco Bay.
The city sits just a mile and a half away, but the icy ocean
currents near the island are treacherous. In 1934 the US
government opened a high-security prison on Alcatraz and
started shipping the country's most dangerous criminals
there—including famous ones like Al Capone and Machine
Gun Kelly. Officials bragged that Alcatraz was escape-
proof, and armed guards watched the inmates' every
move. Some of the prisoners, though, tried to escape. Most
died in the attempt, either shot by guards or drowned in
the ocean. But there was one famous escape attempt that
may—or may not—have been successful.

A DIABOLICALLY CLEVER PLAN

In 1960 convicted bank robbers Frank Lee Morris and
the Anglin brothers started plotting a getaway. Each had a
small vent in his cell, and the men used nail clippers and
spoons stolen from the dining room to pry loose the grills
that covered the vents. The goal was to widen the vents
and dig a tunnel to the outside. Then they would squeeze
through the vents, escape through the tunnel, and use

a makeshift raft to sail across the bay. Each night, they crawled through the vents and crept toward the prison's roof, working to pry away the bolts and bend the bars that blocked access to the outside. They also built a raft out of stolen raincoats and stored it in a corridor below the roof.

SO LONG, SUCKERS!

It took two years, but finally, their work was complete. On June 11, 1962, Morris and the Anglins squeezed through the bars, dragged their raft across the roof, and shimmied 50 feet down a drainpipe to the ground. Then they climbed a 15-foot fence topped with barbed wire . . . and disappeared.

Most people think the trio died in the bay. Men on a Canadian fishing boat said they saw a body floating facedown in the water soon after. None of the prisoners were heard from again, even though all three had been notorious criminals. FBI investigators didn't think they would just stop committing crimes. So what happened after they got into the water, no one knows. The fate of the three men remains a mystery.

 RANDOM FACT:

Richard "The Night Stalker" Ramirez's 1989 murder trial was the most expensive in California history ($1.8 million). Five years later, O. J. Simpson shattered that record when he paid nearly $5 million for his "Dream Team" defense.

Feelin' like a Fool

STUPID FOR 15 MINUTES

"A day after they told their tale of buried treasure on national television, two men were charged with stealing 1,800 antique dollar bills (estimated value: more than $100,000) they said they found in their backyard. As Timothy Crebase, 24, and Barry Billcliff, 27, recounted their story on *Good Morning America, Today,* Fox, and CNN, police noticed the details changed with each appearance. There were discrepancies about when they found the money, how deep it was buried, and more. "When Crebase and Billcliff returned from the New York media blitz, police and the Secret Service were waiting to question them. When it turned out they had found the bills in a barn they were roofing, they were charged with receiving stolen property and conspiracy to commit larceny. The men were unable to raise the $5,000 cash bail."

—*Lawrence* (Mass.) *Eagle-Tribune*

FEELING WANTED

"A suspect in taxicab robberies walked into a New York City police station and failed to notice his picture in a 'wanted' photo on the wall, giving cops one of their easiest busts ever. An alert detective noticed the resemblance and immediately arrested Awiey 'Chucky' Hernandez, 20. Hernandez had gone to the station to inquire about a friend . . . who had been arrested in another investigation."

—*Reuters*

Double Whammy

Sometimes life slaps you upside the head . . . twice.

OWW! Ralph Needs, 80, of Groveport, Ohio, was hospitalized in 2009 after three robbers broke into his home, tied him up, and pistol-whipped him. They broke Needs's nose and stole his truck, computer, and credit cards.
OWW! OWW! Four days later, Needs's son was giving his dad a lesson in self-defense when he loaded up a 9mm pistol—and accidentally shot Needs in the hand. Needs was treated at a nearby (and familiar) hospital and released. His son was not charged with a crime.

OWW! A San Diego, California, Wells Fargo bank was robbed in September 2008. The robber escaped with an undisclosed amount of cash.
OWW! OWW! The same Wells Fargo bank was robbed—on the same day, three hours later—by another bank robber. An FBI spokesman said the robbers were, in order, "The Hard-Hat Bandit," known for wearing a yellow hard hat during his robberies, and "The Chatty Bandit," known for talking on a cell phone as he entered the banks he was about to rob. The two were not working together, the spokesman said. Both of the bandits were later arrested and sent to federal prison.

Poorly Executed

Think your Mondays are rough?

- French officials tried out their new guillotine on a live prisoner, highwayman Nicolas Jacques Pelletier, on April 25, 1792. (It worked.)

- James Rodgers, a Utah murderer who faced a firing squad in 1960, was asked if he had a final request. His response: "Why, yes—a bulletproof vest."

- Only Confederate soldier executed for war crimes: Henry Wirz. He ran the brutal Andersonville military prison, where nearly a third of the Union prisoners died of malnutrition and disease.

- In 1890 murderer William Kemmler of Buffalo, New York, became the first person ever executed by electric chair.

- Being an axe man could be even worse than being a hangman. Take the anonymous beheader of Mary, Queen of Scots in 1587. Rather than one good clean head chopping, his first blow glanced off her lower skull and didn't kill her. A second blow killed her, but her head was hanging on by gristle, so he rocked the axed blade back and forth to cut it. Her head finally detached and he triumphantly lifted it by the hair for the assembled company of nobles . . . but her hair was a wig, and her head fell to the floor.

THE FEDERAL WITNESS PROTECTION PROGRAM

Fun facts about one of the federal government's more mysterious programs.

STARTING OVER

- *Any* relatives or loved ones of a witness are eligible to enter the program if they are potential targets. This includes grandparents, in-laws, girlfriends, boyfriends, even mistresses.
- When a witness enters WITSEC, they get a new name, assistance moving to a new city, and help with rent and other expenses until they find a job. They also get a new birth certificate, Social Security card, and driver's license, but that's about it. The US Marshals Service doesn't create elaborate fake pasts or phony job histories, and it doesn't provide fake credit histories, either.

GETTING A JOB

- It's not easy finding a job without a résumé or job history. "You go to get a job, you got no references and they're not going to lie for you," says former mobster Joseph "Joe Dogs" Iannuzzi. "They don't help you get references for an apartment. You have to go and muscle it for yourself."
- But the Marshals Service does what it can to help. It has compiled a list of companies whose CEOs have agreed to provide jobs to government witnesses.

- When a witness is placed with a company, only the CEO or some other high-level corporate official knows that the employee is a government witness, and even they are not told the person's true identity. They are, however, given details of the employee's criminal history. "You go to the head of the corporation," says retired deputy marshal Donald McPherson, "and you tell him the crimes. You have that obligation. You're not going to help a bank robber get a job as a bank teller."

STAYING IN TOUCH

- Witnesses are forbidden from revealing their new identities, addresses, or the region of the country they live in to friends and loved ones back home. If family members don't know the names and whereabouts of their relatives in the program, criminals are less likely to come after them and try to get the information.

- It's a myth that when witnesses enter the program they are forbidden from ever contacting loved ones outside the program again. They're only forbidden from making *direct* contact—letters and phone calls can be forwarded through the Marshals Service. In-person meetings can be arranged at safe, neutral sites, such as federal buildings or safe houses.

- Does the program work? It's estimated that as many as one in five return to a life of crime after entering the witness protection program. That's about half the recidivism rate of convicts released from prison.

NUDES AND PRUDES

NUDE . . . On Christmas Day 2003, Minneapolis firefighters with sledgehammers knocked down the chimney of Uncle Hugo's Bookstore and rescued a naked man who was trapped inside. The man claimed he had stripped naked in order to fit down the 12-by-12-inch chimney, and that he was looking for some keys he dropped down the shaft. Police didn't buy it—and charged him with attempted burglary.

PRUDE . . . In May 2004, police in Barnsley, England, ordered a local man named Tony Watson to do something about the naked lawn gnomes in his front yard or face arrest for "causing public offense." Watson, an ex-army sergeant, complied by painting bathing suits on the gnomes.

NUDE . . . In 2004, Stephen Gough, known as the "Naked Rambler," accomplished his goal of walking the length of the United Kingdom wearing only socks, walking boots, and a hat. His purpose: to encourage acceptance of the naked body. The 900-mile trip took seven months. Gough was arrested 16 times along the way and served two stints in jail for indecent exposure.

PRUDE . . . In 1998 the US Navy charged an officer with indecent exposure and conduct unbecoming an officer. Why? Lieutenant Patrick Callaghan, 28, had mooned a friend while jogging on the base. "There are people who are real offended when you take your pants down in a public street," Callaghan's commanding officer, Captain Terrence Riley, explained. Callaghan faced dismissal from the Navy, but officials let him off with only a letter of reprimand in the end.

STRANGE CRIME QUOTES

"Squeeze human nature into the straitjacket of criminal justice and crime will appear."
　—Karl Kraus

"Crime seems to change character when it crosses a bridge or a tunnel. In the city, crime is taken as emblematic of class and race. In the suburbs, though, it's intimate and psychological—resistant to generalization, a mystery of the individual soul."
　—Barbara Ehrenreich

"Almost all crime is due to the repressed desire for aesthetic expression."
　—Evelyn Waugh

"A crime persevered in a thousand centuries ceases to be a crime, and becomes a virtue. This is the law of custom, and custom supersedes all other forms of law."
　—Mark Twain

"Commit a crime, and the earth is made of glass."
　—Ralph Waldo Emerson

"Crime is a fact of the human species, a fact of that species alone, but it is above all the secret aspect, impenetrable and hidden. Crime hides, and by far the most terrifying things are those which elude us."
　—Georges Bataille

"It is certain that stealing nourishes courage, strength, skill, tact, in a word, all the virtues useful to a republican system and consequently to our own. Lay partiality aside, and answer me: is theft, whose effect is to distribute wealth more evenly, to be branded as a wrong in our day, under our government which aims at equality? Plainly, the answer is no."
　—Marquis de Sade

Whoops, Wrong Skull

When you're guilty of murder and feeling the heat, make sure the evidence against you is actually from your crime.

MUMMY SOLVES A MURDER

In 1983 Andy Mould was working the peat shredder at the Lindow Moss Peat Company in Cheshire, England, watching for rocks or large pieces of wood that might jam the shredder, when he came across the skull of a middle-aged woman. Police were sure Andy had helped solve a local murder. Poor Mrs. Reyn-Bardt, who lived near the Lindow bog, had been missing since 1960. Authorities had long suspected her husband of doing her in—now, they'd have the evidence to arrest him.

AN OLD LADY, BUT NOT HIS

Frightened by Andy's find, the husband confessed that he'd killed his wife, cut her up, and tossed her in the bog. Though Mr. Reyn-bardt was convicted of murder, the skull was never used as evidence against him. Oxford scientists determined that it belonged to a woman who'd been in the bog since AD 210 and therefore could not be that of his Mrs. Reynbardt. But it was too late . . . the police already had the confession they had been looking for.

Crooked as a Dog's Hind Leg

These New York politicians tried to
buck the system . . . and got caught.

REDEFINING NONPROFIT

Who: State senator Pedro Espada Jr. (D-Bronx)

What He Did: The unraveling of Senator Espada began in 2009, when he defected to the Republican side of the aisle, taking majority control of the state senate away from the Democrats. A five-week legislative deadlock ensued, after which Espada agreed to rejoin the Democratic fold—in exchange for being named majority leader.

Attorney General Andrew Cuomo investigated Espada, and there was plenty to find. Cuomo filed a civil suit accusing Espada of draining $14 million from a group of nonprofit health clinics that he owned in the Bronx and using the money for personal expenses (including $20,000 worth of sushi delivery). Another lawsuit accused Espada of running a bogus job-training program that let him pay janitors at the clinics only $1.70 per hour, far below the minimum wage. He was also being investigated by the federal government and the IRS for his connection to a consulting firm allegedly involved with tax fraud and money laundering. The Bronx district attorney was after him too . . . for not actually living in the Bronx.

Result: In the 2010 Democratic primary, a 34-year-old unknown named Gustavo Rivera defeated Espada.

HELPFUL COP

Who: Bernard Kerik

What He Did: In 1994 Bernie Kerik was an NYPD detective assigned to Mayor Rudy Giuliani's "protective detail" as bodyguard and driver. The mayor trusted Kerik so much that he appointed him as head of the Department of Corrections and then, in 2000, promoted him to NYPD commissioner. As commissioner on September 11, 2001, Kerik happened to meet—and impress—President George W. Bush at the disaster site. In 2004, the Bush administration named Kerik as the next Secretary of the Department of Homeland Security.

Kerik, a highly decorated police officer, had always been a tough guy and a bit of a loose cannon, but when he was vetted by White House officials about his career, he assured them he was squeaky-clean. He wasn't: A New Jersey construction company had paid for $255,000 of renovations on Kerik's Bronx home in hopes that Kerik would help them get a New York City building license. Kerik had contacted city officials on the company's behalf.

Result: Kerik was convicted and sentenced to prison after pleading guilty to eight felony charges. His plea agreement recommended a maximum of 33 months in jail, but the angry judge slapped him with 48, calling him a "toxic combination of self-minded focus and arrogance."

You'd Think She'd Know Better

A WILLING ACCOMPLICE

In February 2011, a friend of Jennifer Green, 28, of Washington, DC, told her he knew about a house that had drugs and cash in it, and that the owners of the house were out of town. If Green sat lookout for him, the man said, he'd burglarize the house and split the loot with her. Green agreed, so the two drove to the house, and she waited in the car while the man broke into the home with a crowbar. He came back with $1,050 in cash and what looked like crack cocaine in a Ziploc bag. Green took $600 and said she didn't want any drugs.

GOTCHA!

Little did the man know that Jennifer Green was a cop! Oh, wait—yes, he did. The Internal Affairs Department of the DC police department had sent the man (a confidential informant) to see if Green, whom they suspected of criminal activity, would go along with the burglary plot, which she did. She was arrested, eventually pleaded guilty to second-degree burglary, and was sentenced to seven months in prison and two years' probation.

Lord High Executioner

THE RISE: Albert Anastasia worked as a longshoreman, where his anger problem became apparent when he killed a fellow workman. Anastasia served only 18 months for the crime because the witnesses "disappeared." Anastasia often worked alongside Lucky Luciano. When Luciano made his bid for power, it was rumored that Anastasia was the executioner. When the commission, La Cosa Nostra, was set up, Anastasia helped head up its "enforcement" arm: Murder, Inc.

THE REIGN: Murder, Inc. is said to have killed hundreds of people in the service of La Cosa Nostra. Anastasia was never prosecuted for any killings because witnesses always disappeared. In 1951 Anastasia became boss of the Gambino crime family, one of the largest in New York. He managed it by killing the family's former boss and by staying in the good graces of Mafioso Frank Costello, who probably allied himself with Anastasia out of fear.

THE FALL: Anastasia's ties with the longshoreman's union helped him grow rich and powerful, but he got too murderous, even for the Mob. His enemies whispered that he was too crazy to be a boss. Vito Genovese wanted to be the boss of all bosses, and Anastasia was in his way. In 1957 Anastasia was shot and killed while he sat in a barber's chair. Newspapers proclaimed that the Mob's worst murderer finally "got the chair."

Are Wii Having Fun Yet?

In September 2009, narcotics investigators in Polk County, Florida, searched the home of a known drug trafficker. While removing weapons, drugs, and stolen goods, several officers passed the time by taking part in a

virtual bowling tournament on the suspect's Wii video-game system. The cops competed fiercely, stopping their search when their turn came up. Little did they know their activities were being recorded by a wireless security camera that the drug dealer had set up to watch for intruders. A local TV station got hold of the footage and aired clips of the cops giving each other high-fives and distracting their fellow bowlers with lewd gestures. "Obviously, this is not the kind of behavior we condone," Lakeland Police Chief Roger Boatner said. Despite his attorney's claims that the search was improper, the career criminal was still sentenced to three years in prison.

To Tell the Truth

Can we ever really know for sure if someone is telling a lie? Most experts agree that the answer is no—but that hasn't stopped people from trying.

ANCIENT LIE DETECTORS

- The Bedouins of the Arabian Peninsula forced suspected liars to lick red-hot pokers with their tongues, on the assumption that liars would burn their tongues and truth tellers wouldn't. The method was cruel but may have had merit, since the procedure measured the moisture content of the suspect's mouth—and dry mouths are often associated with nervousness caused by lying.

- The ancient British used a similar trick: They fed suspects a large "trial slice" of bread and cheese, and watched to see if they could swallow it. If a suspect's mouth was too dry to swallow, he was declared a liar and punished.

- The preferred method in India was to send the suspects into a dark room and have them pull on the tail of a sacred donkey, which was supposed to bray if the person was dishonest . . . at least that's what the suspects thought. The way the system really worked was that the investigators dusted the donkey's tail with black powder. Innocent people, the investigators reasoned, would pull the tail without hesitation . . . but the guilty person, figuring that no one could see them in the darkness, would only pretend to pull the tail but would not touch it at all.

LET'S GET PHYSIOLOGICAL

The first modern lie detector was invented by Cesare Lombroso, an Italian criminologist, in 1895. His device measured changes in pulse and blood pressure. In 1914, another researcher named Vittorio Benussi invented a machine that measured changes in breathing rate. But it wasn't until 1921 that John A. Larson, a medical student, invented a machine that measured pulse, blood pressure, and breathing rate simultaneously. His machine became known as a polygraph, because it measured three types of physiological changes. Today's polygraphs use these methods, as well as more sophisticated measurements.

BEATING THE SYSTEM

Modern-day lie detectors are pretty sophisticated, but they have the same flaw that the ancient methods did—they assume that liars will have some kind of involuntary physical response when they lie. That isn't necessarily the case, according to most experts. Still, many people believe that the polygraph is a useful tool when used in concert with other investigative methods. "It's a great psychological tool," says Plato Cacheris, another defense lawyer. "You take the average guy and tell him you're going to give him a poly, and he's concerned enough to believe it will disclose any deception on his part." (Cacheris is famous for having represented Aldrich Ames, a CIA spy who passed a lie detector test in 1991 and then went on to sell more than $2.5 million worth of secrets to the Russians before he was finally caught in 1994.)

Instant Justice

Sometimes crooks get a dose of instant karma—
and sometimes that's just funny.

CRIME: In 2003 two men attempted to break into a bank in Kansas City.

INSTANT JUSTICE: Cops saw the two thieves running down a street with crowbars in their hands and drove after them into a grassy field. When they lost sight of the fleeing suspects, the officers got out of the car—and then heard moans. One of the robbers was hiding in the tall grass and the cops drove over him. The lucky thief suffered only a scrape on his forehead.

CRIME: An inmate in Missouri jail tried to flee.

INSTANT JUSTICE: The escapee ran into the prison's darkened parking garage and headed for an open door. He turned around, gave the approaching deputies a salute, and dashed through the door . . . running smack into the brick wall behind it. Deputies took the unconscious man to a nearby hospital.

CRIME: Wanton Beckwith, 27, stole a car in May 2003. After a high-speed chase by police, he ran into a house to hide.

INSTANT JUSTICE: The home's occupant pointed a samurai sword at the intruder, led him back outside, and held him at sword's length until police arrived.

BEHIND THE (MOB) HITS

Pro tip: when gambling with ruthless gangsters,
be ready to pony up, win or lose.

Background: Arnold "the Brain" Rothstein was one of the earliest leaders of American organized crime. He wasn't a gun-toting mobster—he was a planner, bankroller, and political fixer. Instead of muscle, he used brains to forge alliances among underworld factions and crooked politicians. He kept a low profile and financed bootlegging operations. Rothstein was also a compulsive gambler. In September 1928, he bought into a high-stakes poker game run by a man named George McManus. The game lasted two days; Rothstein lost $320,000. Claiming the game was fixed, he refused to pay up.

The Place: On November 4, Rothstein received an urgent phone call from McManus to meet him at the Park Central Hotel. The Park Central was located across the street from Carnegie Hall. This ritzy hotel was one of Manhattan's most popular spots. It was a very public place—a place where Rothstein would have felt safe.

The Hit: Hotel employees later found him in the stairwell holding his abdomen—he'd been shot. Was it because of the debt, or had one of his rivals simply found a viable excuse to eliminate him? No one knows for sure, because in the one day that Rothstein lived, every time police asked him who shot him, he answered, "Me mudder did it."

Bible John

*The haunting tale of one of England's most
mysterious serial killers.*

Between 1968 and 1969, three women, aged 25, 29, and 32,
were murdered in Glasgow, Scotland. Each had been raped
and strangled. The clue that tied them together: All three
victims were menstruating at the time of their deaths. Sanitary
napkins or tampons had been placed near their bodies, and their
purses—but not the contents of the purses—were stolen by their
killer. Most bizarrely, they had all met their murderer at the very
same venue—the Barrowland Ballroom. According to police
reports, several people actually saw the killer on the night of the
third murder. Hellen Puttock, 29, had gone to Barrowland with
her sister Jean. They met a man there who introduced himself as
"John." After spending more than an hour together at the club,
they left in a taxi. The taxi first dropped off Jean at her home and
then dropped off Helen and the man at Helen's home. Helen
was found dead in her backyard the next day. Jean told police
that the man had quoted the Old Testament during the taxi ride,
leading the media to dub him "Bible John."

In 2007 a Scottish man named Peter Tobin was convicted
of the murders of three young women in Scotland and
England between 1991 and 2007. Many people believe that
Tobin—who lived in Glasgow until 1969 (he turned 23 that
year)—is Bible John. However, this has not been confirmed.

HAIRPIN TRIGGER

The controversial case of Sacco and Vanzetti.

THE CRIME: In April 1920, witnesses saw the guard of a shoe factory gunned down by two men who stole $15,773 in cash.

THE PERPS: Nicola Sacco and Bartolomeo Vanzetti, two Italian immigrants, were known anarchists. When cops stopped them on a streetcar, they were armed and evasive when questioned. When the cops learned that Sacco hadn't gone to work on the day of the shoe factory killings, they were both arrested for murder.

THE TRIAL: At the trial, prosecution witnesses placed Sacco and Vanzetti at the scene of the crime, and the prosecution's gun experts said that the men owned the type of guns used in the murders. The defense countered with alibis—Sacco was seen in Boston getting a passport, and Vanzetti was seen selling fish. Experts for the defense contradicted the prosecution's gun experts and insisted that the defendants' guns hadn't been used in the murders. The trial became international news when defense lawyers claimed Sacco and Vanzetti were being targeted because they were poor immigrants who held unpopular political views.

THE VERDICT: Both were found guilty, which caused an uproar in the United States, Europe, and South America.

HISTORIC CONSEQUENCES: Over the years, researchers have continued to question the verdict. But modern ballistic tests reveal that a bullet from Sacco's gun did kill the guard. Many historians contend that Vanzetti was likely innocent—but refused to turn in his guilty comrades, including Sacco.

Dahlia M for Murder

Elizabeth Short moved west to chase stardom but never found success as an actor. She did, however, become famous for one thing—being the murder victim in one of Hollywood's most notorious unsolved cases.

On the morning of January 15, 1947, a woman was walking near an abandoned field in Los Angeles. As she passed it, she spotted what she thought was a broken mannequin lying in the overgrown weeds. She took a closer look. It wasn't a broken mannequin at all. It was the body of young aspiring actor Elizabeth Short. The battered corpse had been cleanly cut in half and laid carefully posed in the grass. Not a drop of blood was found at the scene; it appeared the nude body had been washed before being brought to the lot and abandoned. Her clothes were missing, and no personal belongings were found. It was the beginning of one of Hollywood's most gruesome mysteries, the unsolved Black Dahlia murder.

THE INVESTIGATION

The murder caused a sensation in Los Angeles. Police were baffled, and the press sensationalized the case by covering every angle and detail. It was nicknamed the Black Dahlia murder because that was Short's nickname, in reference to her jet-black hair and fondness for dark clothing.

A month after Short's body was found, the *Los Angeles Examiner* received a strange package with a note: "Here is the Dahlia's belongings. Letter to follow." Inside they found Short's Social Security card, birth certificate, business cards, address book, photographs of her with various men, and claim checks for suitcases she had stowed at the bus depot. The police determined that all the items in the package had been washed with gasoline to remove any fingerprints. Nevertheless, they painstakingly hunted down every lead to no avail. The letters, when they came, contained no usable clues.

At first, the leading suspect was Robert Manley, the last person to see Short alive. They had spent the night together in a hotel. The next day, Short told Manley that she was returning home to Massachusetts and asked him for a ride to the Biltmore Hotel, where she was meeting her sister. Manley dropped her off there and last saw her speaking on the lobby telephone. After extensive interrogation and two passed polygraph tests, the police cleared Manley. Nevertheless, the interrogation took a serious toll on Manley, who eventually suffered a nervous breakdown and was committed to a psychiatric hospital. To complicate matters, the police were inundated with false confessions. More than 50 "Confessing Sams" confessed to the murder and cost the police valuable time trying to rule them out. No strong leads emerged, and the case has remained open ever since.

URBAN LEGEND: CRIME EDITION

The real scoop behind a popularly circulated crime story.

THE STORY: A young woman finishes shopping at the mall and walks out to her car to go home. But there's an old lady sitting in the car. "I'm sorry ma'am, but this isn't your car," the woman says. "I know," the old lady replies, "but I had to sit down." Then she asks the young woman for a ride home. The young woman agrees, but then remembers she locked the car when she arrived at the mall. She pretends to go back into the mall to get her sister, and returns with a security guard. The guard and the old lady get into a fight, and in the struggle the old lady's wig falls off, revealing that she's actually a man. The police take the man away, and under the car seat, they find an axe.

THE TRUTH: The modern form of the tale comes from the early 1980s and places the action at numerous malls . . . New York, Las Vegas, Milwaukee, Chicago, and even Fresno, California, depending on who's telling the story. Folklorists speculate the tale may date all the way back to an 1834 English newspaper account of "a gentleman in his carriage, who on opening the supposed female's reticule [handbag] finds to his horror a pair of loaded pistols inside."

What, Is That a Crime?

UNWITTING ACCOMPLICE

In 2013 a mental-health caseworker was driving a patient named Nicholas York around to do some errands. York had been kicked out of a motel the night before, so the caseworker was taking him to another one. On the way, York said he needed to withdraw some money from the bank. The caseworker pulled into the parking lot and waited while York went inside. A few minutes later, York got back in the car, and the two men drove away. Strangely, the bank workers came outside and were watching them. The caseworker waved as he pulled onto the street and headed for the motel. A few minutes after he dropped off York, the caseworker received a phone call: the bank had been robbed, and the getaway car was a county-issued vehicle. The confused caseworker led police to the motel, where they found York and all the money. York was arrested without incident.

PIPE DREAMS

In the midst of a bitter divorce in 2013, Randolph Smith came up with a unique way to annoy his soon-to-be ex-wife. When she arrived home one afternoon, she discovered a pipe bomb on the kitchen table, with a note that read: "This is an explosive. It's a bomb." Written directly on the table: "Boom!" His wife called 911. The police determined the bomb was fake, and tracked down Smith at a nearby Burger King. When asked, he explained, "She pissed me off. What? Is that illegal?" (Yes.)

GUILTY UNTIL PROVEN INNOCENT

In 1985 Kirk Noble Bloodsworth, 23, went on trial for the 1984 sexual assault and murder of a nine-year-old girl in Maryland. Bloodsworth pleaded innocent. No physical evidence linked him to the crime, and he had witnesses who put him somewhere else at the time of the crime. Despite all that, Bloodsworth was convicted and sentenced to death.

TRIED AND TRIED AGAIN

The original conviction was overturned on appeal—but the second trial saw Bloodsworth convicted again. Seven years passed. In 1992, Bloodsworth read a book that had a reference to DNA testing in it. He told his lawyer about it, who then contacted the Innocence Project.

The team was able to determine that biological evidence had been taken in the case. In April 1992, the prosecutor agreed to have DNA testing done. The DNA test conclusively proved that Bloodsworth could not have been the person who committed the crime for which he'd been convicted (twice) and for which he had already served eight years— two of them on death row. His conviction was overturned.

The real rapist and killer in the Bloodsworth case wasn't discovered for another ten years after Bloodsworth's exoneration. When Bloodsworth heard the man's name— Kimberly Shay Ruffner—he said, "My God. I know him." Ruffner had spent five years in the same prison as Bloodsworth. "I gave him library books," Bloodsworth said, "and he never said a word."

Ye Olde Crime and Punishment

From "No Parking" zones to "No Smoking" areas, sometimes it seems as if our society operates under too many rules and regulations. Life didn't used to be like that, did it?

MAKING THE PUNISHMENT FIT THE CRIME

Public humiliation was a favorite way of teaching those darn miscreants a lesson during the Middle Ages. You may have heard about the practice of putting people in stocks or in the pillory in the town square for their offenses, but have you heard of these variations?

The Baker's Cage

Bakers who sold loaves of bread that were too light for the advertised size were placed in something called a "baker's cage" or "baker's chair," a seesaw device that dunked the baker in a pond. The number of dunkings was determined by the difference between the wrong weight and the right weight.

The Ass of Shame

Women who beat their husbands had to ride an ass through town facing backward. If the husband hadn't tried to defend himself, he had to lead the ass.

The Wheelbarrow

Lovers whose lascivious conduct had gone too far for the town authorities were sentenced in this way: the seducer had to push the object of his lust through the streets in a wheelbarrow while onlookers were encouraged to throw garbage at them.

The Barrel

Men who spent too much time and money on drink were paraded through town wearing a barrel painted with humiliating pictures.

The Neck Violin

A double iron collar, it was fastened around the necks of quarreling women who then had to stand locked together in the public square until they agreed to stop bickering and keep the peace.

The Shame Flute

Pity the bungling musician who committed the terrible crime of playing music badly. He was tied to the pillory in the town square with his neck encased in the shame flute, an iron neck restraint with an instrument attached.

The Masks of Shame

These iron masks came in a variety of shapes, each designed to portray the person's offense. A gossip wore an iron mask with a long tongue. A person who stuck his nose into his neighbors' business wore a mask with a huge nose. If one behaved like a pig, he wore the pig's mask in public. The masks hid the wearer's face, but in the small towns of the Middle Ages, where everyone knew everyone else—they did not provide anonymity. And to make sure that the townspeople came out for the public humiliation, the masks were fitted with large bells on top to announce the presence of a new victim.

AW, QUIT YER BELLY-ACHIN'

So the next time you play an instrument poorly, have a little too much to drink, or mis-weigh your bread, be happy you live in the 21st century, the century of "It's my own darn business."

The Boss of All Bosses

THE RISE: Born in 1897, Lucky Luciano moved to New York from Sicily when he was nine. His Sicilian heritage put him in good stead with Joe "the Boss" Masseria, head of one of the most powerful gangs in New York. In 1929 Masseria was at war with Salvatore Moranzano, the leader of a rival gang. Each man wanted to be *capo di tutti capi,* or the "boss of all bosses." Since Luciano worked for Masseria, Moranzano's men attacked him and left him for dead. But instead of seeking revenge, Luciano cut a deal: he arranged Masseria's execution in 1931, took over for Masseria, and let Moranzano become the boss of all bosses— for about six months. Then Luciano had Moranzano killed.

THE REIGN: With both old bosses gone, Luciano revamped what became known as La Cosa Nostra (LCN). Nixing the "boss of all bosses" position, Luciano allowed New York's five bosses to run their own crime families. Crime bosses from across the country each held a place on the "Commission," which had settled disputes. Under Luciano, LCN concentrated on making money from gambling, extortion, arson, and labor racketeering—and started investing in legitimate businesses.

THE FALL: Lucky's luck ran out in 1935, when the authorities convicted (some say framed) him for running a prostitution ring. Luciano controlled his crime family from prison until he was deported to Italy in 1946. He died of a heart attack in Naples in 1962.

Big Payoffs

STICK 'EM UP!

"A man with two sticks demanded money at a food mart in San Antonio, Texas. Employees and customers did not think the man was serious, so they laughed at him. He then left, went to a beauty supply store down the street, and demanded money there. When a female employee said she didn't have any money, the man started hitting the cash register with his sticks. The woman told him to stop, and gave him two dollars just to make him leave, which he did. No one was hurt."

—WOAI-TV (San Antonio, Texas)

ARMED BOOBERY

"Armed robbers . . . pursued a money courier at high speed before shooting at his vehicle and forcing him to stop on a road in Gronau, Germany. Forcing the trunk open, one of the crooks snatched a case before fleeing again. But instead of taking the money, he made off with a first-aid kit. Police spokesman Johann Steinlitz said: 'If there was an award for the dumbest crooks, they would certainly be in the running.'"

—Ananova

A Long and Lonely Road

*The story behind the many disappearances
along the Highway of Tears.*

Dotted along a desolate stretch of freeway in northern
Canada are billboards that read "Girls Don't Hitchhike
on the Highway of Tears, Killer on the Loose!" From the
1970s to the present day, numerous women have been
murdered or have simply gone missing on what has been
dubbed the "Highway of Tears," a remote 450-mile-long
stretch of Highway 16 between the towns of Prince George
and Prince Rupert in British Columbia. Royal Canadian
Mounted Police say the number of women killed or
missing there is 18, but native leaders in the region (several
victims were First Nations people) say the number is much
higher—possibly even in the fifties. While no one believes
all of the murders are linked, police have indicated they
believe a single serial killer is responsible for at least some,
and possibly several, of the attacks. Some even believe the
many disappearances are the result of multiple serial
killers operating in the same area. And while there have
been many suspects in the case, nobody has ever been
arrested. The resources invested in solving this mystery
have been drastically reduced over the years, but the case
remains open.

Hey, I Recognize That Butt Crack!

Well, I do. What do you want me to say?

- In 1997, Minneapolis native Tom Tipton got the thrill of his life when he was invited to sing the national anthem before a Minnesota Vikings football game. Across town, an off-duty sheriff was watching the pregame show—and recognized Tipton's name. Tipton, it turned out, was wanted on two warrants in Minneapolis. He was arrested during the game.

- In 2006 Robert Russel Moore of Maryland, was charged with the robbery of an Arby's restaurant where he was recently employed. At the subsequent trial, four of his former fellow employees testified that, although he was wearing a mask, they recognized Moore in surveillance tapes—especially when he bent over and they recognized his "butt crack" above the top of his pants. A former manager also testified that he had talked to Moore repeatedly about his "butt crack problem." Moore was sentenced to 10 years in prison.

- In 1999 a man wearing a long dark coat and a mask walked into the Royal Casino in Aberdeen, South Dakota, pointed a gun at the clerk, and demanded money. The next day, local man Jerold Nissen, 44, was arrested for the crime. Nissen was a regular at the casino, and the clerk had recognized the distinctively powerful odor of his cologne. He was sentenced to seven years in prison.

Did the Punishment Fit the Crime?

They don't give judges awards for creativity—
but maybe they should. You be the judge.

THE DEFENDANT: Edward Bello, 60, a vending machine repairman and small-time crook

THE CRIME: Conspiracy to use stolen credit cards, with which he racked up more than $26,000 in charges

THE PUNISHMENT: Federal district court judge Alvin K. Hellerstein sentenced Bello to 10 months of home detention . . . *with no TV.* The tube-free environment would "create a condition of silent introspection that I consider necessary to induce the defendant to change his behavior." Despite a 30-year history of committing petty crimes, Bello has never spent a day in prison and says he's grateful to the judge for sparing him from the slammer one more time. But he's appealing the no-TV sentence anyway, claiming that it's a form of censorship and violates his First Amendment rights. "Let's face it," he says, "a television is sort of like your umbilical cord to life."

THE DEFENDANT: Albert Brown, a repeat drug offender in San Francisco, California

THE CRIME: Selling drugs to an undercover cop

A NOVEL APPROACH: Rather than decide the sentence himself, Judge James Warren of San Francisco handed Brown one of his judicial robes and told him to put it on.

"This is your life," he told Brown. "You are your own judge. Sentence yourself."

THE PUNISHMENT: Brown, in tears, gave himself six months in jail. Then, according to news reports, he tacked on a "string of self-imposed conditions such as cleaning himself up for his kids, and steering clear of the neighborhood where he got busted."

"The Probation Department recommended six months and a good lecturing," Judge Warren told reporters. "But I figured, I'm not that good at lecturing. He, on the other hand, was very good at lecturing himself. And maybe this time it will stick. I had the transcript typed up and sent over to him. Just in case he forgets."

THE DEFENDANT: Alan Law, 19, of Derwent, Ohio

THE CRIME: Disturbing the peace by driving through town with his truck windows rolled down and the stereo blasting

THE PUNISHMENT: Municipal court judge John Nicholson gave Law a choice: pay a $100 fine or sit and listen to polka music for four hours. Law chose to face the music. A few days later, he reported to the police station and was locked in an interview room, where he listened to the "Blue Skirt Waltz," "Who Stole the Kishka," "Too Fat Polka," and other hits by Cleveland polka artist Frankie Yankovic. Law managed to sit through it and has since abandoned his plans to buy an even louder stereo for his truck.

HELLO, 911?

A quick lesson in what does not constitute an emergency.

GAS LEAK

Officers in Janesville, Wisconsin, responded to a 911 call about a domestic disturbance after a husband and wife got into an argument. When they arrived at the home, the wife explained to the officers that the argument had started after the husband had "inappropriately passed gas" while they were tucking their son into bed. (The man was not charged with a crime.)

IT'S A *LOVE* EMERGENCY

In July 2006, a sheriff's deputy in Aloha, Oregon, responded to a noise complaint at the home of Lorna Jeanne Dudash. He spoke with the woman for just a moment and then left. A short time later Ms. Dudash called 911—and asked if that "cutie-pie" officer could return. "He's the cutest cop I've seen in a long time. I just want to know his name," she said. The confused dispatcher asked again what her emergency was and Dudash responded, "Honey, I'm just going to be honest with you, I'm 45 years old and I'd just like to meet him again." The dispatcher sent the officer to Dudash's home—and he promptly arrested her for abuse of the emergency-dispatch system.

Who Was D. B. Cooper?

Possible suspects from the infamous hijacking.
Continued from page 98.

POSSIBLE SUSPECT #1. In 1972, four
months after Cooper's successful
hijacking, another hijacker
stole a plane in Denver, using
the same MO as D. B. Cooper.
The Denver flight was also a
727 with a rear stairway, from
which the hijacker made his
getaway by parachute. A tip led
police to Richard McCoy Jr., a
man with an unusual profile: married
with two children, a former Sunday school
teacher, a law enforcement major at Brigham Young University,
a former Green Beret helicopter pilot with service in Vietnam,
and an avid skydiver. When FBI agents arrested McCoy two
days after the Denver hijacking, they found a jumpsuit and
a duffel bag containing half a million dollars. McCoy was
convicted and sentenced to 45 years.

POSSIBLE SUSPECT #2. In August 2000, Jo Weber told *US
News and World Report* that shortly before her husband Duane
died in 1995, he told her, "I'm Dan Cooper." He'd talked in
his sleep about jumping out of a plane, so she looked into his
background and discovered he'd spent time in an Oregon

prison. She also found a Northwest Airlines ticket stub from the Seattle-Tacoma airport among his papers. She found a book about D. B. Cooper in the local library—it had notations in the margins matching her husband's handwriting. She relayed her suspicions to FBI agent Ralph Himmelsbach, chief investigator of the D. B. Cooper case. He insists Weber is one of the likeliest suspects. More recently, facial recognition software was used to find the closest match to the composite picture of Cooper. Of the 3,000 photographs used (including Richard McCoy's), Duane Weber's was identified as the best match.

POSSIBLE SUSPECT #3. In 2017 a new theory emerged that D. B. Cooper had been identified . . . and was living in San Diego, California. Robert Rackstraw was a former helicopter pilot for the US Army. Though the case was officially closed by the FBI in July 2016, armchair detectives everywhere continued to investigate, claiming they had found almost 100 pieces of evidence that linked him to the crime, most of it circumstantial. Rackstraw was identified as a possible suspect in the initial investigation, but was cleared because he was only 28 at the time—much younger than the description given by the flight attendants. Rackstraw denies any involvement in the 1971 skyjacking.

> "A recent police study found that you're much more likely to get shot by a fat cop if you run."
> —**Dennis Miller**

You Don't Know Jack

Jack the Ripper is among history's most infamous killers. Between August and November 1888, five prostitutes in London were violently murdered. Despite the participation of London's city police and Scotland Yard, interviews with over 1,500 witnesses, and investigation of hundreds of possible suspects, the case was closed in 1892—unsolved.

THE PROFILE

In 1988 the FBI came up with a criminal profile of Jack the Ripper. Supposedly, he was . . .

- A resident of Whitechapel.
- From a broken home.
- Someone with training in medicine, such as a butcher or a mortician's assistant.
- Single—since he could stay out all night stalking women.
- Someone with a regular job—since he killed on the weekends or in the early morning hours.
- Between the ages of 28 and 36.
- Neat, shy, a loner, and a man who hated women.

THE SUSPECT POOL

Based on those criteria, the BBC came up with the following most likely suspects in 2008:

1. **Montague Druitt.** He did not match descriptions of the killer. However, he was the son of a doctor, had a history of mental problems, and played cricket tournaments near Whitechapel around the time of several of the murders. In December 1888, just weeks after the last victim was found, Druitt drowned himself in

the Thames River. After his death, the murders stopped.

2. **Prince Albert Victor Christian Edward ("Prince Eddy").** The grandson of Queen Victoria, Prince Eddy wasn't a suspect until 1970, when a surgeon named Thomas Stowell published an article that implicated him in the crimes. According to Stowell, the prince was driven crazy by syphilis and committed the murders while consumed by madness. The author also believed that the royal family knew the prince was Jack the Ripper and covered it up. None of the papers Stowell cited can be corroborated, and according to logs kept by the royal family, Prince Eddy had alibis for most of the murders. (Of course, that could've been part of the cover-up.)

3. **Nathan Kaminsky ("David Cohen").** A few weeks after the last Whitechapel murder, police in the East End discovered a man wandering the streets and muttering to himself in Yiddish. He was taken to a lunatic asylum and named "David Cohen." He attacked a guard with a lead pipe, spat out food, and kicked people who walked by him. Eventually, Cohen was confined to his bed and died in the asylum. It turned out that "David Cohen" was probably a man named Nathan Kaminsky, a cobbler and tailor who had syphilis and was treated in an infirmary that was right in the center of the murderer's domain. Supposedly, Kaminsky was "cured" in May 1888 and released. Their evidence is pretty good: He was released into the East End population at the right time (the murders started that August) and fit witness descriptions. Once incarcerated at the lunatic asylum as David Cohen, the murders stopped.

Over 120 years later, the true identity of Jack the Ripper remains a mystery.

ANTI-HERO

Sometimes, doing the right thing can blow up in your face.

THE ACCUSED: Richard Jewell, a security guard at the 1996 Olympics in Atlanta, Georgia

STORY: Jewell was patrolling Centennial Park at 1:00 a.m. when he noticed a suspicious bag near where thousands of people were enjoying a concert. The bag contained three pipe bombs and shrapnel. Jewell called the bomb squad and immediately started evacuating people. Minutes later, the bombs exploded. Two people were killed and dozens more were injured, but it could have been much worse. The press called Jewell a hero as the manhunt for the bomber began. The FBI was under a lot of pressure, which may be why they leaked a "lone bomber" criminal profile, with a note that Jewell was a "person of interest." For the rest of the summer, the FBI and the press followed Jewell wherever he went. Editorials called him a "failed cop" who planted the bomb and then called it in so people would think he was a hero.

OUTCOME: In 1996 the FBI announced Jewell was no longer a suspect. Jewell sued four news outlets for libel. "This isn't about the money," he said in 2006. "It's about clearing my name."

In 2003 the FBI arrested Eric Rudolph, who had also bombed an abortion clinic and a lesbian nightclub in Atlanta. Investigators were able to link him to the Olympic bombing because of similarities among the three bombs.

Criminal Minds

Most common reason for hiring a private detective in the United States: tracking down someone who owes you money.

In 1976 Bruce Springsteen was arrested for trying to climb over the gates of Graceland.

John Dillinger was the first criminal designated "Public Enemy Number One" by the FBI.

Pro wrestler and actor Dwayne "the Rock" Johnson has a degree in criminology.

Confucius's job: he became China's minister of crime in 501 BC.

As with movies and TV today, many people in 19th-century London blamed the growing crime rate on violence in the theaters.

Alibi means "elsewhere" in Latin.

In 1969 Neil Young and Jimi Hendrix stole a truck to get to Woodstock in time to perform.

The first law school in the United States: the Litchfield Law School in Connecticut, established in 1773. Its graduates included Aaron Burr, Horace Mann, and John C. Calhoun.

The original Draconian (someone who's extremely harsh or cruel): Draco of Athens, executed people for stealing cabbage.

Mary Jenkins Surratt was the first woman executed by the US government. She was hanged in 1865 for conspiracy in the assassination of President Abraham Lincoln.

What crime led to Billy the Kid's first run-in with the law? Stealing cheese. He was 15.

BUSTED ON FACEBOOK

UNFRIEND

Friend: Dylan Osborn, 37, of Buckinghamshire, England

Story: Shortly after Osborn joined Facebook in 2007, a window appeared on the screen asking if he wanted to send "friend requests" to everyone on his email list. He clicked "Yes." Result: a friend request went to his estranged wife, Claire Tarbox . . . with whom he was under court order to not have any contact.

Busted! Tarbox called police, and Osborn was arrested for sending the friend request and then sentenced by a judge to 10 days in jail. Osborn claimed that he hadn't understood how Facebook works and had no idea the request would be sent to Tarbox. "I didn't even know she *had* a Facebook account," he told reporters after his release. "To be honest, I don't think the judge understood how it works, either."

LUNCH LIZARDS

Friend: Vanessa Starr Palm, 23, of Illinois, and Alexander Daniel Rust, 24, of Indiana

Story: While Palm and Rust were on vacation in the Bahamas in 2009, they saw a wild iguana. They killed it. And then they cooked and ate it. And they took photos of the whole process— and posted them on Facebook.

Busted! Iguanas are endangered species in the Bahamas. Someone contacted authorities about the photos, and Bahamian police tracked down and arrested the couple. They were released from jail on $500 bail and eventually paid fines for their illegal meal.

THE DOCTOR IS IN (YOUR WILL)

Decades before Jack Kevorkian, John Bodkin Adams earned the moniker "Doctor Death" for being a suspected serial killer and master manipulator. He convinced his elderly patients (or victims) to change their wills so that he could benefit from their deaths, resulting in a doozy of a conflict of interest.

In 1922 Adams took up a general practice in the sleepy British town of Eastbourne, known as a pleasant retirement location for the well-to-do. Over the course of more than 20 years, he managed to treat 163 patients who suffered suspicious deaths. Of those, 132 left him money or items in their wills. It was suspected that through his treatment, he managed to "ease the passing" of his patients by keeping them in suspended states of disability through drugs. In one case, utilizing a cocktail of heroin and morphine to supposedly remedy a woman's discomfort after a stroke. Although that particular patient, Edith Alice Morrell, left Adams out of her will, he still managed to claim a small amount of money, cutlery, and a Rolls-Royce.

By 1956 Adams was one of the wealthiest doctors in England. In July of that year, police were finally tipped off to the dirty dealings of Doctor Death, thanks to an anonymous call from the friend of a victim. The police quickly learned about Adams's preferred technique of

administering "special injections" to his patients, which never took take place in the presence of a nurse; nor did he ever explain to anyone what was in those concoctions. Adams's trial began in March 1957, splashed across the front pages of newspapers worldwide as the "murder trial of the century." After 44 minutes of deliberation, Adams was found not guilty. He was convicted of lesser charges in a separate trial. But at least he was stripped of his license to practice medicine.

In 1961 he was reinstated as a general practitioner. His authority to prescribe dangerous drugs was restored a year later. He died in 1983 from complications due to an injury suffered while shooting clay pigeons.

On December 8, 1980, John Lennon was shot and killed while walking in to his New York City apartment building. Before that tragic night, Lennon had claimed the building was haunted. And Yoko Ono, who still lives there today, says that her late husband has become one of the Dakota's resident ghosts. One night, she saw an apparition of him sitting at his piano. He turned to look at her and said, "Don't worry, Yoko. I'm still with you."

Don't Take It at Face Value

NO CENTS AT ALL

In 2012 Dakoda Garren and Elizabeth Massman, both 19, were hired to clean a house in Vancouver, Washington. After they left, the homeowner noticed her valuable coin collection was missing. Garren denied everything. "You don't have any evidence on me," he told police indignantly. They let him go, but asked the public to be on the lookout for any rare coins. A week later, a movie-theater employee called police to report that a young couple had paid for their tickets with quarters . . . from the 1930s. It turned out they'd been using the coins—worth between $1,000 and $18,500 each—at face value to buy pizza and play video games. Garren and Massman were arrested. Most, but not all, of the valuable coins were recovered.

THREAT LEVEL: ZERO

In 2012 Wade Radzinski, 25, a hotel worker in Scottsdale, Arizona, reported a bomb threat. When the cops arrived, he said there was no longer any danger because the person who'd made the threat promised to leave in exchange for a large sum of money. Radzinski said he gave the man $290 of the hotel's money and he was long gone. "So you guys can leave." Officers didn't believe it. They asked Radzinski if they could search his car; he said yes. And—lo and behold—when officers removed the gas cap, the $290 fell out. "I don't know why I thought this was a good idea," Radzinski said afterward.

At Their Fingertips

Ever wonder how fingerprinting came about?
Wonder no more.

Crime: In 1905 store manager Thomas Farrow lay dead from a beating, and his wife Anne, who was unconscious, would die a few days later. The shop and living space above the shop were ransacked, and police found an empty cashbox with a greasy fingerprint lying on the floor.

The Perps: Suspicion fell on Alfred (22) and Albert (20) Stratton. Neither had an arrest record, but locals claimed they were thieves. A milkman thought he'd seen them

nearby at the time of the murders, but failed to identify them after their arrest. Authorities thought there was little chance of convicting the brothers of murder—until they took their fingerprints and discovered that Alfred's print matched the one on the cashbox.

The Trial: In 1905 fingerprints were a new forensic tool and prosecutors weren't sure that a jury would accept them as sufficient evidence, let alone evidence that could hang two men. The trial hinged on testimony from forensic expert Inspector Collins, who explained how Alfred's prints had been carefully matched to those on the cashbox by tracing and comparing the ridges, and how the two impressions corresponded exactly.

The Verdict: Guilty

Historic Consequences: With fingerprints accepted as a method of identification in a murder case, this was the beginning of using forensic science to establish guilt or innocence. Both Alfred and Albert were hanged.

What was the only physical evidence that linked serial killer Ted Bundy to his crimes? Bite marks.

Judges on the Loose

*Proof that being a judge is no guarantee
that a person has good judgment.*

Judge: Sharon "Killer" Keller, the presiding judge on the Texas Criminal Court of Appeals

Background: In 2007 the Supreme Court agreed to hear a case on the constitutionality of lethal injection to execute condemned prisoners. Michael Richard was to be executed in Texas that night. Richard's lawyers wanted to request a stay of execution based on the Supreme Court's action, but they had computer problems, and shortly before 5:00 p.m. they called the Court of Appeals and asked if it could remain open a few minutes past closing time so they could file their papers. "Tell them we close at five," Judge Keller replied. The lawyers missed the deadline, and Richard was executed a few hours later.

What Happened: Keller was charged with five counts of misconduct relating to the case. Keller's other claim to fame: authoring a 1997 opinion that denied a new trial to a man serving 99 years for aggravated rape after DNA tests *excluded* him as a suspect in the crime. "We can't give new trials to everyone who establishes, after conviction, that they might be innocent," Keller explained to an interviewer.

Update: In 2010 Keller was fined $100,000 for failing to list more than $2.8 million in assets on financial disclosure forms.

The Milkshake Murder

Her milkshake brought all the boys to the . . . graveyard.

KILLER DRINK!

In the early 1960s, Rene Castellani was working for radio station CKNW in Vancouver, Canada. He was known for his publicity stunts. To help the BowMac car dealership sell more automobiles, Rene stayed perched on top of the 10-story BowMac sign for eight days, vowing not to leave until every car was sold. He also once posed as an Indian prince and drove around town in a limousine with bodyguards and dancing girls.

APPEARANCES ARE DECEIVING

Rene was a "devoted" husband. He brought his wife, Esther, a daily treat of a vanilla milkshake. In 1965 Esther's health began to fail with each shake she drank. She started to get stomach and lower-back pain that kept her out of work. Around this time, she found a love letter in Rene's pocket and confronted him about it. But Esther's health was the bigger concern. She began to have bouts of nausea, diarrhea, and intense vomiting. Her fingers and toes went numb. She couldn't walk or use her hands.

For two months, Esther was hospitalized as doctors puzzled over her condition, but they couldn't find the answer or cure. In August of 1965, Esther died at age 40, leaving behind her husband and their 12-year-old daughter.

KILL HER WITH KINDNESS

Rene was carrying on an affair with a strawberry-blonde receptionist at the radio station. He intended to marry her. But to do so, he needed Esther out of the way. Instead of asking for a divorce, Rene opted for murder.

The autopsy revealed that Esther had 1,500 times the normal level of arsenic in her body. The medical examiners determined that she was ingesting it for more than six months—including while she was in the hospital. Where was she getting it? Those daily milkshake deliveries from her husband.

A HAIRY SITUATION

Police searched the Castellani home and found Triox weed killer beneath the kitchen sink. It was missing the exact amount of poison that was estimated to have been in Esther's body. Esther's hair held more evidence. Scientists could chart the amount of arsenic Esther consumed each day from a strand of her long black hair. Curiously, the hair revealed that during the eight days that Rene was on top of the BowMac sign—when the milkshake deliveries were interrupted—there was no sign of poison in her system. About three months after the murder, Rene applied for a license to marry the receptionist. Two days later, the police arrested him. He was convicted of murder and sentenced to life in prison.

DNA Landmark Cases

DNA evidence has come a long way since the late 1980s and early '90s. Here are two significant events that helped push DNA testing along.

- In 1987 the West Virginia Supreme Court ruled that DNA evidence could be used in a trial (it was a rape case), giving the use of DNA evidence in a courtroom its first major legal precedent.

- In 1989 Gary Dotson of Chicago became the first person in history to have a conviction overturned through the use of DNA testing. It was a heartrending case. Dotson had been convicted in 1979 of the violent rape of a 16-year-old girl and sentenced to 25 to 50 years in prison. Six years into his sentence, the "victim" admitted she'd made up the whole thing. Earlier that day, she'd had sex with her boyfriend for the first time, and was afraid she'd become pregnant. Yet even with that recantation, it took another four years—and, finally, DNA evidence proving that semen taken from the girl's underwear was her boyfriend's, not Dotson's—for him to be exonerated.

Between setting the legal precedent and demonstrating the immense potential that DNA testing had within the criminal justice system, these two cases set the course for the rapid development of forensic science.

★ STARS BEHIND BARS ★

STAR: Charles S. Dutton, who had a recurring role on *House* as the father of Dr. Foreman

BEHIND BARS: In 1967 the 16-year-old Dutton killed a man in a knife fight and served time for manslaughter. Caught with a deadly weapon while on parole, he was sent back to prison. He attacked a guard, and more time was added to his sentence. While in solitary confinement for refusing a work assignment, Dutton read a book of plays from the prison library. He credits *Day of Absence,* by Douglas Turner Ward, with inspiring him to turn his life around. After getting paroled in 1976, Dutton acted in local theater, earned a college degree, and won admission to the Yale Drama School. That led to a career on Broadway, in film, and on TV. "I consider myself a living testament to the power of the arts," he says.

STAR: Tim Allen, stand-up comedian, film actor, and star of *Home Improvement*

BEHIND BARS: In 1978 Allen was arrested for drug trafficking after he tried to sell 1.4 pounds of cocaine to an undercover cop. That was enough to get him sent away for life, but Allen copped a plea and testified against other drug dealers, so he served a little over two years in federal prison. While awaiting sentencing, Allen made his first appearance as a stand-up comedian, at the Comedy Castle in Detroit. "The judge suggested I get my act together, and I took him seriously," he says.

Strange Lawsuits

These days, it seems that people will sue each other over practically anything. Here are more real-life examples of unusual legal battles.

The Plaintiff: Toshi Van Blitter

The Defendant: Harrah's casino

The Lawsuit: After losing $350,000 playing blackjack, Van Blitter decided to sue the Las Vegas casino. She filed to have her debts canceled, claiming that Harrah's was negligent—they should have told her that she was an incompetent blackjack player.

The Verdict: The gamble didn't pay off. A federal judge dismissed her claim.

The Plaintiff: Timothy Ray Anderson, an armed robber

The Defendant: John Hobson, a security guard at a McDonald's restaurant

The Lawsuit: Anderson was robbing a McDonald's at gunpoint; Hobson ordered him to drop the weapon. Anderson spun around, aiming his gun at Hobson, but Hobson shot first, hitting Anderson in the stomach. Anderson was subsequently convicted of armed robbery and sentenced to 15 years. Anderson then sued Hobson, the firm Hobson worked for, and the owner of the McDonald's, claiming "excessive force" was used against him. His argument: "The mere fact that you're holding up a McDonald's with a gun doesn't mean you give up your right to be protected from somebody who wants to shoot you."

The Verdict: The case was thrown out of court.

It's an Open and Shut Case, Johnson

*These crooks might as well handcuff
themselves and close their own cell door.*

EGG ON HIS FACE

One night in July 2009, 18-year-old Daniel Barr of Strasburg, Pennsylvania, and a bunch of his friends were driving around and decided it would be fun to throw eggs at a police car. They found a parked cruiser and hurled a dozen eggs at it. They might have gotten away with the crime . . . had they not chosen a police car that was occupied by a police officer.

TAKE THE MONEY AND (DON'T) RUN

In January 2008, a 53-year-old man and his 20-year-old accomplice (names were withheld in police reports) set out to rob the Vernon, British Columbia, branch of the CIBC Bank. The older man went into the bank to commit the actual robbery, while the younger man stayed in the getaway car, listening to the radio. When the older man returned, the car wouldn't start—the battery was dead. They quickly got out of the car and ran down the street, but were apprehended a few minutes later. Why? The CIBC Bank is located next door to a police station.

LIQUID COURAGE

Thirty-three-year-old Shawn Lester stormed into a Charleston, West Virginia, convenience store, filled up a cup at the soda fountain, then demanded all of the money in the register,

claiming he had a gun. But before the clerk could get any money out, Lester got cold feet and didn't want to go through with the robbery. He started to walk out of the store . . . with his drink. The clerk told Lester he had to pay for it, so he did—with his debit card. Even though he signed the receipt "John Doe" (and didn't actually steal any money), police easily traced the debit card and arrested Lester at his home.

IT'S JUST POLITE TO LEAVE A NOTE

One day in June 2009, an employee at Ziggy's, a hardware store in Spokane, Washington, found a plastic bag filled with small, crystallized rocks on the floor near the checkout. Thinking that it was crystal methamphetamine, the employee called the police. But before they arrived, 34-year-old Christopher Wilson walked in and asked if anyone had found a bag of crystal meth he thought he may have lost in the store. The employee lied and told him they hadn't, so Wilson left his name and phone number, just in case the drugs turned up. Wilson returned home . . . where police arrested him a few minutes later.

CUFF 'EM, DAN-O

In 2009 a Massachusetts man showed up at a police station and asked to have a pair of handcuffs removed. Earlier that day, the man's sister had put the cuffs on him as a joke, but then lost the key. On a whim, the police decided to run the man's name through their computer and discovered that he had several outstanding warrants. (He was promptly given a brand-new set of handcuffs.)

INVESTING IN THE FUTURE

*Helpful politicians personally invested
in positive foreign relations.*

THE RUSE: In 1978 two wealthy Arab sheiks started inviting US government officials to meetings. The purpose of the meetings: the sheiks had a ton of money, and they wanted help making "investments" in the United States.

THE HOOK: Several government officials happily took the sheiks' money and "invested" it into their own pockets, in exchange for helping secure purchases of casinos, mining companies, and other American businesses.

GOTCHA! The sheiks weren't sheiks—they were undercover FBI agents. It was all part of the agency's "Abscam" operation (from "*Ab*dul," the name of the fictitious company the "sheiks" owned, and "scam"). And the government officials? They included eight members of Congress. Five members of the House of Representatives went to federal prison, as did Senator Harrison Williams of New Jersey, who was videotaped promising the "sheiks" he'd secure them contracts to open a titanium mine in exchange for shares in the company. Williams remains one of only two US senators in history who went to prison for crimes committed while in office.

Canadian Gangsters, Eh?

A 2008 report by the Royal Canadian Mounted Police said that gang members involved in international drug smuggling had infiltrated airports in major cities around the country. Most were working as baggage handlers.

Canada's Criminal Intelligence Service estimates that more than 11,000 Canadians are members of street gangs.

More than 130 gangs are based in Vancouver alone, vying for a drug business estimated to be worth more than $6 billion per year.

In the late 1990s, Toronto police arrested four members of the Spadina Girls, a short-lived, all-female gang led by a 16-year-old girl. The gang, charged other students for protection. The arrests came after gang members brutally assaulted a fellow student at a billiards hall.

A much more dangerous all-female gang has formed in recent years: the Indian Posse Girls, an offshoot of Indian Posse. They're believed to be in control of the sex trade in Winnipeg and Edmonton.

DRAKEN TO THE CLEANERS

BACKGROUND: In 1913 thousands of people with the last name Drake received a letter from the "Sir Francis Drake Association," an organization founded for the purpose of settling the estate of the legendary British buccaneer who had died 300 years earlier. Any Drake descendant who wanted a share of the estate was welcome—all they had to do was contribute toward the $2,500-a-week "legal expenses" needed to pursue the case. The fight was underway and any Drake descendant who hesitated risked being cut out entirely.

EXPOSED: The scam was the work of Iowa con man Oscar Merrill Hartzell. Hartzell got the idea for his version after his mother was conned out of several thousand dollars in another Drake estate scam. When he tracked down the crooks who had swindled her and realized how much money they were making, Hartzell decided that rather than call the police, he would keep quiet . . . and launch his own scam. Using the money he'd recovered for his mother, Hartzell promptly sent out letters to more than 20,000 Drakes.

FINAL NOTE: By the time the feds caught up with him 20 years later, Hartzell had swindled an estimated 70,000 people out of more than $2 million. Rather than admit they'd been duped, many of the victims donated an additional $350,000 toward his legal defense. Hartzell was convicted of mail fraud and sentenced to 10 years in federal prison; a few years later he was transferred to a mental institution, where he died in 1943.

The Cutthroat World of Texas Cheerleading

Cheerleading is serious business in Texas. Deadly serious.

WHO WAS "THE TEXAS CHEERLEADER MOM"?

Wanda Holloway, who in 1991 lived in Houston, worked as a secretary, and played piano for her church.

WHAT DID SHE DO?

She tried to hire a hit man to kill the mother of a rival cheerleader at her daughter's middle school.

WHY ON EARTH WOULD SHE WANT TO DO THAT?

Wanda really, *really* wanted her daughter, Shanna Harper, to be a cheerleader. Young Shanna had failed to make the cheerleading squad because of "improper campaigning." Her mother had given away pencils and rulers with Shanna's name on them to promote her (apparently a big no-no), thus disqualifying Shanna.

Wanda wanted to give her daughter an extra edge the following year. By helping her with a routine? Well, no. Wanda decided to murder their neighbor, Verna Heath, whose daughter Amber was also trying to make the cheer squad. Wanda thought that Amber would be so distraught at the death of her mother that she wouldn't be able to cheer—thus opening the door for her own little Shanna to make the team.

DID VERNA HEATH GET BUMPED OFF?

No. Before the deed could be done, the police arrested Wanda.

HOW DID THAT HAPPEN?

Because Wanda Holloway chose her co-conspirators poorly. The twice-married Holloway approached her former brother-in-law Terry Harper about finding someone to do the deed; Harper informed the authorities about Holloway's ambitions. He then wore a wire when he went to talk to her.

Holloway toyed with the idea of killing both Verna and Amber Heath, but balked at Harper's $7,500 asking price. She chose instead the more economical route of bumping off only the mom, a bargain at a mere $2,500. Holloway said, and this is a direct quote from the tape: "Maybe I should go with the mother. Ah, the kid, she can just be screwed with the murder. Maybe it would mess with her mind." Later Holloway met with her undercover "hit man" and handed over a pair of diamond earrings in payment—which is solicitation for capital murder.

WHAT HAPPENED TO "THE TEXAS CHEERLEADER MOM"?

She went on trial in 1991, was convicted, and sentenced to 15 years in the slammer. But wait! A mistrial was declared when it was discovered that one of the jurors was improperly impaneled. Turned out he was on probation for cocaine possession, which apparently is enough to fling a fella out of the jury pool in Texas.

In 1996 Wanda pleaded no contest to solicitation of capital murder and was sentenced to 10 years in prison. However, after just six months, she was released on probation.

DID SHANNA MAKE THE CHEERLEADING TEAM?

No. But Amber Heath was on the cheerleading squad throughout high school.

The First Rule About Fight Club . . .

In the 1999 movie *Fight Club*, Tyler Durden (Brad Pitt) runs an underground club where men have bloody fistfights with each other. They also belong to "Project Mayhem," a terrorist cell that blows up symbols of corporate America, including, in one scene, a Starbucks coffee shop. The film has garnered a huge cult following, and one of the biggest fans was 17-year-old Kyle Shaw, who maintained that he actually wanted to *be* Tyler Durden.

In 2009 Shaw started his own fight club in New York City, but fighting his fellow teenagers wasn't enough. So, following the model of Project Mayhem, Shaw built a crude homemade bomb and set it off in front of a Starbucks in the middle of the night, destroying an outdoor bench. Ignoring the first rule of Fight Club, which is that you do not talk about Fight Club, Shaw bragged about it to his friends, one of whom tipped off the police. (Coincidentally, the jail that Shaw went to had its own version of a fight club, called "The Program." While he was on a pay phone, a much larger inmate walked up and hit Shaw in the face, giving him a black eye for his appearance in court the next day.)

Court Transquips

The verdict is in! These were actually said,
word for word, in a court of law.

Judge: I know you, don't I?

Defendant: Uh, yes.

Judge: All right, how do I know you?

Defendant: Judge, do I have to tell you?

Judge: Of course, you might be obstructing justice not to tell me.

Defendant: Okay. I was your bookie.

Judge: Please identify yourself for the record.

Defendant: Colonel Ebenezer Jackson.

Judge: What does the "Colonel" stand for?

Defendant: Well, it's kinda like the "Honorable" in front of your name—not a damn thing.

Judge: You are charged with habitual drunkenness. Have you anything to say in your defense?

Defendant: Habitual thirstiness?

Plaintiff's Lawyer: What doctor treated you for the injuries you sustained while at work?

Plaintiff: Dr. J.

Plaintiff's Lawyer: And what kind of physician is Dr. J?

Plaintiff: Well, I'm not sure, but I remember that you said he was a good plaintiff's doctor.

Defendant: If I called you a son of a bitch, what would you do?

Judge: I'd hold you in contempt and assess an additional five days in jail.

Defendant: What if I thought you were a son of a bitch?

Judge: I can't do anything about that. There's no law against thinking.

Defendant: In that case, I think you're a son of a bitch.

In 2012, Michelle Chapman reported to police that her family members had been trolling her online, relentlessly bombarding her social media with vile and menacing comments. When police investigated, they discovered that Michelle had set up "catfish" accounts and had posted the insults on her "real" account herself. She was the first person in Britain to be arrested for trolling herself.

Who Wants to Sue a Billionaire? (Everyone)

THE PLAINTIFF: Hollywood producer Steve Bing

THE DEFENDANT: Movie-studio mogul Kirk Kerkorian

THE LAWSUIT: Kerkorian's ex-wife, Lisa Bonder, sued for $320,000 *a month* in child support for their four-year-old daughter. Billionaire Kerkorian claimed he couldn't possibly be the father—he was sterile. He also said he had proof that the real father was Bonder's ex-boyfriend, multimillionaire Bing. His private detectives had collected DNA evidence—they went through Bing's garbage and found some used dental floss. Probability that Bing's the dad: 99.993%. Bing sued for invasion of privacy, asking a staggering $1 billion in damages.

THE VERDICT: They settled quietly out of court and the suit was dropped.

> I've always thought I'd been pretty good with people, and I basically have spent a conflict-free life, you know?
>
> —O. J. Simpson

GPS: GREAT POLICING SERVICE

When you're leading a life of crime,
GPS isn't quite as nifty as it is for the rest of us.

Games People Play

In 2009, 22-year-old Jeremiah Gilliam stole an Xbox from
a home in an affluent section of Westchester County,
New York, just north of New York City. He took it to his
grandmother's apartment in the Bronx and decided to
play a game. But to do so, Gilliam had to log on to the
victim's Xbox LIVE account. That made it easy for police
to track down the IP address, which led them straight to
Grandma's. When they showed up to question Gilliam, they
found 50 other stolen gadgets, and in one swoop solved
dozens of unsolved burglaries in Westchester County.

GaPS in Judgment

Police sirens blared behind William Bowen as he drove a
car full of stolen contraband through Steens, Mississippi.
He didn't know how the cops tracked him down, but
figured that one of the stolen items had a GPS device, so
he started flinging stuff out of the car—purses, wallets,
guns—but couldn't elude the police, who were keeping
a safe distance. If only Bowen had tossed the stolen cell
phone, he might have gotten away. But he kept it. "This is
one of the few cases where someone stole a cell phone with
GPS, and all of his movements led us right to him," said
police investigator Tony Cooper.

Legal Landmarks for Forensic Science

*Forensic science, and by extension,
the criminal justice system, has come a long
way with the assistance of technology.*

1901 Human blood groups are identified and described by Austrian doctor Karl Landsteiner, who subsequently codified his discoveries into the blood types we know today. This discovery was useful in the field of forensics, as well as in medicine in general, and it lands Landsteiner a Nobel Prize in 1930.

1910 Rosella Rousseau confesses to the murder of Germaine Bichon. Why? Because her hair is matched to hairs at the crime scene, a technique pioneered by Victor Balthazard, a professor of forensic medicine at the Sorbonne. The same year, another French professor of forensic medicine, Edmund Locard, helps create the first police crime lab. The first US crime lab was founded in 1925 by Los Angeles police chief August Vollmer.

1921 The portable polygraph (lie detector) is invented. In 1923 polygraph testimony is ruled inadmissible in US courts.

1925 Blood is not the only bodily fluid you can type, suggested Japanese scientist K. I. Yosida, as he undertook studies to determine serological isoantibodies in other bodily fluids. He's right.

1960 An arsonist's job gets harder as gas chromatography is used for the first time in a lab to identify specific petroleum products.

1977 Japanese forensic scientist Fuseo Matsumur notices his fingerprints popping up as he prepares a slide for examination and tells his friend Masato Soba. Soba would use this information to help develop the first process to raise latent prints with cyanoacrylate, or, as it's more commonly known, superglue. Yes, superglue. Now you know why not to get it on your fingers.

1984 Yes, 1984. An ironic year for the first successful DNA profiling test, created by Great Britain's Sir Alec Jeffreys.

1986 Jeffreys uses his DNA profiling method to help convict the ominously named Colin Pitchfork for murder. Interestingly, in this same case, DNA is used to clear another man accused of the crime.

1987 DNA profiling makes its debut in the United States and nails Tommy Lee Andrews for a number of sexual assaults in Orlando, Florida. However, in the same year, the admissibility of DNA profiling is challenged in another case, *New York v. Castro*, in which the defendant was accused of murder. This set the stage for many years of back-and-forth argument on the standards and practices of the labs that perform DNA profiling.

1996 In Tennessee, a fellow named Paul Ware is accused of murder, but the only physical evidence is a few hairs. Investigators use those hairs to extract DNA from mitochondria, a small structure within human cells. It's the first use of mitochondrial DNA to convict someone of a crime.

She's a Liar! (Whew!)

A case where everyone sighed in relief when they found out it was a hoax.

A woman wearing a bandana over her face posted a video on an Internet site in January 2010 in which she claimed that she had HIV/AIDS—and that she had infected more than 500 men in Detroit, Michigan, with the disease. And, she said, she planned to infect more, because she wanted to "destroy the world." Within a few days, more than half a million people had watched the video. Detroit police were able to quickly identify the woman: Jackie Braxton, 23, a Detroit adult-film actress. After she was arrested, she admitted to making the video—and said it was a hoax. (She volunteered to take an HIV test, and it came back negative.) Braxton said she started the hoax to raise awareness about AIDS. Police decided she had not committed a crime.

BONUS: Braxton apparently *did* raise awareness in Detroit: Michael McElrath, a spokesman for the city's health department, said that after the video went viral, the number of men who went to clinics for HIV testing in Detroit more than doubled.

Assault on the Senate Floor

*Even the prestigious Senate floor has been
the scene of some unruly behavior.*

On May 22, 1856, South Carolina senator Andrew Butler was ridiculed on the Senate floor by antislavery advocate Charles Sumner of Massachusetts during a debate over whether Kansas should be admitted to the Union as a slave or free state. During his speech, entitled "The Crime Against Kansas," Sumner accused Butler of leading the effort to spread slavery to Kansas, for Butler, he said, had taken "a mistress, who, though ugly to others, is always lovely to him . . . I mean, the harlot, Slavery."

Butler's response is not recorded, but by all accounts, Sumner concluded his speech and the day's session continued. Meanwhile in the House of Representatives, Butler's cousin, Congressman Brooks, was preparing his own response to what he considered a grievous slander against a kinsman and fellow Southerner. Sumner was sitting at his desk putting stamps on copies of his speech to send to constituents. Slamming his metal-tipped cane onto Sumner's head, Brooks proceeded to beat the man viciously. Then he turned on his heels and walked out.

To their partisans, each man became an instant hero. The stunned and bloodied Sumner was carried away by friends. It took him months to recover from his wounds, but he returned to the Senate and served another 18 years. Brooks survived a Senate censure vote and was even reelected to office, but died six months later at the age of 37.

SON OF SAM

How the notorious killer got his nickname(s).

David Berkowitz murdered six people, wounded several
others, and committed arson around New York City in
1976 and 1977. He was first known in the press as the
".44 Caliber Killer," after the weapon he used in most of
his attacks. In April 1977, Berkowitz left a letter at the
scene of a double murder in the Bronx. A month later,
he sent another letter to *New York Daily News* columnist
Jimmy Breslin. In both letters, he referred to himself as
"Son of Sam," explaining that "Sam" was an evil spirit that
compelled him to kill: "Sam loves to drink blood," one read.
"'Go out and kill' commands father Sam." (Berkowitz later
said "Sam" was a demon that possessed his neighbor's
dog.) Police eventually released that information to the
press—and the rest is serial-killer history. Berkowitz was
captured in August 1977 (his first words to police: "You got
me. What took you so long?"), and is now serving 25 years
to life for each murder.

Update: Berkowitz became a born-again Christian in
prison in 1987. On his personal website—yep, he has one,
reportedly administered with the help of friends outside of
prison—he says he no longer wants to be known as "Son of
Sam," but now goes by the name "Son of Hope."

Cold Comforts

How cold was it during the January 2014 "polar vortex"? It was so cold that the Chicago Zoo had to put its polar bears and penguins inside. And in Kentucky it was so cold that an escaped prisoner decided to go back to prison just so he could warm up. The ex-ex-con, Robert Vick, had run away from the minimum-security Blackburn Correctional Complex where he was serving a six-year sentence for burglary and possession of a forged instrument. But he picked a bad day to escape: the temperature in Lexington was only 3°F, and the wind chill made it seem like -17°F. (Kentuckians aren't used to those kinds of temperatures.) So Vick, who had no money and spent the night in an abandoned house, went to a motel the next morning—but not to check in. "He walked in and told me to call the law on him. He was frozen," said manager Maurice King. "I don't think the police even believed me. I had to call again." Vick was scheduled to go before a parole board in only two months, but instead he had another five years tacked on to his sentence.

THE REAL FUGITIVE?

Director Roy Huggins denied that he based his movie *The Fugitive* on a true story, but the events in the series are suspiciously close to the murder trial of Sam Sheppard. One July morning in 1954, Dr. Sheppard called police to tell them he'd been attacked by a bushy-haired man who'd broken into his Cleveland home. The intruder knocked the doctor unconscious, and when Sheppard came to, he discovered that his pregnant wife Marilyn had been murdered.

The shocked public was sympathetic, but police were suspicious. They wondered why Sheppard couldn't find the T-shirt he'd worn that night. They said the crime scene didn't look like a typical burglary—it looked staged. Nobody found the murder weapon or the bushy-haired intruder. Public feeling turned against Sheppard after he admitted to an adulterous affair that he'd previously denied. Sheppard was found guilty and sentenced to life in prison.

While Sheppard was serving time, police arrested a thief in possession of Marilyn's wedding ring. The suspect, Richard Eberling, admitted that he'd burgled

the home of Marilyn's sister-in-law, who inherited the ring after Marilyn's death. Eberling also said he'd worked on Marilyn's home days before her murder and that he'd cut his finger while he was there.

The police released Eberling after he passed a lie-detector test. Meanwhile, the US Supreme Court was reviewing prejudicial press coverage against Sheppard—a "carnival" that the judge never tried to control. In 1966 the high court granted Sheppard a new trial. At that second trial, the doctor was acquitted.

FASHION POLICE:

CRIME: In 1907 Australian swimming star Annette Kellerman wore a one-piece bathing suit that revealed her knees and exposed her elbows.

PUNISHMENT: She was arrested for indecent exposure.

A Case of Mis-mistaken Identity

THE ACCUSED: Eric Nordmark, 35, a homeless man in California

STORY: In 2003 Nordmark was walking down the street when two cops stopped him. They brought him to the station and took his mug shot. Then he was released. A few weeks later, as he walked out of a store, the police were waiting for him. They cuffed and arrested him. The charge: the assault of three 11-year-old girls. A few days earlier, the girls had claimed they were attacked by a homeless man on the way home from school, but escaped. Nordmark's disheveled appearance matched their description, and two of the three girls identified him in a photo lineup. Bail was set at $50,000, but Nordmark didn't even have $50, so he was forced to remain in jail until his trial began . . . eight months later. At the trial, one of the accusers took the stand. "He started choking me," she testified. "I couldn't breathe, and I felt like I was going to black out." Nordmark told his lawyer that if he was convicted, he'd kill himself before he ever got to prison.

OUTCOME: The following day, Nordmark was brought back into the courtroom. The judge told him, "All charges have been dismissed." The girl apologized and explained that they made up the story because they got home late from school that day and didn't want to get in trouble. All three girls were arrested for the false accusation.

GRAND THEFT AUTOS

November 10, 2017, turned out to be quite a day for Chandra Bourelle. That morning, the 33-year-old Berkshire, Massachusetts, woman stole a car, got caught, got arrested, posted bail, and then stole another car. It wasn't even 10:00 a.m., and Bourelle was just getting going. While police were looking for the Toyota Highlander that she'd driven off in while it was idling, they received a call about a stolen Lexus. When officers arrived at the scene of the Lexus theft, they found the abandoned Highlander. Meanwhile, Bourelle decided she wanted something classier, so she ditched the Lexus and stole a BMW, her fourth car theft of the day (a Berkshire record, said cops). The officers in pursuit—across several jurisdictions by this point—finally spotted the stolen Lexus that evening. "She took off at speeds over 100 miles per hour and ended up losing control of the car near Duke's Sand and Gravel," said Cheshire Police Chief Timothy Garner. "She didn't crash, but, and here's the other thing, she almost hit a flatbed wrecker that was just coming back from returning the Highlander she stole earlier in the day." Bourelle was eventually caught and sent to jail. A flight risk if there ever was one, she was denied bail.

Haunted Crime Scenes

THE BORDEN HOUSE: The home in Fall River, Massachusetts, where Lizzie Borden (most likely) murdered her parents is a B&B today. You can stay in the same room where Lizzie's stepmom Abbie was killed. It looks the same as it did in 1892. Making it even creepier: There's a crime-scene photo of Abbie's corpse hanging on the wall right next to the spot where she was found. Guests have reported hearing a woman whisper in their ears, seeing a human-shaped indentation on the bed, and even glimpsing a full-bodied apparition of Abbie. But the scariest claim is the disembodied maniacal laughter that many people attribute to Lizzie herself.

THE CHELSEA HOTEL: Sex Pistols lead singer Sid Vicious and his girlfriend Nancy Spungen were living at the trendy New York hotel in 1978. One night, Sid and Nancy took a lot of drugs and got into a huge fight. When Sid woke up the next morning, Nancy was dead on the bathroom floor, the victim of a stab wound. After giving police conflicting accounts of what happened, Sid was arrested, and died of a drug overdose while out on bail. Unable to rest peacefully, Nancy's ghost is said to roam the

halls of the hotel to this day.

THE OMAN HOUSE: The Beverly Hills, California, house where members of the Manson family brutally murdered actress Sharon Tate is gone. Another house, built 30 years after the 1969 killings, stands about 200 feet away. The owner, David Oman, insists that the ghost of Tate has taken up residence there. His claims have been backed up by such paranormal investigation shows as *Ghost Hunters* and *Ghost Adventures*. According to Oman, the "geomagnetic energy" of his house makes it a "containment vessel" for spirits. Skeptical? You can rent it out for a night and conduct an investigation yourself.

THE AMITYVILLE HOUSE: In 1974 Ronald "Butch" DeFeo Jr. murdered his family in their Long Island, New York, home. A year later, George and Kathleen Lutz moved into the house. Twenty-eight days later, they moved out. Among their claims (which spawned a popular book and movie series) the horrors at Amityville included green slime coming out of the walls, putrid odors, and a "pig-like creature with red eyes." Though dogged by claims of a hoax, the Lutzes stuck to their story. And Defeo, who is still in prison, once said that voices in the house told him to carry out the murders.

Snowballistics

One snowy afternoon in December 2009, about 200 office workers took part in a snowball fight on 14th Street in Washington, DC Everyone was having a good time . . . until someone threw a snowball at a Hummer SUV driving down the road. The Hummer slid to a halt; a large, imposing man got out. "Who threw that damn snowball?" he shouted. When no one answered, the man pulled out a pistol, sending people running for cover. A few tense moments later, a uniformed police officer arrived and ordered the man to drop his weapon. That's when the gunman identified himself as Detective Mike Baylor. With the danger passed, the crowd started chanting: "You don't bring a gun to a snowball fight." At first, the DC police department denied that the detective, a 28-year veteran, pulled out his gun. But the incident was caught on several cell phone cameras and soon made the rounds on YouTube . . . and then the local news. DC police chief Cathy Lanier called Baylor's actions "totally inappropriate." He was placed on desk duty.

CLOSE ENCOUNTERS MAKE BAD THERAPY

Do you have to be mad to treat a psychopath?

NO ROUND TRIP

In 1968 Elliott Barker, a psychiatrist at the Oak Ridge Hospital for the criminally insane in Penetanguishene, Ontario, thought that he could cure psychopaths. His solution: nude psychotherapy sessions, fueled with LSD, lasting for 11-day stretches. The patients, all male, volunteered to be placed in a windowless, 8 x 10-foot room. The soundproof room had a sink and toilet and a one-way mirror in the ceiling. There were no beds or privacy—patients had to sleep on a small rug over a foam mat.

THERAPY CAN BE VERY REVEALING

Dr. Barker procured batches of LSD, as well as the approval of the Canadian government. With no windows and lights on around the clock, patients were unable to tell day from night. Confusion, disorientation, and confrontations between the men ensued. The psychopaths were encouraged to go to their rawest emotional places by screaming

and clawing at the walls and confessing fantasies of forbidden sexual longings. Barker thought his technique would summon the madness so patients could be "born again" as empathetic human beings.

At first, the results seemed promising. The tough, young prisoners were slowly transforming and seeming to care for each other. Psychopathic murderers were now gentle. Many were declared cured and were freed. On average, 60 percent of criminal psychopaths released into the outside world will become repeat offenders—but Dr. Barker's patients hit 80 percent. The treatment actually made patients worse.

"But if you go over the line, you don't want to get stuck in a Nevada state courtroom. Honestly, because Nevada has been doing a good job of putting California criminals in jail. I mean, we couldn't put O. J. in jail, but they did. We couldn't put Paris Hilton in jail, but they did."

—**James Belushi**

LEGISLATING IRONY

Legislatin' ain't easy.

- A new anti-pornography law could not go into effect in Winchester, Indiana, because the editors of the town's only newspaper refused to print the wording of the law on the basis that it was pornographic. For a new law to be official, it had to be printed in the newspaper.

- New York state assemblywoman Nancy Calhoun pled guilty to charges that she harassed her ex-boyfriend in 1999. According to testimony, she "burst into his home in the middle of the night, tailgated him in a car, and posed as a cosmetics seller to get his new girlfriend's phone number." Calhoun was co-sponsor of the state's new anti-stalking legislation.

- On October 30, 2003, Congress released findings of a study that said toy guns don't have any relationship to crime. That same day, the Capitol was locked down for an hour because two workers had brought toy guns to work as part of their Halloween costumes.

STRANGE CRIME

DUMB JOCK CRIMES

POWER PLAY

In March 2000, three security guards at The Mansion on Turtle Creek, a hotel in Dallas, responded to a noise complaint about a guest, Dallas Stars goaltender Eddie Belfour. The caller told the guards that Belfour had become drunk, angry, and violent, and she feared for her safety. When three guards arrived and attempted to subdue him, Belfour reacted as if they were charging forward on an opposing team—he kicked two of them in the chest and spat in the other's face. Thanks to a hefty dose of pepper spray, the guards apprehended Belfour. By the time the police arrived, the hockey player's violent rampage had dwindled to pathetic pleading: "If you let me go," he slurred, "I'll give you a *billion* dollars!" The cops rejected the bribe and placed Belfour in the back of a squad car, where he puked all over himself. He received a $3,000 fine.

PICTURE IMPERFECT

In 2009 Miami Heat forward Michael Beasley used Twitter to show off a picture of a tattoo he'd just gotten. The photo depicted Beasley's back, decorated with the tattoo of angel wings and the words "Super Cool Beas" ("Beas" is his nickname). Also depicted in the photo: a baggie containing a green, leafy substance. After a few readers pressed him on it over the next few days (he'd had problems with the NBA, and the law, over drugs), Beasley closed the Twitter account and checked into a Houston drug treatment facility.

THE EVIL TWIN & THE GOOD TWIN

Sunny and Gina Han seemingly had it all. The identical twins were co-valedictorians at their San Diego high school, they were beautiful, and they were inseparable . . . until the falling-out. In 1996 Gina became convinced that Sunny had stolen some of her stuff. Despite Sunny's denials, Gina couldn't let the matter go. According to several witnesses, she openly discussed wanting her sister dead. Then one night, Sunny and her roommate, Helen Kim, were in their apartment when two teenage boys pretending to be magazine salesmen barged in and tied up Helen. Sunny hid in her bedroom and called 911. Police arrived just in time to prevent a double homicide. When questioned, the teens said they were acting on behalf of Gina, who orchestrated the crime.

Gina was convicted of conspiracy to attempt murder. At her sentencing hearing, she said through tears, "I am deeply sorry for everything that has happened." But she didn't confess: "I had absolutely no intent to kill my twin sister." The judge didn't buy it, though, calling Gina a "danger to society, particularly her own family." She received the maximum sentence: 26 years to life in prison. Gina was granted parole in 2017, but that could still be overturned.

The Real Jekyll & Hyde

Robert Louis Stevenson fascinated the world with his story The Strange Case of Dr. Jekyll and Mr. Hyde—*inspired by a fellow Scotsman.*

THE TWO SIDES OF DEACON BRODIE

William Brodie was born into an upright 18th-century Edinburgh family and grew up as the model of respectability. He was the deacon of the local chapter of the Mason's guild as well as an Edinburgh city councilor. Brodie loved to gamble. And he had ongoing relationships with two prostitutes. Inevitably the gambling debts started to pile up and, when his two mistresses began to produce little Brodies, the good deacon found himself in desperate financial straits.

CASING THE JOINT

In the course of his legitimate daytime activities, Brodie visited his rich clients in their homes. He started making wax impressions of the house keys he came across, and checking out the houses for items of interest. He'd return in the evening to gather up the goods.

Brodie teamed up with a locksmith, and together they stole everything they could find that wasn't nailed down. In contrast to his elegant and cultured cohort, his partner George Smith, was a small-time crook with few redeeming qualities. When two more local criminals with similar dispositions were recruited into the gang, the undoing of William Brodie began.

THE HEIST

His most daring job—an attack on the headquarters of the Scottish Customs and Excise—was plagued with inefficiency. Brodie, dressed

in black and acting as if he were playing a role in a pageant, stood guard outside as two other members of the gang made their way inside. One of his partners got cold feet and the usually cool Brodie canceled the job. Someone told disbelieving authorities that the man behind the raid was none other than the highly respected Deacon William Brodie. The police were dispatched to Brodie's apartment—but only so they could officially discount the preposterous suggestion that he could be involved.

THE EVIDENCE

But what they found there substantiated the accusation. Skeleton keys, a burglar's black suit, and several pistols were cataloged and taken to headquarters for further examination. Brodie himself was nowhere to be found. He'd fled to Holland, intending to set sail for America. But as he boarded the ship (in top hat and tails), he was approached by two Dutch police officers. They escorted him back to dry land and extradited him to Edinburgh. He seemed completely untroubled by the fate that awaited him— death by hanging.

THE EXECUTION

As he stood on the gallows that he himself—in his role as city councilor—had designed, Brodie offered up his own prayer (which is too hypocritical for us to repeat). Then he bravely beckoned for the hangman to perform his task. The night before, he'd rigged his clothes with wire to take the jerk of the rope; the silver tube he'd stuck down his throat was supposed to prevent his neck from breaking. However, the trick failed, and Deacon Brodie breathed his last on October 1, 1788.

Cyclical Crime

During routine cleanups of homeless encampments, police often make some strange discoveries. One of the strangest took place in Santa Ana, California, in 2017. While clearing the typical trash, needles, and whatnot from a concrete riverbed, a public-works crew ventured into a six-foot-high spillway tunnel and saw a stash of bicycles. At first, it looked like there were only a few dozen bikes in there, but as they investigated further, the tunnel kept going, and so did the bikes. In all, more than 1,000 bicycles were hauled out of there. Sheriff's Lieutenant Jeff Puckett told the *Orange County Register*, "Common sense would usually dictate if you have a thousand bikes in a tunnel, some of them could be stolen." Ya think?

> "It's about time law enforcement got as organized as organized crime."
>
> **–Rudy Giuliani**

Murder, He Wrote

How did New York City, a famous cigar girl, and Edgar Allan Poe combine to create one of the world's first murder mystery stories?

PART ONE: THE BODY

In 1841 the body of 21-year-old Mary Cecilia Rogers was found floating in the Hudson River near Hoboken, New Jersey. The discovery was shocking, not just because the body was battered beyond recognition, but because Rogers was famous in New York City. One of America's first celebrities, she was nicknamed the "beautiful cigar girl." Until shortly before her death, Rogers had worked at a huge tobacco and cigar shop on Broadway. According to legend, she was so beautiful that men would come inside just to see her, and wouldn't leave without buying tobacco . . . including New York City newspaper reporters and a writer named Edgar Allan Poe.

PART TWO: THE DISAPPEARANCE

By July 1841, Rogers had quit her job at the tobacco shop to help her mother run a boardinghouse on Nassau Street. She had plenty of admirers there, too, including a sailor named William Kiekuck, clerk Alfred Crommelin, and the dashingly handsome (but hard-drinking) Daniel Payne. To her mother's dismay, Rogers chose Payne and accepted his marriage proposal, though there were rumors later that the young woman was planning to leave him.

On Sunday, July 25, Rogers told her fiancé that she was going to visit her aunt, who lived uptown. She never made it. That Wednesday, her body was pulled from the river.

PART THREE: THE REVELATION

Despite having several leads, police couldn't find Rogers's killer. Every suspect they questioned (including her fiancé, Daniel Payne) had an alibi. But events began to take a strange turn. In October 1841, a few months after Rogers's death, Payne walked to the thicket near Hoboken where Rogers's clothes had been found. There, he penned a vague note about his "misspent life" and drank a fatal overdose of laudanum, a liquid form of opium.

Then, in the fall of 1842, a woman named Frederica Loss lay on her deathbed, the victim of an accidental gunshot by her son. A delirious Loss confessed that on that fateful Sunday, Mary Rogers and a doctor had rented a room in the tavern. Rogers was pregnant, Loss said, and she died in the rented room from complications after the doctor performed an abortion.

Police found nothing to corroborate the confession, but the case was back in the spotlight. A botched abortion contradicted the coroner's report that Rogers had died of strangulation. Maybe Mary Rogers was planning to leave Daniel Payne after all, and when he found out about that and the abortion, he killed her in a fit of rage. No one knew, and no one ever figured it out. To this day, Mary Rogers's murder remains unsolved. It was the basis of one of Edgar Allan Poe's early stories, "The Mystery of Marie Roget," and helped launch detective genre of literature.

The Becker Scandal

THE PERP: Lieutenant Charles Becker of the New York City Police Department

THE STORY: On July 15, 1912, Herman "Beansy" Rosenthal, owner of an illegal casino in New York's notorious Tenderloin district (near what is now Times Square), told a district attorney a sensational story: Manhattan's top anti-vice cop, Lieutenant Charles Becker, was part-owner of his casino. Even worse, Becker and his "Strong Arm Squad," who were supposed to be cleaning up the Tenderloin, were instead allowing hundreds of casinos and brothels to flourish—while extorting huge amounts of cash from them. Just hours later, four men jumped out of a gray Packard and shot Rosenthal dead on a Manhattan street.

OUTCOME: The men who carried out the murder were arrested, and they all said that Becker had ordered the hit. The ensuing investigation revealed that Lieutenant Becker had taken more than $100,000 (about $2 million today) in extortion money in just nine months as head of the anti-vice unit. The story was a national sensation—and a major NYPD embarrassment—as the case dragged on for three years. The four hit men were convicted of murder and executed. Becker was also convicted, and on July 30, 1915, he became the first police officer in US history to be executed for murder.

IF YOU CAN'T BEAT IT, EAT IT

- In 2014 Kenneth Desormes, 40, got pulled over for speeding on Interstate 95 in New York. He appeared intoxicated, so he was taken to the police station for a Breathalyzer test. When an officer held up the printout to show Desormes the results—a 0.13 percent blood alcohol level, well over the legal limit of 0.08—Desormes grabbed the piece of paper and ate it. Amazingly, his cunning plan didn't work: he was charged with a DUI . . . and criminal tampering.

- On a train traveling through Mumbai, India, a man grabbed a necklace from a female passenger and tried to run away but was quickly apprehended. There's nothing weird about a "grab-and-run" jewelry theft. Unfortunately, it's pretty common. What's weird is what happened next. When confronted, the crook swallowed the evidence and then denied he'd done anything wrong. So, the police were called. They took him to a hospital to be X-rayed, but the X-ray failed to reveal the chain. "See?" he said. "I told you." Then doctors ran an ultrasound . . . and the gold chain showed up clear as day. To recover the stolen chain, the cops fed the thief bananas—96 of them over a period of 24 hours—until the gold chain showed up again.

FOR SALE:

A Bridge in Brooklyn

"If you believe that, I have a bridge to sell you"
has insulted gullible people since the 1800s.

SWINDLER: Reed C. Waddell

SALE DATE: 1880s through mid-1890s

PRICE: Unknown

DETAILS: Waddell moved to New York in 1880 and started conning people immediately. He offered the Brooklyn Bridge to gullible folks and pioneered a "gold-brick scandal" in which he passed off lead bricks plated with gold as solid-gold ones. Over several years, he made about $250,000.

CLOSING COSTS: In 1895 Waddell was shot and killed by fellow criminal Tom O'Brien, with whom he'd been arguing.

SWINDLER: Brothers Charles and Fred Gondorf

SALE DATE: Early 1900s

PRICE: $200 to $1,000

DETAILS: The brothers were professional con men who had a surefire way to avoid detection: as soon as police officers crossed the bridge one way on their beat, the Gondorfs whipped out "Bridge for Sale" signs, chose their marks, and collected cash. They knew roughly the length of a beat path, and always broke down the enterprise before the cops returned.

CLOSING COSTS: The men also ran a horse-racing scam. In

1915 Charlie was caught and imprisoned for that. Fred soon joined his brother after he was arrested for wire fraud. Neither was ever arrested for the Brooklyn Bridge con.

SWINDLER: George C. Parker
SALE DATE: Twice a week for several years during the 1920s
PRICE: From $50 to $50,000, with payment plans available
DETAILS: Parker convinced his marks that he was a legitimate businessman by presenting them with "official" ownership documents that listed him as the property holder for the Brooklyn Bridge. The documents were forged, but they fooled many people. Sometimes it took months for the duped buyers to realize the bridge wasn't theirs—and often they figured out they'd been conned only after they tried to set up toll booths and were stopped by police. Parker went on to "sell" Madison Square Garden, General Ulysses S. Grant's tomb, and even the Statue of Liberty.
CLOSING COSTS: Parker was caught when he scammed three Texans who had him arrested. Facing his third fraud conviction, he got a life sentence. He died in Sing Sing in 1936.

Reportedly, North Korea has a very liberal and tolerant policy towards cannabis. Journalists and defectors have said that you can buy it in markets and smoke it in public.

DAD?
IS THAT YOU?

STICK 'EM UP!

Stephanie Martinez was working in the Pizza
Patron restaurant in Denton, Texas, in July 2008
when a man in sunglasses and a bushy wig walked
in, pointed a gun at her, and demanded money.
She started getting cash out of the register—when
fellow employee Rudy Sandoval jumped on the
man and started punching him. In the melee, the
robber's wig and glasses flew off.

HI, SWEETIE

When the wig and glasses flew off, Martinez
recognized the robber: it was her father. "I dropped
the money," Ms. Martinez said afterward. "I said,
'Don't hit him again! That's my dad!'" Her father
ran out of the store and to a getaway car—in which,
it turned out, Martinez's husband and mother were
waiting. They were all in on the plot, though police
later determined that Stephanie Martinez knew
nothing about it. Her father, husband, and mother
were captured and arrested.

One-Man Band

Stephen Lutz might have gotten away with his strange crime had he decided to steal something small, like harmonicas. But Lutz, 45, had his eyes on bigger prizes. When a police officer in Exeter Township, Pennsylvania—responding to a late-night burglar alarm at a music store—caught up with Lutz, he was riding his bike away from the store while trying to balance a large trash bag on the handlebars. The cop stopped Lutz and had a look in the bag. Inside was a saxophone, two trumpets, and a toolbox (for percussion, perhaps). Lutz tried to explain that he found the bag on the sidewalk, and he was just taking it home. But the store's security footage proved otherwise, and Lutz was sent to jail.

Medieval Due Process

No DNA. No fingerprints. No jury. These justice systems surely made criminals think twice.

1. GLOWING IRON

An iron rod was heated until it was red-hot and, after a series of prayers and blessings, the accused carried it a distance of nine feet. His hands were then wrapped and inspected three days later. The logic was that God protected the innocent and his hands would be healing.

2. BOILING WATER

The accused would be asked to plunge his hand into a cauldron of boiling water (that had been blessed by a priest) and pull out a pebble or another object. As with the glowing iron, the accused's hand would be bound and inspected three days later. If it was healing, he was found innocent; if it wasn't, the verdict was guilty.

3. THE CROSS

This ordeal was used to settle disputes. Both parties faced the cross and extended their arms to the sides, imitating the shape of the cross. Whoever was the first to tire and put his arms down was in the wrong, since God would give strength to the righteous.

THE TRIAL OF THE CENTURY

The infamous case of the Lindbergh baby.

(Continued from page 131.)

MAKING A CASE

Prosecutor David T. Wilentz asserted that greed was the motive for the Lindbergh kidnapping. Hauptmann had lost a lot of money in the stock market. He used a homemade ladder to break into the Lindbergh home, took the baby, and left behind a ransom demand. According to Wilentz, Hauptmann killed little Charlie immediately so he wouldn't cry out, though he also suggested the baby died from a fall when the ladder broke as the kidnapper fled. Afterward, Hauptmann buried the body in nearby woods on the side of the road.

Flashy defense attorney Edward "Big Ed" Reilly was hired by Hearst newspapers to keep the media circus going. Reilly asserted the kidnapping was actually a conspiracy between Hauptmann's shadowy business partner, furrier Isidor Fisch, and someone on Lindbergh's staff.

WITNESSES FOR THE PROSECUTION

- In Germany, Hauptmann served time for burglary. In one of his crimes, he had used a ladder.
- The Lindbergh bills were found in his house. The ladder used in the kidnapping was partly constructed from a beam in the attic. Jafsie Condon's phone number was written inside a closet.
- Handwriting experts testified that Hauptmann's writing matched the ransom notes. Hauptmann's private papers also revealed some of the same grammar mistakes and misspelled words that the kidnapper used.

- A taxi driver and Condon had both seen Cemetery John. Lindbergh had heard his voice. All three testified that Hauptmann was Cemetery John.
- At the same time that Cemetery John picked up his money, Hauptmann quit working as a carpenter.

REASONABLE DOUBT

- The defense claimed that the police had written the phone number on the wall and stolen the board from Hauptmann's garage to claim it was part of the kidnapper's ladder.
- Hauptmann was roughed up by police and forced to imitate the handwriting on the ransom notes for the prosecution's handwriting experts.
- Hauptmann wouldn't know which was the nursery window at the Hopewell estate—a huge house with 20 rooms. He couldn't know that the Lindbergh baby would be there, since the family usually spent weekdays in Englewood.
- Anna Hauptmann testified that she'd been with her husband on the night of the kidnapping.

VERDICT IN

The jury found Hauptmann guilty. He was taken to the prison in Trenton, where he was executed on April 3, 1936.

IS THE JURY STILL OUT?

Hauptmann never confessed, despite being offered plea bargains. The Lindbergh family believed that justice was served. Meanwhile, Anna Hauptmann campaigned to clear her husband's name. Many began to believe her. To this day, authors, historians, and crime buffs continue to debate the trial's verdict.

A Tale from the Mounties

Royal Canadian Mounted Police officers got an odd
call in September 2009: A 20-year-old Vancouver man
phoned his parents from Cancún, Mexico, where he
claimed he'd been kidnapped, forced into a fight, shot
at, and then dumped in a lagoon . . . only to be gnawed
on by crocodiles. His family, understandably upset,
called in the Mounties to investigate. After talking
with the man and the Mexican authorities, though, the
police came to a different conclusion. As it turned out,
the man had been drunk and stumbled to the lagoon
to go to the bathroom. There, he tripped, fell into the
water, and was bitten by several crocodiles. Oh, and
those crocs? They were each only about 25 centimeters
(10 inches) long, and the lagoon was plastered with
signs warning that they were there.

> After he murdered his son,
> Ivan the Terrible had himself rechristened
> as a monk to atone for his crime.

CRIME-FIGHTING FAKE TV

For when you want to fool people into
thinking you're a couch potato.

Uncomfortable keeping a gun around the house? Unable to figure out the buttons on one of those fancy alarm systems? The Hydreon Corporation has developed the perfect solution: FakeTV, a timer-operated device that tricks potential home invaders into thinking you're home when you're not. Crime prevention and TV: two great tastes that taste great together!

It's about the size of a coffee cup, but it emits an LED light pattern as bright as a big-screen television, with shifting colors and motion to simulate—when seen through a window outside the house—an actual TV in action. Sensors turn it on at dusk and operate it for four hours (if you feel like pretending to turn in early), seven hours, or all the way until dawn (if you want to make robbers think you stayed up all night for a *Growing Pains* marathon). No matter which setting you choose, you'll convince potential robbers—not to mention your neighbors—that 1) you're always home, and 2) you never stop watching TV.

A Tip for Stupid Criminals

TODAY'S TIP: When you decide to re-embark on a life of crime, don't leave your ID at the scene.

We don't know for sure, but we expect that "Joaquin" did not spend his free time in California's Folsom Prison in job-training courses. Nine days after being released, Joaquin was lurking around homes in Los Angeles, searching for that certain special domicile to break into.

Eventually Joaquin found one that appeared just right. Like an older, scruffier, more Y chromosome laden Goldilocks, he just wandered right in. Whereupon he found the homeowner, who just happened to be home on that day. This particular homeowner, incidentally, happened to be Rocky Delgadillo, city attorney for Los Angeles. In the entire city of LA, there may be worse houses to break into, but off the top of our heads we can't think of any.

So, there they are, the just-released inmate and the guy who represents the second-largest city in the United States in court (although Joaquin, who is proving himself to be kind of an "always the last to know" sort of guy, is not up on this little fact). But Joaquin is not entirely without guile, and suggests that he's part of a work crew. Delgadillo would probably know if he was expecting people to work at his house, so he calls 911. Joaquin runs away, but leaves a backpack with identifying information. Soon enough, the LAPD hustles him away.

The Singing Detective

Sometimes, criminals are weak to the persuasive and unconventional techniques of law enforcement.

In May 2004, an off-duty police detective named Dave Wishnowsky noticed Willie Mitford sitting in a karaoke bar in Palmerston North, New Zealand. Wishnowsky had worked a case that resulted in theft charges against Mitford, and Mitford had already beaten one of the charges. The detective went over to Mitford, and the two started chatting over a few beers. Before long, Mitford made a surprise offer: "You get up there and sing a song, and if you're good, I will go guilty." So Wishnowsky, who— unbeknownst to Mitford—was a former singer in a pub band, got up and started belting out "Better Man" by Robbie Williams. "I had only sung two lines," he said later, "and he came over to me and said 'I'm guilty.'" Mitford lived up to his word and changed his plea to guilty later that month because, he said, the singing cop was so good.

LEGALLY SPEAKING

Maybe you find yourself in court (we won't ask why), and you realize you have no idea what the judge and lawyers are talking about. Here's a handy guide to legal mumbo jumbo.

DEPOSITION. Testimony of a witness, usually taken in a lawyer's office.

ARRAIGNMENT. The first court appearance of a person accused of a crime, usually when a plea is entered.

AFFIDAVIT. A written statement made under oath.

BAIL. Money accepted by the court for the release of a defendant, given as a guarantee they will show up for trial.

STATUTE OF LIMITATIONS. The window of time during which someone can be charged with a crime.

VOIR DIRE. The process of questioning prospective jurors or witnesses. Old French for "to speak the truth."

BENCH WARRANT. If a defendant out on bail doesn't show up for trial, the judge issues this to order that person's immediate arrest.

SUBPOENA. An order to appear in court to testify.

HABEAS CORPUS. A court order used to bring a person physically to court.

NO CONTEST. A plea in a criminal case that allows the defendant to be convicted without an admission of guilt.

PLEA BARGAIN. An agreement the defendant makes, usually involving pleading guilty to lesser charges in exchange for a lighter sentence.

CAPITAL CRIME. A crime punishable by death.

New Bedford Highway Killer

Someone was prowling New England highways committing heinous acts until they simply stopped . . . and no one ever found out who it was.

For eleven harrowing months between July 1988 and June 1989, people in and around the town of New Bedford, Massachusetts, grew increasingly terrified as they heard over and over about the murder of yet another young woman. Before the killing spree ended, the bodies of nine women between the ages of 24 and 36 had been discovered along highways in the region. Two other women went missing in the same time period, and have never been seen since. All of the victims are believed to have been in rough circumstances: All were either prostitutes or drug addicts. Collectively, their deaths left behind 15 orphans. There have been a handful of suspects in the case over the years, and one man, Kenneth Ponte, an attorney who had represented several of the women before their deaths, was charged with one of the murders. But, due to lack of evidence, Ponte was never brought to trial, and he died in 2009. The murders remain unsolved today.

Exonerated!

These people almost spent their lives behind bars, until a vote of confidence and forensic science set them free.

- **The Ford Heights Four.** In 1996 DNA evidence proved that Dennis Williams, Willie Rainge, Kenneth Adams, and Verneal Jimerson were not guilty of the 1978 rape and murder of a young couple in the Ford Heights neighborhood of Chicago. Williams, Rainge, and Adams spent almost 18 years in prison for that crime, Jimerson almost 11. In 1999 they settled with Cook County, Illinois, in a $36 million wrongful conviction lawsuit—the largest civil rights settlement in history at the time. During the investigation that fréed them, it was revealed that a witness had told police that four *other* men were seen running from the crime scene—but police never investigated that claim. In 1998 DNA evidence proved that those four other men had committed the crimes. One was in jail for having murdered another woman.

- **Marvin Anderson.** In 2001 Anderson was exonerated in the violent 1982 rape of a young woman in Hanover, Virginia. He was 18 when he was convicted, and he had no criminal record. The victim, who was white, told police that her assailant was black, and that he had a white girlfriend—and Anderson was the only black man in the area that the police knew of who had a white

girlfriend. He was convicted by an all-white jury in about 45 minutes—and sentenced to 210 years in prison. In 1988 John Otis Lincoln, also from Hanover, admitted in a courtroom that he'd committed the crime—but the judge said he was lying. Anderson was freed on parole in 1997, after serving more than 15 years. It took another five years to get a DNA test done, which proved his innocence. In 2002 he was granted a full pardon. He was the 99th person in the United States exonerated, post-conviction, through the use of DNA evidence. Further testing showed that John Otis Lincoln *had* committed the crime. He was convicted of the 1982 rape in 2003.

- **James Bain.** In December 2009, James Bain of Brooklyn, New York, was proven by DNA testing to be innocent of the kidnapping, burglary, and rape of a nine-year-old boy—for which he had spent 35 years in prison. It's the longest sentence served by any person exonerated by DNA evidence. The victim had picked him out of a police lineup. The boy admitted years later that he'd been directed to pick Bain.

In 1994 the FBI began operating CODIS (Combined DNA Index System), a massive database of DNA profiles for millions of people who have been convicted of violent and sexual crimes, which has been instrumental in the exonerations of many people.

When the Bullet Hits the Bone

Another headline that writes itself: "Hot Dog Stand Robbery Suspect Shoots Himself in Wiener." The suspect was 19-year-old Terrion Pouncy. One night in 2016, he barged into Original Maxwell Street Polish in Chicago's South Side, pulled out a small pistol, and ordered a worker to empty the cash register. Cash in hand, Pouncy started running away, but it turns out he's not a very good multitasker. While trying to stuff the pistol back in his pants, it discharged twice. One bullet hit him in the thigh, the other hit him in a very tender spot a few inches higher. Pouncy made it as far as a nearby car wash, and then—in excruciating pain—called 911. He was arrested on two counts of armed robbery. It's a good bet that whatever punishment the judge laid down wasn't nearly as severe as the instant karma Pouncy served upon himself.

"One way to make sure crime doesn't pay would be to let the government run it."
—**Ronald Reagan**

DUMB DOGNAPPER

In January 2013, 18-year-old Christopher Young walked up to a woman walking her Yorkshire terrier on a street in Washington, DC "Give me your dog," Young demanded. "Yorkies cost a lot of money." Young was right: Yorkies go for as much as $1,500. But when he was counting his potential take, he didn't take into account his own clumsiness. As he snatched the dog, Young dropped his cell phone. While he scrambled to find it, the Yorkie slipped out of his grasp and ran for home. Young fled, but the dropped cell phone led police to information about another valuable device: the GPS-enabled ankle bracelet he was wearing for committing another crime. The bracelet not only pinpointed his exact location but—because it had been tracking his every step—gave law enforcement the evidence needed to lock up Young.

Half-Baked Schemes

These plots weren't quite cooked in the middle.

BAG MAN

"Clenzo Thompson, 45, was arrested in New York City in January 2007 after allegedly robbing the same Commerce Bank branch twice in three days. The first robbery ended when the chemical dye in the money bag exploded and spooked him. He apparently failed to learn from that, because the dye in the second robbery's money bag also exploded. (And three years earlier, Thompson had been caught after another bank robbery after having accidentally dropped his ID on the bank floor.)"

—*News of the Weird*

WENT TO THE WELL ONCE TOO OFTEN

"A scofflaw who came to be known as the 'gin and tonic bandit' went to the same O'Charley's restaurant in Bloomington, Indiana, every Wednesday for a month, ordered two gin and tonics and a rib-eye steak, then skipped out on his $25.96 bill. At the end of each meal he would excuse himself to use the restroom, then skip out without paying. Amazingly, the man returned a fifth time. This time the restaurant was ready for him. When his server presented the bill, he again claimed he needed to use the bathroom. But when he walked out of the restaurant, four employees were waiting to confront him. He immediately offered to pay the bill . . . with a check. Told the restaurant didn't accept checks, the man 'got nervous and ran,' according to police. He was quickly caught and arrested."

—Associated Press

NO SUCH THING AS A FREE LUNCH

"Richmond Heights police Sgt. Chuck Duffy has long known that Joan Hall is a habitual scammer and thief. After all, he is the detective who spearheaded the case charging the 65-year-old woman with bilking department stores out of millions of dollars through shoplifting and merchandise-return schemes. But even Duffy could hardly believe it when he saw Hall and her co-defendant, Roger Neff, stealing food from the Justice Center cafeteria during the lunch break from their trial. He reported the incident to cafeteria managers, who summoned sheriff's deputies. Minutes later, they found Hall and Neff lunching at a table—the defense table in Judge Nancy Fuerst's courtroom, where the two are on trial. The judge ordered Hall and Neff to stay out of the cafeteria for the rest of their trial. 'You bring your lunch,' Fuerst told them."

—*Cleveland Plain Dealer*

WILD CARD

"A hapless German thief snapped his credit card in two while prying open his neighbor's lock, inadvertently leaving behind his name and account details. 'He tried to copy what he'd seen them do on television, but the flat-owner woke up and the criminal ran away,' a police spokesman said. 'The victim called up and read us the details off the card. When we got to the burglar's house, the other half of his credit card was sitting on his kitchen table.'"

—Reuters

CRIME QUESTION

Do the police really outline a murder victim's body in chalk?

At one time, maybe, but according to investigators we surveyed, it's really not done anymore. Why? While chalk or tape might make for dramatic TV, they also contaminate the crime scene, and contamination is a major headache for crime scene investigators.

Mega Trials

Some trials make bigger splashes than others.

HENRY ORCHARD TRIAL (1907)

In 1905, Idaho governor Frank Steuenberg was killed by a bomb strapped to the front gate of his home. James McParland, an agent for the Pinkerton Agency (well known for busting union activity) conducted an investigation and arrested miner and union member Harry Orchard. Orchard entered a plea bargain in which he implicated as conspirators the Western Federation of Miners general secretary Bill Haywood and president Charles Moyer, and labor organizer George Pettibone. The trio were arrested in Colorado in 1906 and tried in 1907. The plea backfired; Pettibone and Haywood were acquitted, charges against Moyer were dropped, and Orchard got life in prison, where he died in 1954.

CHICAGO SEVEN (1969)

Seven people were charged with conspiracy for inciting a riot at the 1968 Democratic National Convention in Chicago. Bobby Seale, a founding member of the Black Panther Party, was ultimately tried separately and convicted of contempt of court after calling the original trial's judge a "racist pig." Hoffman and Rubin were consistently disruptive, showing up in court wearing judicial robes and blowing kisses at the jury. The trial became a critical examination of the 1960s countercultures. All seven were found innocent of conspiracy, Froines and Weiner were acquitted, and the other five were convicted of intent to riot and sentenced to five years in prison and fined $5,000. (The convictions were reversed on appeal due to the original judge's refusal to screen jurors for political and racial prejudices.)

"When I went to the prosecutor's office, I wanted to be one of the good guys that the defense could trust. I'd try fair, clean cases, pull no punches, no below-the-belt stuff. Honorable. Because that's the kind of prosecutor I wanted to deal with."
—Marcia Clark

Holes in the Plan

BOOK 'EM!

Buffalo, Oklahoma: "The only explanation police have is that the two teenagers must have gotten the bank mixed up with the library. 'It's the first attempted library robbery I ever heard of,' policeman Ray Dawson said Thursday. Dawson said the teenagers held out an empty pillow case and told the library attendant, 'Put it in.' 'Put what in?' the attendant asked. 'The money. Put it in and nobody'll get hurt,' the youth demanded.

The attendant, who said there was less than $1 in collected library fines in his petty cash box, ran out the door and escaped. The teenagers were arrested hours later in Garden City, Kansas."

—United Press International, 1975

OH, THAT

Wandsworth, England: "On July 20, 1979, an armed robber dashed into a little grocery store and told the proprietor, 'Give me the money from your till or I will shoot.' The owner was perplexed. 'Where's your gun?' he asked. There was an awkward silence . . . Then the robber replied that he didn't actually have a gun, but if the owner gave him any trouble, he'd go out and get one and come back. After a moment, the crook quietly left."

—*The Return of Heroic Failures*

Angel of Death

This guy needs a refresher on the Hippocratic oath.

End-of-life decisions are difficult for the family of a terminal patient. So, for ten years, a nurse at a hospital in Glendale, California, was generous enough to make those decisions for his patients. Efren Saldivar was a respiratory nurse at Glendale Adventist Medical Center. In 1998 police questioned him after several co-workers reported his suspicious behavior. Saldivar confessed to killing 50 patients by administering drugs to stop their breathing, but said he did so as an act of mercy. Soon after, he denied his confession. Police were forced to exhume 20 of the more than 1,000 patients who had died during Saldivar's shift. Six of those showed traces of the drug Saldivar allegedly used.

In 2002 the "Angel of Death" pled guilty to those six counts of murder to avoid the death penalty. But at his sentencing, the judge unsealed a second confession in which Saldivar claimed to have killed well over 100 patients, including some at two other hospitals where he moonlighted. In that confession, he also said he killed patients simply to lighten his workload, and likened it to shoplifting. "After that moment, you don't think about it the rest of the day, or ever," he said. To this day, nobody knows exactly how many victims he claimed.

TORONTO'S FIRST (BOTCHED) HANGING

A city isn't a city until it executes its first prisoner . . . or comes close.

IN OLD YORK

In 1798 Toronto was just a five-year-old hamlet called York. The city was growing, and so was its crime rate. In October 1798, an unthinkable, heinous crime took place. An illiterate tailor named John Sullivan and his friend, Michael Flannery, got rip-roaring drunk in one of the town's first taverns. Out of cash with their thirst not yet slaked, the two men conspired to fake a banknote for three shillings, which they used to buy more whiskey.

HANGING AROUND

The crime was quickly discovered. Flannery escaped and crossed the US border to freedom. Sullivan, however, was caught. In short order, Sullivan was tried, convicted, and sentenced by the unforgiving judge to pay with his life.

Trouble was, the city did not yet have a hangman (and it wouldn't, for another century). Nobody in town was eager to step up. Fortunately, a fellow inmate known only as "McKnight" offered to end Sullivan's reign of terror—for a price. He wanted $100 (about $1,400 in today's money) and a pardon. The judge accepted the offer. Unfortunately, McKnight had no idea what he was doing, and two attempts to tighten the noose and hang Sullivan failed to achieve the desired result. The story goes that Sullivan's last words were something like, "McKnight, I hope to goodness you've got the rope all right this time." The third time was, in fact, a charm.

STRANGE EVIDENCE

At one point during the 1893 Lizzie Borden ax-murder trial, prosecutors presented into evidence the skulls of her parents, which were secretly removed during the autopsy. Upon seeing them, Borden nearly fainted and had to be taken out of the courtroom.

Wasn't Expecting That

When man's best friend turns out to be a snitch.

TAKE A BITE OUT OF CRIME

On Thanksgiving Day 2001, police were called to the Ohio home of Nandor Santho. While searching the premises, they found 150 marijuana plants growing in the basement. Who called the cops? Santho's dog Willie—the pointer apparently stepped on his master's cell phone in such a way that it auto-dialed 911—*twice*. Dispatchers mistook Willie's whimpering for a female in distress, which is why they sent the police to the home.

PIG-HEADED

In 2003, a burglar broke into Richard Morrison's apartment in Liverpool, England, and began ransacking it. But when he saw a big jar with the human head floating in it, he went straight to the police, turned himself in, and told them what he found. Police sped over to the apartment, kicked down the door and discovered . . . that Morrison is an *artist,* not a psycho—the object in the jar was a mask he'd made from strips of bacon.

That's Awkward

In 2017 two undercover cops from Detroit's 12th Precinct, posing as drug dealers, were trying to ensnare wannabe buyers at a drug house. At the same time, two undercover cops from Detroit's *11th* Precinct showed up, posing as buyers, and tried to arrest the fake dealers. And then all hell broke loose. Fists flew, guns were drawn, and an ambulance was called out to take one of the quarreling cops to the hospital. No actual drug dealers or buyers were arrested in the botched raid. Officials from both precincts were tight-lipped about what happened, saying only that an investigation was underway. A neighbor who witnessed the debacle summed up the problem: "You gotta have more communication, I guess."

Queen of the Jail

Jack and Ed were "the Biddle Boys"—leaders of a gang who relied on brains to commit their crimes. In 1901, the gang was robbing a house next to a grocery store. An accomplice kept the grocer distracted while the boys robbed the house. The distraction didn't work—the grocer heard noise and went to investigate. A struggle ensued, shots were fired, and the grocer was killed. The Biddle brothers fled, but the police soon caught up with them. After a violent shootout, the outlaws were arrested, but not before a policeman was killed. The Biddle Boys were sentenced to death.

The jail's warden, Peter Soffel, and his wife Katherine were in the midst of a divorce when the Biddles arrived. Katherine spent most her time visiting the prisoners, offering them spiritual advice. They called her "Queen of the Jail." She went to see the Biddles out of curiosity; their exploits had made them notorious. Ed's charm and good looks swooned her. The warden knew his wife had taken an interest in the outlaw—but didn't realize how keen an interest. After a few months, Ed and Jack convinced Katherine they were innocent and to help them escape.

Ed's cell could be seen from Katherine's bedroom window. The two designed a secret alphabet code with

which they could spell out messages about the warden's movements. They asked Katherine to smuggle in two saws and a revolver.

On January 29, 1902, the boys broke free. As they were leaving the prison, they were met by Katherine, which was *not* part of the plan. Katherine, mad with love, chloroformed her husband. The warden awoke to a headache and an empty house. When he was told the Biddle Boys had escaped, he knew Katherine was involved and immediately put out an all-points bulletin on the fugitives.

Ed agreed to let Katherine come. They stole a horse and a sleigh from a nearby farm. They had only traveled a few miles when a posse met them head-on. Ed and Jack jumped off the sleigh, each with gun in hand. The lawmen responded with a hail of bullets.

Ed was shot twice, Jack 15 times, and Katherine once, by Ed, after pleading for him to take her life. Katherine's wound was treatable; Ed and Jack were not so lucky. As they lay on their deathbeds, they told police varying accounts of what happened. Ed claimed he'd never loved Katherine, that he used her to help him escape. Katherine claimed that Ed was saying that to protect her. Love letters he wrote her while still in prison backed her up, but only Ed knew for sure. He and Jack both died on February 1, 1902. Katherine survived, and died a lonely and disgraced woman in 1909.

THE GREAT PUMPKIN MYSTERY

It remains the most infamous prank ever pulled off at Cornell University in Ithaca, New York. On an October morning in 1997, students noticed a 50-pound pumpkin speared through the spire of the 173-foot-high bell tower. How it got up there, and by whom, is still a mystery. But the real star of this story is the pumpkin, which somehow stayed atop the tower through the winter. It became one of the Internet's first viral sensations, even spawning a "Pumpkin Watch" live webcam (also among the first). Stories of the great pumpkin's resilience spread around the world. MTV even sent a crew to cover it. The pumpkin finally fell the following spring during an attempt to remove it.

But its story didn't end there: parts of the carcass were taken to Cornell's biology lab for testing, to no avail. And then, according to *Atlas Obscura,* "Its remains were freeze-dried and kept in a glass case in the visitor's center, then added to a display of brains in the psychology department, and finally found a permanent perch in the office of professor Barbara Finlay." Long since decayed, its legend lives on today. Despite pleas on the prank's 20th anniversary for the perpetrators to come forward (they wouldn't be charged with a crime), no one took credit.

Whodunit?

*Here's a murder mystery that's ripped
from the headlines . . . of 1799.*

A SENSATIONAL MURDER

In December 1799, Gulielma "Elma" Sands got dressed and left
her home—a boardinghouse owned by Elias and Catherine Ring.
She was never seen alive again. According to Catherine, Elma
was planning to get married that night. Instead, her body was
pulled out of the Manhattan Well.

Suspicion fell on a carpenter named Levi Weeks. Levi lived
in the same boardinghouse and had been courting Elma—a
scandalous situation in that day. After Catherine claimed that
Levi was the man Elma had planned to elope with on the night
she disappeared, Levi was indicted for murder.

LOOKING BAD FOR LEVI

The trial began on March 31, 1800. A *New York Evening Post*
editor wrote a transcript of the proceedings, making the Weeks
spectacle America's first recorded murder trial. After the jury
was chosen, the prosecutor presented his case: Weeks moved
into the Greenwich boardinghouse and seduced Elma Sands. He
had promised to elope with her in December, but when the time
came, he changed his mind and killed her instead.

Boarders at the Rings' home testified that Levi had been in
Elma's room overnight several times. Catherine Ring testified
that the two had exited the house within a short time of one

another. Witnesses said they'd seen a horse and sleigh near the crime scene that resembled Levi's brother Ezra's. Richard Croucher, a fellow boarder, claimed Levi's accomplice in New Jersey had confessed to the murder.

THE DEFENSE TO THE RESCUE

The defense portrayed the carpenter as "an injured and innocent young man" who'd never treated Elma badly. Plus, Levi had an alibi—several people had seen him at Ezra's house on the evening in question. Other witnesses said Ezra's horse and sleigh never left the barn.

Other boarders contradicted the prosecution's portrayal of Elma as a happy, innocent girl. They claimed that Elma used drugs and talked of killing herself. One boarder said Levi wasn't her lover. According to him, Elias Ring, the owner of the boardinghouse, spent the night with Elma when his wife was away. As for the prosecution's star witness, boarder Richard Croucher, the defense showed that he personally hated Weeks.

A VERDICT AND A CURSE

The judge bluntly informed the jury that the prosecution's case was a flimsy basis for conviction. The jury returned its verdict: not guilty. New Yorkers disagreed with the verdict, and Weeks was run out of town. Less than a year after the trial, Richard Croucher was found guilty of raping a young girl in the Ring boardinghouse, changing public opinion. Levi Weeks settled in Natchez, Mississippi, where he became an architect, married, and had a family. Today, the Manhattan Well where Elma Sands met her end still exists—in the basement of the Manhattan Bistro in Soho.

The Stoner Report

BURNING QUESTION

Robert Michelson of Farmington, Connecticut, called 911 one day in February 2011. When the dispatcher asked if there was a crime in progress, Michelson said, "Possibly. I was just growing some marijuana and was just wondering how much trouble you can get in for one plant." After a long pause, the dispatcher replied, "It depends on how big the plant is." "It's only a seedling," said Michelson. The dispatcher informed him that having a plant *does* constitute possession of marijuana. Michelson thanked her and hung up. The dispatcher alerted the police, who arrived at Michelson's house a short time later. However, there was no plant. Michelson told police he was only thinking about growing marijuana. However, he was still arrested, as he was in possession of marijuana, marijuana seeds, and several bongs.

GREEN GIANT

Ramiro Gonzalez, 30, of Progreso, Texas, was driving a tractor-trailer filled with papayas in the far south of the state one day in January 2011. A sheriff's deputy pulled the truck over and found 3,103 pounds of marijuana underneath the papayas. Gonzalez was arrested on felony drug-trafficking charges. He probably would have gotten away with it, too, if it hadn't been for the expired tags on his truck, which was the only reason he'd been stopped in the first place.

IN THE BIG HOUSE

In most of New York's prisons, inmates are known for the single worst crime they've committed . . . or been caught for. But a few prisoners also made names for themselves for what they did while they were doing time.

Inmate: Lil Wayne, Grammy winner and self-proclaimed "Best Rapper Alive"

Locked up in: Rikers Island

While in Prison: In 2010 Lil Wayne released the album titled *I Am Not a Human Being* (which shot to #1 on the Billboard charts), collaborated on a song with rappers Drake and Jay-Z, was sued by a record producer, and posted regular blog entries. The last month of his incarceration was spent in solitary confinement because he was caught with contraband—not drugs or weapons, but an iPod charger and earphones.

Inmate: John Colt, brother of revolver inventor Samuel Colt

Locked up in: The Tombs

While in Prison: The day before Colt's execution in 1842, he married his housekeeper. Hours later, he committed suicide in his cell by stabbing himself through the heart. At the same time, a candle (or lamp) ignited a fire that swept through the prison and destroyed part of the roof. Several prisoners escaped, and Colt's bride was never seen again,

sparking a rumor that she set the fire while Colt faked his death, substituted another body for his own, and escaped.

Inmate: Drifter Eddie White
Locked up in: Rikers Island
While in Prison: By 1994 White had broken out of Rikers Island three times. (He'd been locked up for the murders of two people and sentenced to 200 years to life.) The breakouts earned him the respect of inmates, who dubbed him "Rabbit Man" for his quickness. In one escape, he allegedly killed two more people, but those charges were dismissed when the judge noted that he was already going to die in jail.

Inmate: Con artist Tuvia Stern
Locked up in: The Tombs
While in Prison: In June 2009, Stern threw a lavish bar mitzvah for his son . . . behind bars. Held in the prison gym, the gala had 60 guests, a band, and catered kosher food. Attendees were even allowed to keep their cell phones, a big no-no in prison, and the jail paid officers overtime for the event. Four months later, Stern threw another party, this time for his daughter's engagement. When the city's corrections commissioner found out about the parties, he suspended the prison rabbi who'd overseen the bar mitzvah and took away the vacation benefits of four corrections officers who'd been in on the event.

The Night Guard Whistle-Blower

In 1997 Christoph Meili was employed as a night guard by an outside security firm responsible for protecting the Union Bank of Switzerland headquarters in Zurich when he discovered that bank officials were destroying documents related to the assets of Nazi Holocaust victims. Meili took home some files that were to be shredded; he intended to save the documents and expose the bank's activities. At the time, investigations were underway concerning Switzerland's activities during World War II, in particular what happened to the dormant bank accounts of Holocaust victims. By law, those records were supposed to have been turned over to the victims' heirs. Meili gave his files to a Jewish organization, which revealed to the public what the bank was trying to do. In 1998 Swiss banks and Jewish officials agreed to a $1.25 billion settlement, of which Meili received a reported $750,000. Meili was vilified by many in Switzerland for violating the laws of bank secrecy, and was granted political asylum in the United States.

SOCIAL MEDIA MAYHEM

SMOKIN'

Friend: Rachel Stieringer, 19, of Keystone Heights, Florida

Story: In 2010, she posted a photo of her 11-month-old son on her Facebook profile. In the picture, the diapered boy appears to be smoking a bong. The photo became an Internet sensation.

Busted! A concerned citizen called a Florida child abuse hotline. A police investigation was started, and Stieringer turned herself in to police. She said the photo was just a joke . . . and that the bong was "only used for tobacco." Stieringer was arrested, and Florida children's services ordered that both Stieringer and her son be tested for drugs. The baby tested negative, but Stieringer did not. She was arrested for possessing drug paraphernalia and was ordered to attend both drug and parenting classes.

POOR JUDGMENT

Friend: Steven Mulhall, 21, of Coral Springs, Florida

Story: Mulhall was in a Broward County, Florida, court on February 23, 2012, on a theft charge. That same day, someone noticed that the nameplate from the door of Judge Michael Orlando had disappeared. Who could have stolen it?

Busted! In March an anonymous tipster called Broward County Sheriff Al Lamberti. The tipster advised him to go to a certain Facebook page. Lamberti did, and saw a photo of Steven Mulhall . . . proudly displaying the nameplate of Judge Michael Orlando. Mulhall was arrested. "The nameplate is like only $40," Lamberti told reporters, "not that big of a crime—but what an idiot. He's got multiple convictions for petty theft, so now this is a felony."

Dog, the Bounty Hunter

Duane Lee Chapman, a.k.a. Dog, was a member of a
biker gang called the Devil's Disciples. They gave Dog his
nickname. In 1976 Dog was involved in a drug deal that
went bad; the other gang member killed a drug dealer
while Dog sat in a car half a block away. Dog served 18
months in Texas's Huntsville State Prison for his role in the
murder. He caught his first fugitive while still incarcerated,
when he ran down a fleeing inmate nicknamed Bigfoot to
prevent guards from shooting him. Saving Bigfoot's life
earned Dog the nickname "Bounty Hunter," and helped
him win early release from prison. Dog was soon back in
court, this time for nonpayment of child support—he's
been married five times and has 14 children. While looking
over Dog's criminal file, the judge found a letter from
the warden of Huntsville Prison praising Dog for saving
Bigfoot's life. That gave the judge an idea: he showed Dog
a mug shot of a fugitive wanted by the court for skipping
bail, and told him that if he caught the guy, the judge
would personally pay $200 toward his child support. Dog
caught the fugitive within days and began a new career as
a bounty hunter and bail bondsman. An appearance on the
2003 A&E reality show *Take This Job* landed Dog his own
series, which debuted in 2004 and was soon the top-rated
program on that network.

The Murder of Julien Latouche

Even before the days of tabloid journalism, the public heard the grisly details of bizarre crimes of the day. One such crime occurred in the 1670s.

CHILD BRIDE—OR NO?

Although the legal age for marriage at the time was 12, most families didn't encourage their children to marry at such a young age. One person who seemed to have a different opinion on the subject was Jacques Bertault, who had four daughters he was apparently anxious to rid himself of. Two of his older daughters were both married young, at age 12 and 14, and he had another young daughter, Isabelle, to marry off.

He settled on 29-year-old Julien Latouche, a man who seemed to have a bright future. Isabelle's mother, Gillette, had concerns and let her husband know she was opposed to the marriage. But Bertault asserted his right as "master" of the house to make the decision, and Isabelle was married at age 12.

NOT A MATCH MADE IN HEAVEN

Julien turned out to be a lazy, uncaring, and abusive man that couldn't provide the basic necessities for himself or his bride, and often beat her. Her parents tried to provide them both with food and resources, but it's not hard to imagine that both Gillette and Bertault felt guilty about the situation.

THE MAN WHO WOULDN'T DIE

Something inspired Gillette to try and poison Julien with a plant that had killed some of their pigs. She prepared some soup for Julien, who ate it all, but nothing happened. The next day, Isabelle's parents visited Isabelle and Julien, and Gillette entered the barn where Julien was doing something it seemed he rarely did: working.

In a burst of anger, Gillette picked up a hoe and struck Julien in the head with it. He responded by attacking Gillette. Bertault entered the barn and grabbed the hoe from Gillette and repeatedly struck Julien with it while Gillette screamed "Kill him! Kill him!"

SELF-DEFENSE OR RETRIBUTION?

They dragged Julien's body out and threw it in a nearby river. Neighbors had heard the commotion and traveled to the barn where they saw the horrific sight of blood everywhere, and even some teeth. After a brief investigation, Isabelle and her parents were arrested for Julien's murder.

Gillette and Bertault confessed their role in the crime. They both claimed that Isabelle was only a bystander. Isabelle claimed that Gillette was defending herself against Julien's attack. Unfortunately, the court decided that all three were guilty of murder. Gillette and Bertault were executed, and just as Isabelle had watched the death of her husband, she was forced to watch her parents' execution.

What happened to Isabelle afterward isn't clear . . . except that she lived with the notoriety of the murder for the rest of her life.

HOME SWEAT HOME

In February 2015, a light dusting of snow fell on the Amsterdam suburb of Haarlem. Concerned neighbors in a row of town houses called police to report that one of the town houses had no snow on its roof. Dutch police had seen this happen before, and they had a pretty good idea what the cause was. Upon investigating, their suspicions were confirmed. The hot lights from a large-scale cannabis grow operation in the attic had melted the snow. The occupants of the home were arrested, and the cannabis plants were confiscated. If only they'd waited until spring . . .

> "Going to trial with a lawyer who considers your whole lifestyle a crime in progress is not a happy prospect."
> —Hunter S. Thompson

THE FAKE McCOY

In 2013 a Brooklyn entrepreneur/con man named Howard Leventhal convinced investors that he had invented a medical tricorder—the device that *Star Trek*'s Dr. McCoy used to scan his patients. Leventhal, 56, called it "Heltheo's McCoy Home Health Tablet." The wireless device supposedly worked something like this: you scan yourself, and then vital information about your health is instantly sent to the company's "nurse-staffed call center." Though Leventhal had no prototype or even schematics, he received $800,000 to develop the device. But there was nothing to develop, because Leventhal made the whole thing up. He was arrested. At his hearing, he pleaded guilty, lamenting, "I'd like to move to Mars but the option isn't open."

LITTLE-KNOWN FACT: Dr. McCoy actor DeForest Kelley's final role was a voice in the 1998 animated feature *The Brave Little Toaster Goes to Mars*.

THE POWER OF THE PEN

If you wrote *The Turner Diaries,* you'd keep your identity secret, too. That's why William Luther Pierce used the name Andrew Macdonald in 1978 when he published the book dubbed "the bible of the racist right" by the FBI.

A bizarre, racist sci-fi adventure, *The Turner Diaries* is set in the year 2099. In diary form, its protagonist, Earl Turner, describes how he and fellow members of a terrorist group known as "The Organization" have brought down the American government and instituted a worldwide race war that ultimately eliminated all Jews and nonwhites. It's unhinged, paranoid stuff—and it's sold about 500,000 copies to date.

Dr. William Luther Pierce III (1933–2002) was an assistant professor of physics at Oregon State University in the 1960s and onetime leader of the National Alliance, a white separatist group associated with the American Nazi Party, whose racist rhetoric made the Ku Klux Klan look tame. Pierce was also the founder of Cosmotheism, a religion based on white racial superiority and eugenics.

Among other things, *The Turner Diaries* is credited with influencing acts of violence and terrorism, including the 1995 Oklahoma City bombing by Timothy McVeigh, a known admirer of the book. When Pierce died of cancer in July 2002, he was hailed as a prophet by some and as an inflammatory racist scaremonger by others. For a man who saw life in black and white, he wouldn't have expected anything less.

The term *Mafia* muscled its way into dictionaries in the late 1860s. But long before, in Sicily, everybody knew the word. It originated in the tough streets and slums of Palermo. A man who was a *Mafioso* was a "man of respect," prepared to take the law into his own hands. Americans learned the word *Mafia* when it traveled to America along with the flood of immigrants from Italy in the late 19th and early 20th centuries. *Mafia* meant organized crime.

TOUGH PILLS TO SWALLOW

- In August 2017, police in the town of Osnabrück, Germany, pulled over a 51-year-old father and his 17-year-old son for suspect license plates. The pair were acting suspicious, so the police searched the car and discovered 5,000 orange Ecstasy pills in the shape of President Donald Trump's head.

- In 2015 more than 120 statues of Shaun the Sheep, the beloved British cartoon character from *Wallace & Gromit,* were scattered throughout Bristol and London, urging people to donate to local children's hospitals. Give enough money and you could own one of the sculptures. But for only £10, you could own a Shaun the Sheep Ecstasy pill. That was not a part of the charity drive, but rather an attempt by some deranged drug dealers to cash in on the campaign. Several Shaun tablets were seized by detectives, but the culprits were never caught.

MAKING A MONSTER

Ted Kaczynski, the man whose case the FBI dubbed UNABOM (for "UNiversity and Airline BOMber"), set off 16 homemade explosive devices between 1978 to 1995 that killed three people and maimed nearly two dozen others. His infamous manifestos shed light on two predominant themes that bounced around his brilliant but sick brain: a disdain for technology and a love of nature. After abruptly leaving academia in the 1970s to live in a cabin in the woods, Kaczynski might have stayed there had bulldozers not razed the land around his Montana homestead. That's when the bombings began.

But the bad seed that led to the bombings may have been sowed much earlier. As a Harvard sophomore in 1959, Kaczynski participated in a twisted research study led by famed psychologist Henry Murray—who in World War II had trained US spies to withstand intense interrogation. In the Harvard study, Murray's 22 subjects were told to write an essay outlining their personal philosophy, which would later be debated by a fellow student. Instead, Kaczynski, a 17-year-old "child genius," was strapped to a chair under

intense lights, and electrodes were hooked up to his head. Then, from behind a one-way mirror, a camera recorded his angry facial expressions as a lawyer read back his essay, exploiting every perceived weakness, and insulting and berating him relentlessly. Later, the footage of Kaczynski's reactions was played back to him ad nauseam. Murray's method of "destructive psychology" was by design "vehement, sweeping, and personally abusive."

Opinion is divided as to how much this three-year study directly led to Kaczynski's crimes, but consider this: Henry Murray's theory of personality states in part that "an individual's personality develops dynamically as each person responds to complex elements in his or her specific environment." And Kaczynski's response to "complex elements" was bizarre, to say the least. His targets, whom he called "agents of antihuman technology," were university and airline officials with nature-themed names like Thomas Mosser, Percy Wood, and Leroy Wood Bearson. Included in Kaczynski's crude bombs were pieces of wood and moss.

Who knows how many more people would have suffered had the FBI not published the Unabomber's manifesto in 1995? Kaczynski's estranged brother David read it and recognized it as Ted's writing. He contacted the FBI, and the Unabomber was arrested and later sentenced to life in prison without the chance of parole.

Miami Vice

THE PERPS: Several officers in Miami, Florida

THE STORY: On July 29, 1985, a group of men were attacked on a boat on the Miami River in the city's Little Havana district. Several of the men were thrown (or jumped) overboard; three died by drowning. An investigation found that the men had been unloading roughly 400 kilos of cocaine when the attack occurred. Further investigation revealed that the attackers were Miami cops, and they were in uniform when they made the raid. But instead of arresting the suspects and taking the cocaine as evidence, they took the cocaine and sold it, making about $116,000 in the process. Still more investigation revealed that the same group of corrupt cops had been pulling off similar drug heists, as well as a host of other crimes, for years.

OUTCOME: Thirty-four members of the Miami PD were arrested, some of whom agreed to testify against the others in exchange for immunity. During the course of the trial, several of the arrested cops hired a hit man to murder the key witness against them. (The plot fell through.) When it was all over, 24 Miami cops were convicted, and 17 went to prison. The longest sentence went to the leader of the group, Officer Osvaldo Coello, who got 35 years.

EXTRA: Writers for the television crime drama *Miami Vice* based several episodes on the scandal.

A Meaty Case

It was all going according to plan for Gilberto Escamilla. Until 800 pounds of fajitas came crashing down on him (figuratively, anyway).

Usually when people steal things from their workplace, they take pens or paperclips. When you're Gilberto Escamilla, you take fajitas—and lots of them. Escamilla had been working in the kitchen of a South Texas juvenile justice department for over 9 years when he decided to take a day off work for a medical appointment. While Escamilla was out, a driver from Labatt Food Service called the kitchen to let them know he had 800 pounds of fajitas to deliver. The employee who answered the phone was confused: the kitchen didn't serve fajitas. The driver informed her that he had been delivering fajitas to the department for nearly a decade.

When Escamilla returned to work the next day, he was questioned about the food delivery. That's when he admitted that he had been stealing the fajitas (food funded by the county)—for the past 9 years! Apparently, Escamilla would sell the food to his outside "customers" the day he ordered it. Officials obtained a search warrant and searched his home, only to find packages of the fajitas in Escamilla's refrigerator. Escamilla was fired from his job and arrested for stealing somewhere between $2,500–$30,000 worth of fajitas. The ex-kitchen employee posted bond and was released from jail.

But it wasn't over yet—after reviewing documents such as purchase orders and invoices from the past 9 years, the district attorney's office determined that Escamilla had scammed the justice department out of $1,251,578 in fajitas. That's a first-degree theft felony. "If it wasn't so serious, you'd think it was a *Saturday Night Live* skit," said Cameron County district attorney Luis V. Saenz. "But this is the real thing."

Escamilla was arrested once again. You could say justice was served—and it was delicious.

BEANE'S CANNIBAL FAMILY

Dinnertime in this household ran a little differently.

Some swear the tale of this Scottish cannibal clan is true. Others call it the ultimate urban legend, but the tales about Sawney Beane and his family refuse to die. According to legend, Sawney Beane raised three inbred generations on the coast of Gallows in Scotland in the 15th century. He sustained his huge family by attacking, robbing, killing, and eating travelers who passed by the family cave. At first Beane took only the odd traveler. But as the decades passed and his clan grew, the death toll began to rise.

When local villagers discovered odd, preserved bits of bodies washing up on the shore near the cave, they hunted for the murderer. Beane and his family were discovered, and publicly burned for their crimes on the order of King James of Scotland. The story may be hard to believe, but Scottish and British kids know all about it. Their mums used tales of the Beanes to scare their kids into being good. The story was also the basis for Wes Craven's 2006 film *The Hills Have Eyes*.

Easy Busts

SHORTCHANGED

While officers were investigating a 2012 bank robbery in Syracuse, New York, the robber, Arthur Bundrage, 28, returned to the bank and tried to get in the front door, which police had locked. Why'd he come back? The teller had shortchanged him, giving him less than the $20,000 he'd demanded.

NAME THAT CROOK

In 2012, a Twin Falls, Idaho, police officer stopped a man who was acting suspiciously and asked him for his name and birthday. He answered, "Emiliano Velesco," and gave a date. A search of that name came up empty. Then the cop saw the name "Contreras" tattooed on his arm. So he ran that name with the birthday given, and up popped Dylan Edward Contreras, 19, who had three outstanding warrants for failure to appear . . . and for giving false information.

Munchausen by Proxy

Her name is Gypsy Rose Blanchard. "Gypsy" because
her mother, Dee Dee, had always liked that name, and
"Rose" because her father, Rod, had always liked Guns &
Roses. That dubious reasoning marked the beginning of a
tumultuous life that would land Gypsy Rose in prison for
the murder of her mother, who was found stabbed to death
in her Missouri home in 2015.

The events that led to the murder read like something
out of a twisted David Lynch movie. Rod split not long after
Gypsy was born, leaving Dee Dee to raise her daughter
alone. Although Gypsy was a healthy girl, her mother
convinced her that she wasn't healthy at all, that though
she was a teenager, she only had the mental capacity of a
seven-year-old. She also convinced Gypsy—and her entire
family—that she had leukemia, asthma, and muscular
dystrophy. She even fooled a few doctors into performing
unnecessary surgeries on the girl. At the height of the ruse,
the Make-A-Wish Foundation was sending Gypsy—who
was wheelchair bound—to Disney World and to Miranda
Lambert concerts.

But there was nothing medically wrong with Gypsy,
and every time she'd tried to say that, Dee Dee physically
abused her. Even worse, Dee Dee put Botox in Gypsy's

saliva glands to make her drool, and stuck tubes in her ear to give her ear infections.

It wasn't until Gypsy was in her early 20s that she was able to break free. She met her boyfriend at a science-fiction convention, and eventually decided that the only way to be free was to kill Dee Dee and flee the state—so they did. They were later caught and sent to prison.

POSTSCRIPT: Dee Dee Blanchard "suffered" (for lack of a better word) from an actual condition known as Munchausen syndrome by proxy. In the more common Munchausen syndrome (named for an 18th-century German man who embellished his life story), the sufferer believes they suffer from one or more chronic illnesses. In this rare case, the proxy was Rose, whom Dee Dee was convinced was sick. And she managed to convince everyone else as well. As Gypsy put it during an interview she granted in prison, "I think Dee Dee would have been the perfect mom for someone that actually was sick."

> "History is nothing but a parade of crimes and adversities."
> —**Voltaire**

Kooky Crooks

Some lawbreakers make it difficult to classify them.

WHEN ART REALLY BOMBS

In 2002 Luke Helder, a University of Wisconsin art student, was arrested for planting 18 pipe bombs in mailboxes in a half-dozen states. It was all part of a bizarre "art" project: when plotted on a map, the bomb sites formed a "smiley face," with the "eyes" in Nebraska and Iowa and the left side of the "mouth" in Colorado and Texas. The right side remained unfinished because police caught Helder after his father turned him in. (Nobody died.)

STRESSLING

Simon Andrews of Osbaldwick, England, was sentenced to six months' house arrest in 2003. The crime: Andrews had attacked four random men on the street, wrestling them to the ground and taking off—but not stealing—their shoes and socks. Why'd he do it? Andrews, an accountant, says he was "stressed out."

HE JUST WANTED TO WATCH TV

A couple living in Dorset, England, called the police in 2001 when they realized their home had been broken into while they were out. An investigation revealed that the thief hadn't actually stolen anything, but had left behind a new television and an unopened bottle of Zima.

Creativity in the Courtroom

THE PLAINTIFF: Robert Lee Brock

THE DEFENDANT: Robert Lee Brock

THE LAWSUIT: Brock, an inmate serving 23 years for grand larceny, filed a $5 million lawsuit against himself. He claimed that he violated his own religious beliefs and civil rights by forcing himself to get drunk. Because of this self-induced drunkenness, he perpetrated several crimes. He claimed, "I want to pay myself $5 million for violating my own rights, but ask the state to pay it since I can't work and am a ward of the state."

THE VERDICT: Case dismissed.

THE PLAINTIFF: Ned Searight

THE DEFENDANT: The State of New Jersey

THE LAWSUIT: In a $14 million lawsuit, Searight claimed he had suffered injuries while in prison in 1962. He charged that he was injected with a "radium electric beam" against his will. As a result, he began hearing voices in his head.

THE VERDICT: Claim dismissed . . . on the grounds that the statute of limitations had run out. The judge also offered this strange lesson in physics: "Taking the facts as pleaded . . . they show a case of presumable unlicensed radio communication, which comes within the sole jurisdiction of the FCC. . . . And even aside from that, Searight could have blocked the broadcast to the antenna in his brain simply by grounding it . . . Searight might have pinned to the back of a trouser leg a short chain of paper clips so that the end would touch the ground and prevent anyone from talking to him inside his brain."

In 2016, Chicago's murder rate rose a whopping 60% higher than the year before, bringing the Windy City's murder rate to 27.7 homicides per 100,000 people. Despite the huge increase, it still trailed far behind St. Louis, MO, which claimed the top murder rate in 2016 at a mind-blowing 60 murders per 100,000 residents.

A Tragic End for a Comic Star

*Movie actor and comedian Thelma Todd was found
dead in her garage. Was she murdered?*

Two days before her body was found in her garage, Thelma Todd
had been at a party at the Café Trocadero on Sunset Boulevard.
Todd was known for her hard-partying ways. She drank heavily
and stayed out until 2:45 a.m. Afterward, her chauffeur drove her
home. He was the last known person to see her alive.

IN OVER HER HEAD

Todd's life was full of drama and crime. She was attracted to
powerful men, and gangsters Pat DiCicco and Lucky Luciano
intrigued her. Todd married DiCicco in 1932. DiCicco introduced
her to Luciano. With her husband often away, Thelma became
Luciano's lover.

A former flame and costar, Roland West, proposed that
Thelma Todd open a joint-venture restaurant on Sunset
Boulevard. In 1934 Thelma Todd's Sidewalk Café opened. A
three-story building housed the restaurant on the main floor, a
private bar on the second floor, and storage on the third floor.
West ran the place and Todd's fame drew the crowds.

HOT TODDY IN HOT WATER

Todd divorced DiCicco in 1934, but her relationship with Luciano
was not so easily dissolved. He insisted on opening an illegal
gambling parlor on the building's third floor, which Todd
vehemently opposed. Luciano tried to "persuade" West and Todd
by sending his associates to repeat his demands.

Todd decided to fight back. She had made an appointment with the district attorney's office for December 17 (coincidently, one day after she died). Todd was ready to spill all she knew about the mobster. She also planned to audit the café's financial records. Busy as it was, the restaurant wasn't making money. West and the café's treasurer weren't giving her the answers she demanded (they were being intimidated by Luciano).

REASONABLE DOUBTS?

Thelma Todd's body was found on December 16, 1935. On December 19, a grand jury convened. With national media camped outside, the jury called more than 40 witnesses to explain the circumstances leading up to Todd's death. The jury ruled her death accidental. The ruling presumed that an intoxicated Todd had taken refuge in her car after having been locked out of her apartment—possibly by Roland West. Perhaps Todd had turned on the engine and fallen asleep. But that wouldn't explain the blood and bruises found on her body, or her cracked ribs.

THE THEORIES

Among the leading suspects were the three men in Todd's life: Luciano, West, and DiCicco. Their motives were all clear. Luciano wanted his illegal casino and orchestrated her murder to get it. He also allegedly knew about Todd's appointment with the DA. Roland West came under suspicion as a jealous ex-lover or greedy business partner. Todd's ex-husband, Pat DiCicco, drew police attention because he tried to convince Todd to involve him in the steak house venture. No hard evidence could link any of them to her death, and no one was ever arrested. The full story behind Thelma Todd's death remains a mystery.

COURTROOM ALL-STARS

Here are a few real-life examples of unusual legal battles involving celebrities.

THE PLAINTIFF: Florence Henderson

THE DEFENDANT: Serial Killer Inc.

THE LAWSUIT: Henderson, the actor who played Carol Brady on the TV show *The Brady Bunch,* sued clothing maker Serial Killer Inc. in 1999 when they put out a T-shirt that showed her picture with the caption "Porn Queen." The suit called the caption "highly offensive . . . and false."

THE VERDICT: Serial Killer pulled all the offending merchandise out of stores the day after the suit was filed.

THE PLAINTIFFS: Anna Kournikova, Judith Soltesz-Benetton

THE DEFENDANT: *Penthouse* magazine

THE LAWSUIT: *Penthouse* published photos it claimed were of Kournikova, a top-ranked Russian tennis player, bathing topless. Kournikova denied it was her and threatened to sue. But the magazine's editors said they had studied the photos in "painstaking detail" and refused to back down. It seemed *Penthouse* might win until Soltesz-Benetton (of the Benetton clothing family) came forward and said *she* was the woman in the photos . . . and then filed a $10 million lawsuit.

THE VERDICT: *Penthouse* settled out of court.

Madoff Madness

Bernie Madoff is known as the mastermind of the largest financial fraud scheme American history. After his empire crumbled, people wanted a piece of the rubble.

Auction Item: A blue satin New York Mets baseball team jacket with "Madoff" stitched on the back in orange. (Team owner Fred Wilpon was one of Madoff's victims.)
Estimated Value: $720
Sold for: $14,500

Auction Items: A Lady Hermès brown suede handbag that belonged to Madoff's wife, Ruth, plus two other purses.
Estimated Value: $210
Sold for: $1,900

Auction Items: Three boogie boards, one with "Madoff" written on it with a black marker.
Estimated Value: $80
Sold for: $1,000

Auction Item: A set of Madoff's personalized golf clubs (irons only).
Estimated Value: $350
Sold for: $3,600

Auction Item: A pair of Ruth Madoff's diamond Victorian dangle earrings.
Estimated Value: $20,000
Sold for: $70,000

Auction Item: A 1960 Hofstra University ring engraved with "BM."
Estimated Value: $360
Sold for: $6,000

Auction Item: A black leather Mont Blanc wallet embossed with "BM."
Estimated Value: $100
Sold for: $2,200

The Murder of Chico Mendes

"At first I thought I was fighting to save rubber trees, then I thought I was fighting to save the Amazon rain forest. Now I realize I am fighting for humanity."—Chico Mendes

As the son of a family of rubber tappers (workers who gather latex from rubber trees) in Brazil, Chico Mendes became a tapper when he was only nine years old. When prices for rubber collapsed in the 1960s, many Amazon landowners began auctioning their land to cattle ranchers, who promptly felled the trees to convert the acreage for grazing. Alarmed, Mendes campaigned to save the trees by running for local office. He proposed creating forest reserves managed by the people who lived there, and founded the Xapuri Rural Workers Union to unite rubber tappers and rally them to resist ranchers. He raised consciousness about the global dangers of deforestation. His effort led to the preservation of 8 million acres of Amazon forests.

In 1988, Mendes led a successful campaign to stop rancher Darly Alves da Silva from logging an area designated to become a reserve. Later that year, Mendes was assassinated at age 44. The murder made headlines across the globe. Alves da Silva's son, and one of their ranch hands were arrested, convicted, and imprisoned for the crime. Prior to his murder, Mendes said in an interview he wanted to live, but "if a messenger from the sky came down and guaranteed that my death would strengthen our struggle, it would be worth it."

THE TRUTH IS IN THERE

In 2002, just a few months after the 9/11 attacks, a bizarre message flashed on a US Army computer screen: "Your security system is crap. I am Solo. I will continue to disrupt at the highest levels." The message appeared on 97 Army, Navy, Air Force, and NASA computers. Officials immediately suspected—and feared—that it was a terrorist attack. It wasn't. Security experts tracked the messages to Scotland, where they'd been sent out by one Gary McKinnon. His lawyer's defense: McKinnon has Asperger's syndrome, a condition marked by an inability to understand simple social cues but an enhanced ability to understand complex systems (such as computer networks). McKinnon had hacked into the military networks because he believed that's where the US government was storing "the truth" about UFOs. The US government asked the UK to extradite McKinnon for trial, but in 2012—after ten years of legal wrangling—the extradition was denied and McKinnon went unpunished.

Let's Dig Up Jimmy Hoffa . . . Again

Jimmy Hoffa was a well-known union leader in the 1960s and '70s, On July 30, 1975, Hoffa had dinner at restaurant in Detroit. Then he disappeared. After seven years, he was declared legally dead. Over 40 years later, federal agents are still looking for him.

1975: Detectives inspected a trash compactor at the Raleigh House, theorizing that mobsters used it to crush Hoffa's body before carting it off in a Mafia-related garbage service. No luck.

1989: Donald "Tony the Greek" Frankos said he'd been part of the hit team that murdered Hoffa. Frankos said they dismembered the body and shipped it to New Jersey in an oil drum, where it was buried under one of the end zones in Giants Stadium. Though the feds never followed up, when the stadium was demolished in 2010, Hoffa was nowhere to be found.

2004: A criminal named Frank Sheeran admitted that he'd killed Hoffa in a Detroit house in 1975. Two retired Detroit police detectives searched the house in question. They claimed to have found traces of blood on some floorboards, so authorities searched the property. They didn't find Hoffa, or any of his blood.

2013: The FBI received a tip from a man (who reportedly had mob ties) who said that Hoffa's body was buried in a field outside of Detroit. Agents conducted a search, but didn't find anything.

The Sane Clown Posse

The Juggalos are a gang of ax-murdering clowns who worship the rap band Insane Clown Posse. Well, that's the general impression of them. But most Juggalos maintain that they are misunderstood. "It isn't fair just because this group depicts violent images and talks about very crude murder scenarios," lamented Juggalo Patrick Flanary. That being said, there have been quite a few strange crimes associated with the group. Two examples:

- A Juggalo cut off a woman's pinky toe and drank her blood.
- Two Juggalos threw feces at Tila Tequila during a concert.

But it's not all fun and games. Roughly 15 percent of America's one million Juggalos are members of actual gangs, and they've been known to commit really gruesome murders with hatchets and other sharp objects. So it's not surprising that, in 2011, the FBI classified the Juggalos as a gang.

At first, Insane Clown Posse cofounder Shaggy 2 Dope thought the classification was "pretty dope." (That means good.) But he changed his tune when he found out that non-gang-affiliated Juggalos were getting hit with harsher sentences for petty crimes. So the band sued the FBI to have their dope name restored, and even held a rally in Washington, DC, in 2017, stating, "We truly are a family that is united by a shared love of music and fellowship." As of last report, however, Juggalos are still on the gang list. So if a scary clown approaches you in a dark alley, just ask, "Are you a good Juggalo, or are you a bad Juggalo?"

FELONY FAILS

Successful felonies aren't as easy as you might think . . . they require a little foresight. Take it from these criminals.

IF CONVICTED, HE WILL A-PEEL

In 2007 a man walked into a 7-Eleven in Monrovia, Maryland, just past midnight and attempted a holdup. The unidentified man didn't have a gun or any kind of weapon at all—he merely demanded that the clerk give him money. The clerk refused, so the man started picking up items off the counter to use as weapons. After repeatedly hitting the clerk with a banana, the attacker fled (empty-handed) before police arrived.

KIDNEY REMOVAL

In 2007 the Seattle Museum hosted "Bodies: The Exhibition," an educational display of preserved corpses and internal organs. One of the display kidneys was stolen. Police are still searching for the culprit, but do not fear the kidney will turn up on the black market, because even though the kidney is real, it's not "usable," as it's been filled and covered with plastic resin.

The Lindow Man

There is no statute of limitations on murder . . .
even ancient ones.

MUMMY COMES OUT

The Lindow Man had definitely been murdered. The victim's skull was bashed in, he was strangled, his neck broken, and his throat slashed. His ultraviolent end stirred international interest. But there was no cry for the cops to find his killer. He'd died around AD 100 and he'd been bogged down (so to speak) in the Lindow Moss bog for nearly 2,000 years.

PETE'S VITAL STATISTICS

Scientists swarmed over the Lindow Man, using modern forensics to follow a crime trail almost 2,000 years cold. Examining the victim, they learned that he was about 5'5" tall and weighed about 160 pounds. He'd been between 25 and 30 years old, muscular, and in good health on his last day on earth. He was naked except for a fox fur armband, but traces of fox fur in the bog made it likely that he'd once worn a fox fur cape.

Pete was likely a man of high rank; he was well fed and sleekly groomed. His close-cropped hair, mustache, and sideburns were all preserved by the bog. His skin was decorated but it was smooth, minus any scars that might indicate that he'd been a warrior. And Pete Marsh was no peasant; he had well-manicured fingernails on hands that had never done much manual labor. He'd eaten burned griddlecakes at his last meal, and there were traces of mistletoe pollen in his stomach as well.

DID THE DRUIDS DO IT?

Some scholars believe that the Lindow Man was a Druid. After they were conquered by the Romans, the Druids disappeared, leaving no written records. Roman writers reported that Druids painted their skin, used the mistletoe plant in their sacred rituals, and sacrificed human beings to their gods to ensure fertility—practices that make the Druids our number-one suspects.

CLUES TO MUMMY'S LAST DAYS

Beginning with his burned meal, his last day went downhill from there. His last vision may have been an ax or hammer raining blows down on his head. Once unconscious, he was strangled or garroted with enough force to break his neck vertebrae. After he was strangled, a blade sliced his throat draining him of blood. Pete was dumped face down in the bog.

Some historical sleuths make the case that the Lindow Man's violent end was a punishment for a crime. But many more believe that his last meal, which included mistletoe (sacred to the Druids), along with his triple killing and burial in the bog, are proof of a human sacrifice to the Celtic gods.

FREEZE-DRIED IMMORTALITY

The Lindow Man's body has been freeze-dried to keep it mummified. His face has been reconstructed based on radiographs of his skull, and he turns out to be a good-looking fellow. His face isn't primitive or savage—he could easily be a guy you meet on the modern streets of London. He stays indoors these days in a dim, quiet corner of London's British Museum.

Noasis

A lookalike was licking windows. Who did the lookalike look like? Noel Gallagher. After several eyewitnesses alerted the Swindon (England) police about the Oasis lead singer's strange doppelgänger in October 2017, the police posted an alert on their Facebook page: "You know it's going to be one of those shifts when you get a report of 'A Noel Gallagher lookalike swigging from a bottle of White

Lightning and licking windows!'" The post drew a lot of attention, amassing several hundred likes and shares. That prompted the department to release an official statement: We received reports of a man resembling Noel Gallagher in Swindon at around 5:30pm yesterday who appeared to be under the influence of alcohol and was licking windows— not a 'Wonderwall,' and he may have been 'Half the World Away.' The incident was nowhere near the Oasis, but in the town centre, near the Wyvern Theatre. If anyone heard or saw anything suspicious in the area, please 'Don't Look Back in Anger' but contact us on 101."

Even the real Noel Gallagher responded to it on Instagram, "Nowt to do with me mate. I'm still away on holiday." At last report, the White Lightning-swigging window licker was still at large.

> "From Jesse James to Charles Manson, the media, since their inception, have turned criminals into folk heroes."
>
> **—Marilyn Manson**

Dumb Crooks: Tech Edition

DUMBPHONE

- British police suspected 23-year-old Emmanuel Jerome of several home burglaries in Huddersfield, West Yorkshire. Although he denied everything, investigators discovered that during one of the break-ins, Jerome had used his iPhone's flashlight to see . . . but didn't realize that he'd also activated the video camera. He recorded his own crime, and was sentenced to 10 months in prison.

SMILE, YOU'RE ON DUMB*SS CAMERA

- In 2009 Kadeem Cook, 18, mugged a college student in Philadelphia and ran off with her purse. Later, he used the woman's cell-phone camera to take a self-portrait holding a gun up to his head. What Cook didn't know was the student had programmed her phone to send the pictures it took to her computer. When she received the photo, she sent it to police. After the photo started appearing on the evening news (and all over the Internet), Cook turned himself in.

- In 2012 Timothy Jackson, 18, of Savannah, Georgia, did the same thing. Only he didn't realize he'd photographed himself. He was just pressing random buttons on a stolen phone when a photo of his face automatically popped up on the victim's Facebook page. She sent it to the police, who recognized Jackson because he was on probation. He was arrested.

The Hot Felon

Steel-blue eyes. Chiseled cheekbones. Scruffy five o'clock shadow. Sad teardrop tattoo. Scary neck tattoos. It was the mug shot shared 'round the world. And it belonged to 33-year-old Jeremy Meeks, who looked as if he jumped from the pages of *GQ* and landed in the custody of the Stockton, California, police department. His rise to tabloid fame began on June 18, 2014, after he was arrested for gun possession and resisting arrest during a gang sweep. His sexy mug shot was posted on the department's Facebook page, and before long, the "Blue-eyed Bandit" had racked up tens of thousands of likes. His fame spread even further after his dear old mother started a GoFundMe page so Meeks could make bail.

His good looks couldn't keep him out of prison. But that's when his modeling career began . . . and he became even more famous. The tabloids were captivated by the neck-tattooed gangster who looked like a supermodel. The paparazzi was there when Meeks, now out of prison, was caught snogging a hot heiress named Chloe Green on a yacht in Turkey. He was still married at the time, and the scandal made him even more famous. He was even a topic of conversation on *The View*: "Is the 'Hot Felon's' modeling career rewarding bad behavior?" (Yes.) Meeks has since launched a successful career as a runway model. And he's still with the heiress. At last report, according to the *Sun*, "Chloe is sending Jeremy to finishing school to iron out his bad-boy mannerisms."

Belle Gunness: The Terror of La Porte

BACKGROUND

Belle Gunness was born in Selbu, Norway, in 1859. At the age of 22 she emigrated to America. She got married and opened a candy shop with her husband. A year later the store burned down, the first of what would be several suspicious fires in Belle's life. The couple collected an insurance payout and bought a new house. Fifteen years later, in 1898, *that* house burned down, and another insurance payment was issued. In 1900 yet another insurance policy was brought into play, but this time it was life insurance: Gunness's husband had died under suspicious circumstances.

MORE SUSPICIONS

In 1902 Belle married a local butcher named Peter Gunness. One week later, Peter Gunness's infant daughter died while alone with Belle, and another insurance policy was cashed out. Eight months later, Peter Gunness was dead. Belle told the police that a meat grinder had fallen from a shelf and crushed his skull. The coroner ruled the cause of death to be murder. Belle denied killing her husband, and a jury found her innocent.

NOT WELL SUITED

Belle placed ads in newspapers around the Midwest, soliciting gentlemen who were interested in "joining fortunes." The ads worked, and suitors began to show up at the farm. John Moo arrived with his life savings. He stayed at the farm for about a week . . . and disappeared. Over the years, several more met the same fate: Henry

Gurholdt who had brought $1,500; Ole Budsburg, who brought the deed to his property, and was last seen in a La Porte bank; and Andrew Hegelein, also last seen in the bank. A few weeks after Andrew's disappearance, his brother, A. K. Hegelein, wrote to Gunness to inquire about him. She replied that he'd gone to Norway. Hegelein didn't believe her—and threatened to come to La Porte to find him.

SUITOR WANTED

Comely widow, who owns a large farm, desires to make the acquaintance of a gentleman with a view to joining fortunes. Must be willing to make a visit in person.

Belle Gunness

FIRE!

In 1908 Gunness's farm burned down. Inside, four bodies were discovered—three of Gunness's children, and a headless corpse. Upon further investigation, it became clear the mystery body couldn't be that of Gunness—she was significantly taller than the corpse, even adding in some height for the missing head. A search of the farm revealed five dismembered corpses buried around the property.

THE AFTERMATH

People reported seeing Belle Gunness at dozens of locations across the country over the following decades. In 1931 a woman named Esther Carlson was arrested for the poisoning murder of her husband in Los Angeles. She reportedly looked a lot like Belle Gunness. Carlson died awaiting trial, but some La Porte residents made the trip to the Los Angeles morgue and viewed the body. They said it was Gunness.

Police Blotters

Don't have a lot of time but still want to read interesting little stories? Just check out the police blotters of your local paper.

A woman reported that someone entered her condo, tied her shoelaces together, tilted pictures on the walls, and removed the snaps from her clothing.

A resident called police after finding a 12-pack of toilet paper on her doorstep on Greenridge Drive, not for the first time.

At 11:50 p.m. police talked to four nude people seen running down Lincoln Street, and advised them not to be nude in public again.

The glass to a snack machine in the Knott Hall commuter lounge was reported to be broken. Campus Police responded and removed all remaining snacks.

Clinton Police responded quickly to an accident in the parking lot of a Dunkin' Donuts. The prompt response time is accredited to there being a squad car waiting in line at the drive-up window.

A man reported a burglary around 10 p.m. Thursday after he returned home and found his 36-inch Samsung TV missing. It had been replaced with an RCA TV. Decorative items were placed around the new TV in an apparent attempt to fool him.

The mother of an adult man called police, concerned he was running with the wrong crowd.

LOONY LAWS

*Rotting fish, manhandling a mango,
and coin management: these are just some of
the subjects covered by Canadian jurisprudence.*

- Your money or your rights: It's illegal everywhere in Canada to pay for something with just pennies if the total is more than 25¢. You can't pay with only nickels for something over $5, or in all dimes if the cost is more than $10.

- Sure, you can fish in some of the lakes and streams of Canada's national parks, but if your catch rots, you've broken the law.

- Check in your old childhood closet: it's illegal to own any comic book that "exclusively or substantially" depicts crimes—real or fictitious.

- You can't "manhandle" fresh produce in British Columbia until after you've paid for it.

- Engaging in a duel is not specifically against the law in Canada. However, challenging someone to a duel, inciting another to challenge someone, or accepting a challenge is definitely breaking the law.

- Keep 'em in the backyard where they belong: Toronto forbids crocodiles or alligators, no matter how small or large, in private homes.

- Got a wound? Don't consider changing your bandage in public or it'll cost you a pretty penny (literally—the maximum fine is 1¢).

- See all those glossy ads for Viagra? An old Canadian law says you can be prosecuted if you advertise a product that enhances or improves sexual performance. There's a big loophole, however: you can skirt the law if you can prove that "the public good was served" by the advertisement.

It's Not Murder if You Kill a Fake Person

Jean Crump, 67, and Faye Shilling, 61, masterminded an insurance scam that was as morbid as it was clever. The two women worked out of the Steward-Pearce Mortuary in Los Angeles. From 2005 until 2009, they took out bogus life insurance policies on bogus people and then staged bogus funerals, which they then billed to real insurance companies. The two elderly women (with the help of two middle-aged women) created elaborate backstories for their dead ringers—such as poor Jim Davis, a contractor who suffered a fatal heart attack at his home on April 2, 2006. Crump and Shilling forged all the necessary documents, and hired a young woman to play Davis's niece and collect from the insurance companies. When the claims adjusters showed up at Davis's small ceremony, it looked as real as any funeral. Crump and Shilling even buried Davis's empty casket. The payoff: a cool $1.25 million.

But the claims adjusters suspected something might be up, so they hired a private investigator. When Crump and Shilling found out, they exhumed the empty coffin to have it cremated. To make sure it weighed the correct amount at the crematorium (so as not to alert the workers), the women filled it with animal bones, raw meat, and a mannequin.

By this point, the FBI was on the case. Agents found the doctor who'd signed the bogus death certificates. He agreed to cooperate and secretly recorded Crump and Shilling offering him $50,000 per policy to keep the scam going. The jig was up.

At the trial, Crump—who was wearing all white—claimed (through her lawyer) that it was Shilling who masterminded the whole thing, and that Crump herself made only $12,000. Unconvinced, the judge sentenced her to a year and a half in prison. As for Shilling, she claimed that she'd renounced her fraudulent ways and was helping a young woman stay out of crime. "Your honor," pleaded Shilling, "I hope to continue helping people and shining a different light on our community." She got two years.

"The Sixth Amendment states that if you are accused of a crime, you have the right to a trial before a jury of people too stupid to get out of jury duty."
—**Dave Berry**

What a Clown

On its July 30 'Family Fun' page, the *Kansas City Star* ran a blurb on National Clown Week. Accompanying the text, naturally enough, was a photo of a clown. But the editor selecting the file photo neglected to look at the flip side, which would have revealed that the clown in question was John Wayne Gacy, a Chicago serial killer (and onetime clown) executed five years ago for killing 33 boys and young men. The *Star* apologized the next day in an editor's note.

FAMILY FUN!

National Clown Week

The Law Sure Did Ketchup with Her

Officials and patrons at the Ada County Library in Boise, Idaho, were perplexed by a bizarre series of crimes in 2009 and 2010: Someone was dumping ketchup, mustard, mayonnaise, and even syrup into the book drop box. After dozens of books had been damaged, police staked out the drop box and busted Joy L. Cassidy, 74, with a jar of mayonnaise in her car. Her motive was unknown, but police did say that she was mentally competent enough to stand trial and she pleaded guilty.

PRISON BUDDIES

In 1999, three of the 20th century's most notorious criminals were housed at a high security federal prison in Colorado: Ted Kaczynski (the Unabomber), Timothy McVeigh (the Oklahoma City bomber), and Ramzi Yousef (the 1993 World Trade Center bomber)—collectively responsible for 177 deaths. Twenty-three hours of each day were spent in solitary confinement, but for one hour, they shared the same outdoor recreation time in a concrete courtyard. Separated by wire cages and not allowed to make eye contact, the three terrorists nevertheless struck up an odd friendship. Although Kaczynski didn't agree with McVeigh's crime, he later said, "On a personal level I like Tim, and I imagine that most people would like him." So what did they all talk about? "They don't discuss how to make a bomb," explained Yousef's lawyer. "For the most part, they discuss what they saw on Turner Classic Movies."

The Pentagon Papers Whistle–Blower

At the behest of Defense Secretary Robert McNamara, Daniel Ellsberg, a Rand Corporation and Department of Defense analyst, compiled a top-secret study of US decision making from 1945 to 1968, in the lead-up to the Vietnam War. The 7,000-page study revealed a series of presidential failures and public deceptions regarding Vietnam and left Ellsberg deeply disillusioned. A summa cum laude graduate in economics from Harvard and a former US Marines infantry commander, Ellsberg made photocopies of the report and turned them over to the Senate Foreign Relations Committee in 1969 in hopes of altering the course of the war. Lawmakers refused to act. When nothing happened and the fighting escalated, Ellsberg leaked the so-called Pentagon Papers in 1971 to the *New York Times*, the *Washington Post*, and 17 other newspapers. Their publication was the beginning of the end of public support for the war.

STRANGE CRIME

The Nixon administration, in an attempt to muzzle and threaten Ellsberg, created a secret team known as the "Plumbers," who broke into the office of Ellsberg's psychiatrist in Los Angeles to search for his medical records. Subsequently, the administration filed espionage charges against Ellsberg that carried a 115-year prison term. Because of the break-in (and an attempted bribery of the judge), however, a federal judge dismissed the case. In 1972 the infamous Plumbers carried out the Watergate burglary of the Democratic National Committee headquarters, which led to the conviction of several White House aides and the resignation of President Nixon.

Over the past 30 years, the per capita cost of incarceration has more than tripled.

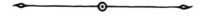

METALHEAD

In November 2002, Portland Trailblazers star Damon Stoudamire skipped the team jet for a return trip home after a game in Seattle, opting to drive himself the 150 miles home. With teammate Rasheed Wallace in the car, Stoudamire's Humvee was stopped by police. Not only was he speeding along at more than 80 mph, he also had the windows rolled down, and marijuana smoke was billowing out of them. Stoudamire was charged with driving under the influence and speeding, and he paid a fine. In July 2003, Stoudamire was again in possession of marijuana, but had the foresight to at least try and hide it from the authorities this time. So before he boarded his flight from Tucson to New Orleans, he carefully wrapped his stash in tinfoil and put it in his carry-on luggage. The foil set off a metal detector, and Stoudamire was detained by airport security. He paid $250,000 in fines and was suspended by the NBA for three months.

The Gang's Last Stand

When the James-Younger gang rode into Northfield,
Minnesota, their plan was to rob a bank.
The townspeople, however, had other ideas.

BROTHERS IN ARMS

After the Civil War ended, Jesse and Frank James were in a bind:
They couldn't surrender for fear of being shot by the conquering
Union army, and they didn't want to ally themselves with their
former enemies. The James brothers teamed up with another group
of brothers that had sided with the South: the Youngers.

Together, the James-Younger gang went on a violent crime spree.
They robbed banks, stores, stagecoaches, and individuals—and even
committed murder. In 1873 they pulled off their first train robbery,
killing the engineer and stealing $3,000 from the passengers. This
crime earned the James-Younger gang a reputation as the most
notorious—and wanted—criminals of their time.

GO NORTH, YOUNG MEN

In 1876 a gang member from Minnesota suggested that his home
state would be an easy target for a bank robbery. The gang cased
various Minnesota cities, deciding on the First National Bank of
Northfield. The bank was rumored to hold a lot of Union money. The
men looked forward to a quick and profitable job.

THE JOB

On the day of the heist, Cole Younger and Clell Miller stood guard
at the front door, while Jesse James, Jim Younger, and Bill Stiles

protected the planned escape route. Inside the bank, they ordered the clerk to open the safe. He refused. A passerby noticed the commotion inside, and ran off yelling, "The bank is being robbed!" Miller and Cole Younger started shooting at him.

The gunfire startled the robbers and the hostages inside the bank. Frank James then shot and killed the bank clerk, who had refused to open the safe. Meanwhile, several Northfield citizens armed themselves and took up strategic positions around the town. As the outlaws made their escape, they were met by a barrage of bullets from the townsfolk.

LIVING ON THE LAM

The wounded outlaws headed for the woods. They were lost. Slowed by their injuries, they grew increasingly tired and hungry. They decided to split up—the James bothers headed for Dakota Territory, while Charlie Pitts and the wounded Younger brothers went west. Posses of angry Minnesotans were hot on Pitt and the Youngers' trail. The search party closed in on them. Pitts was killed, and the Youngers surrendered. They were arrested and tried on four counts, including murder, attempted murder, and robbery. To avoid execution, the brothers pleaded guilty to the crimes.

THE ASSASSINATION OF JESSE JAMES

The James brothers escaped. They kidnapped a doctor to treat their wounds, released him, then traveled to Missouri. There, they formed a new gang and continued their lives of crime. But there was a huge price on their heads, and they knew it. In 1881 Jesse James was shot and killed by the youngest member of the gang. Frank James turned himself in. He was acquitted for his crimes.

Capital Punishment

If you don't read these facts about the death penalty, you will be sentenced to . . . nothing, really. Have a nice day.

From 1851 to 1888, beheading was a legal execution method in the Utah Territory. (In Utah the condemned chose their method of execution and no one ever chose beheading.)

Number of pirates executed, in US history: 68.

First US state to abolish the death penalty: Michigan, in 1846, upon becoming a state.

State with the most executions in the modern era: Texas. Second place: Oklahoma.

The British used "blowing from a gun" for executions in India until the mid-1800s. The condemned was tied to the front of a cannon, and then the cannon was fired.

Youngest person executed in US history: Hannah Ocuish, a 12-year-old Pequot girl. She was hanged in 1786 for the murder of a 6-year-old girl.

140 countries have abolished the death penalty; 57 still have it. Canada officially abolished the death penalty in 1976. Mexico abolished it in 2005.

Crimes punishable by death in the American colonies included witchcraft, adultery, trading with Indians, and stealing grapes.

Crushing or dismemberment by elephant was a commonly used execution method in parts of South and Southeast Asia until the 19th century.

Hidden in Strange Sight

Think of an object—any object. Chances are, at some point someone tried to hide drugs in it. For example, in 2013 Spanish police seized nearly 2,000 pounds of hashish hidden inside frozen sardines. Even grosser, in 2017 a man was arrested in the United Arab Emirates while trying to smuggle 5.7 million amphetamine pills . . . stuffed inside sheep intestines. At an airport in Sydney in 2007, Australian customs agents discovered 293 grams of ecstasy tablets hidden inside a Mr. Potato Head.

In 2010 some Mexican drug smugglers should have tried a little harder to hide their 105 tons of marijuana. According to CBS News, "The marijuana was wrapped in silver, gray, yellow, and red packages, each with a different logo, which authorities said were meant to identify the area in the United States where the shipments were to be sent. Some packages depicted a dog, another a smiley face. One even had a scornful-looking Homer Simpson with the inscription 'Voy de mojarra y que wey!' which roughly translates as 'I'm going to get high, dude!'"

Perhaps the stupidest drug cache award goes to the geniuses who thought that bags of pot wrapped in orange duct tape would look like carrots, but they looked like bags of pot wrapped in orange duct tape.

EARLY FORENSICS

While forensic science made some of its biggest strides in the 1990s and 2000s, some major breakthroughs happened long before then.

AD 700: The Chinese use fingerprints on documents and on clay sculptures. Sometime before this, ancient Babylonians were also pressing thumbprints into clay documents for business transactions. So at least a few civilizations out there are clued into the idea of fingerprints as identifying marks.

1248: We're in China again—this time for the publication of a book entitled *Hsi Duan Yu (The Washing Away of Wrongs)*, which told its readers how to tell the difference between someone who had been strangled and someone who had been drowned. What makes this such a big deal is that it offers medical reasoning instead of just saying something like "if they're floating in the water, there's a good chance

they've drowned." It's the first time anyone recorded medical reasoning being used to solve crimes.

1609: The first stirrings of forensic accounting occur when François Demelle of France publishes the first treatise on systematic document examination.

1784: In Lancaster, England, some guy named John Toms had a torn piece of newspaper in his pocket. The bad news for him was that the torn newspaper nicely fit another torn bit of newspaper found in a pistol that was used to commit a murder. The law puts them together—the first instance of physical matching—and Toms is convicted.

> "Organized crime in America takes in over forty billion dollars a year and spends very little on office supplies."
>
> **—Woody Allen**

STRANGE CRIME

Life After Death

Not everybody gets to rest in peace.

In 1911 Elmer McCurdy held up a passenger train in Oklahoma that he thought was carrying a safe filled with money. It was actually carrying just $46 and a few bottles of liquor. The police caught up with him, shot him, and dropped him off at a local funeral home. Nobody claimed the body. After curious townspeople began dropping by to see McCurdy's corpse, the mortician decided to make some money from it. He embalmed McCurdy and put him on display, telling visitors to put a nickel in the corpse's mouth to cover the cost of admission. Five years later, the corpse was stolen by someone claiming to be his brother but who really worked for a carnival that quickly put the body on display.

Fast-forward to 1976—a camera crew for the TV show *The Six Million Dollar Man* was setting up at a haunted house in Long Beach, California. An assistant moved what he thought was a mannequin . . . but its arm broke off, revealing human muscle and bones. It was McCurdy. How he got to Long Beach remains a mystery, but the coroner found a penny and a ticket for a Los Angeles crime museum in his mouth. It seems McCurdy had been exhibited at carnivals, museums, and haunted houses for more than 60 years. Finally, he was sent back to Oklahoma and buried in Guthrie . . . under three cubic yards of concrete to make sure no one could get at him again.

Crime Time

Twenty thousand silver teaspoons are stolen from the Washington, DC, Hilton each year.

Justice Department prediction: one in 20 babies born today will serve time in prison.

According to criminal law, only three people are necessary for a disturbance to be called a riot.

The retail industry loses more inventory to employee theft than it does to shoplifting.

Items most likely to be shoplifted from a supermarket: cigarettes, beauty aids, and batteries.

Ransom paid for a kidnap victim can be tax-deductible.

A 15-year-old burglar was charged with armed robbery after pointing his pet boa constrictor at a man and ordering him to hand over all his cash.

Half of all crimes are committed by people under the age of 18.

More Americans are arrested for drunk driving than for any other crime.

Russia has almost twice as many judges and magistrates as the United States; the United States has eight times as much crime.

Nearly 50 percent of all bank robberies take place on Friday.

When burglars break into a home, they usually go straight for the master bedroom.

Al Capone's business card said he was a used furniture dealer.

US shoplifters steal an estimated $2 billion worth of merchandise every year.

Odds that someone caught shoplifting is a teenager: 50 percent.

Lewis Keseberg: Donner Party Desperado

In the winter of 1846, when the Donner party was trapped and starving in the Sierra Nevadas, they turned, famously, to cannibalism. Most of those who survived were forgiven. Society understood the terrible desperation of starvation. But nobody ever forgave Lewis Keseberg. Keseberg was one of the few Donner party survivors who managed to reach a set of lake cabins along with a woman named Tamsen Donner. Nobody knows exactly what happened next, but Keseberg is suspected of murder. Rescuers found him at the cabin, boiling parts of Ms. Donner's body in a pot on the fire. He calmly admitted eating her and that he found her delicious, the best flesh he'd ever tasted.

Keseberg wasn't convicted for his suspected crime, but his life went badly anyway. (Surprise, surprise.) He briefly opened a Sacramento restaurant. (What a career choice!) But the restaurant was soon burned to the ground. Keseberg lived out his life in shame and poverty—despised.

STRANGE CRIME

The Watergate Whistle-Blower

William Mark Felt is perhaps the most famous whistle-blower of all time for his role in exposing the break-in of the Democratic National Committee headquarters at the Watergate office complex in Washington, DC, which led to the resignation of President Richard Nixon. In 1972 Felt was the FBI's associate director, working at the agency's headquarters in Washington. He met clandestinely with *Washington Post* reporter Bob Woodward, providing him with critical leads that would unwind the Watergate scandal and Nixon's involvement in the cover-up of the break-in. The *Post*'s coverage of the break-in and its ties to the White House eventually led to hearings before the US Senate and the jailing of White House chief of staff H. R. Haldeman and presidential adviser John Ehrlichman.

Woodward's anonymous key source came to be known as "Deep Throat," a moniker given to him by *Post* editor Howard Simons; the nickname was a reference to a controversial pornographic movie. Woodward refused to reveal the identity of his informant for 33 years. On May 31, 2005, Felt, who was then retired, revealed that he was Deep Throat; he died in 2008 at the age of 95.

CRUSADERS AGAINST CRIME

Role Models: The Texas Commission for the Blind, which was set up to provide workplace support to the visually impaired

Setting an Example: In 1999 it paid $55,000 to settle lawsuits filed by two blind employees. The commission had neglected to make "Braille and large-type employee manuals available to employees."

Role Model: Charles Mahuka, an anger management instructor

Setting an Example: In 1995, 32-year-old Miguel Gonzales was ordered to attend an anger management class after he assaulted his girlfriend. He showed up at the class drunk, which made Mahuka, his instructor, so angry that he beat Gonzales to death.

Role Model: A German youth worker who teaches anger control, identified only as "Herman K"

Setting an Example: In June 1999, Herman K was fined about $1,000 and given a 10-month suspended sentence. What for? He punched a policeman in the face, shouting "Here's something for your mouth!" after the officer ticketed his illegally parked car.

Role Models: Age Concern, a British organization "devoted to concerns of the elderly"

Setting an Example: In June 2000, a 69-year-old Englishman named Hector McDonald applied for a job at Age Concern. He was turned down for the job—because he was too old.

LUDICROUS LAWBREAKERS

TWO WRONGS

A 30-year-old metal thief broke into an abandoned hospital one night in Devon, England. He heard police entering the building, so he hid in an air duct. Meanwhile, a 19-year-old metal thief broke into the same hospital. *He* heard police enter the building, so he hid on the roof. Turned out that the two burglars hadn't heard the police—they'd heard each other. Neighbors heard the commotion and called the *actual* police. Both men were arrested.

THE LONG ARM OF THE LAWLESS

A 17-year-old crook tried to break into a Belfast, Ireland, home by reaching through the mail slot and unlocking the door. But his arm got stuck. The homeowners arrived and called the police. Firefighters removed the door, then removed the mail slot frame from the door, but they still couldn't

free the boy's arm. He was taken to the police station—still stuck in the slot—and booked. His arm was finally freed; he was not.

LACK OF (BRAIN) POWER

In early 2011, a snowstorm knocked out power to thousands of homes in Silver Spring, Maryland. Cody Wilkins, 25, broke into a house (that still had power) and stole jewelry. He also plugged in his phone charger because his place had no power. Someone came home unexpectedly, and Wilkins had to make a quick getaway. The homeowner discovered the strange phone plugged into the wall. That led police straight to Wilkins . . . and pictures on the phone linked him to several more burglaries.

> "Shoplifting is a victimless crime.
> Like punching someone in the dark."
> —**Nelson Muntz**, *The Simpsons*

MAKING FACES

Re-creating a human face from minimal remains may seem impossible, but to forensic artists, it is an art and a science. The results of the painstaking process—putting together clues to reconstruct a face—are astounding.

A NEW KIND OF ARTIST

In matters of history or crime, forensic artists are helping us see the unknown. They're brought in as a last resort, when clues to a crime have dried up and the victim is unknown.

IDENTITY THEFT

Police know they can't expect exact replicas of a deceased person's face without any other evidence—that can be virtually impossible. But they hope the artist can reconstruct enough visual details so that someone who knew the victim will be able to identify him or her. In the United States alone, there are an estimated 40,000 unidentified human remains.

PUTTING IT TOGETHER

Without a skull, forensic artists can't do much to re-create a face. But even an incomplete or badly damaged skull is a start. First, the forensic artist must rebuild the skull using modeling wax. Skulls can be re-created even if significant parts, such as the occipital bone, are missing. Mirror imaging

(mirroring one side of the face after the other) can be used to fill in blanks. (The mandible is the only bone whose absence can cause significant discrepancies in a re-created skull.)

A complex look at the angle and shape of each part of the skull helps the artist determine the shape of the face, pointing to whether the deceased had a round, oval, or square face. Microscopic examination of the pieces of the skull can show scientists where the hairline was and even forehead creases can be seen based on muscular attachments in the area.

MATH MAKES THE DIFFERENCE

Mathematical equations are used to ascertain the shape of the nose. Caroline Wilkinson, in her 2004 book *Forensic Facial Reconstruction,* notes, "The width of the nasal aperture, at its widest point, is three-fifths of the overall width of the nose (at its widest point)." She further explains how to figure out the overall shape and size of the nose based on evidence found in the skull tissue. "A straight, thin nose usually has a weak glabella [the smooth space between the eyebrows]," she notes. A broad nose will show through "broad rounded nasal bones with simple contours and a bell shape." The nasal aperture will even show how far apart the nostrils were.

Dental analysis of the skull shows the thickness of the lips and the width of the mouth. The biggest missing details of the face are hair and eye color. Without any DNA evidence, they are difficult to determine. Forensic artists earn up to $2,000 per skull they re-create. It takes about two weeks for them to do their job.

The Murder of Dian Fossey

She was known as the "Gorilla Girl," and for dedicating her life to these animals, she paid the ultimate price.

Dian Fossey's stepfather wanted her to go to college to get a business degree, but the San Francisco-born Fossey had other ideas, starting with her job as an occupational therapist at a Kentucky hospital. It was there that a lecture by anthropologist Dr. Louis Leakey turned Fossey's attention to Africa. By 1966, she'd gained Leakey's support to carry out research on the endangered mountain gorillas of the Virunga Mountains of Rwanda. She founded a research center dedicated to the primates and lived with them for 18 years, earning their trust. When one of her favorite gorillas was killed and beheaded by a poacher, she began a successful international campaign to stop the slaughter. After earning a PhD at Cambridge, she wrote the autobiographical *Gorillas in the Mist,* which became a movie in 1988. She then returned to the Virunga Mountains to continue the struggle to save the gorillas and their habitat.

On December 26, 1985, Fossey's body was found mutilated by the type of machete used by poachers. Her murder remains unsolved, and poaching as well as logging continues in the gorillas' habitat. Fossey may have foreseen her own end: "The man who kills the animal today is the man who kills the people who get in his way tomorrow."

Put Your Phone Where I Can See It

There are worse things you can do with your phone than texting your ex after a few drinks.

DON'T DRINK AND DIAL

An intoxicated car thief in Tacoma, Washington, would have gotten away had he not pocket-dialed 911 . . . twice. On the first call, the dispatcher heard a woman screaming and a man telling her to be quiet, so a unit was sent to investigate. The officer saw a car run a red light and gave chase. The woman was released from the car; the man sped away and was able to elude police . . . until the next morning, when he accidentally dialed 911 again. Police discovered him and a woman, both intoxicated, sitting in another stolen car. The thief had no idea until that moment that he'd been calling 911 on himself.

A FINE METH

In 2012 a Lewiston, Idaho, police detective received a text message on his cell phone: "U know any1 looking 4 meth?" He thought one of his fellow officers was playing a joke on him because who would be stupid enough to text a cop about a drug deal? Aaron Templeton, a drug dealer with a wrong number, that's who. Templeton, 37, knew where he could obtain a large amount of meth, so he was texting friends, asking them to pitch in to buy it. The detective agreed to pay $150. As he drove into the parking lot and approached Templeton, he received one final text: "Well that's weird, cop just pulled up on me so what's up with that?"

Pants on Fire

These people can't handle the truth!

CRIME SPREE

A Florida man called 911 from a store and said that he'd been robbed: He was getting into his car after leaving the store, when a man hit him and took $100 in cash from him. Police watched the store's surveillance video and saw the "victim" walk out of the store, sit in his car, then go back inside to call 911. When confronted, the man admitted he lied . . . because he was afraid to tell his wife that he'd spent the $100. He was arrested.

SURE, THAT WILL WORK

In 2009 more than 100 friends and family of cancer patient Trista Joy Lathern, 24, held a benefit in her honor at a tavern in Waco, Texas. They raised over $10,000 for her . . . which she used to get breast-augmentation surgery. Lathern had lied about having cancer (she even shaved her head so she'd look like she'd undergone cancer treatment). Lathern told police she wanted the boob job in order to save her marriage. Her husband filed for divorce shortly after her arrest.

A DAY OFF (FROM THINKING)

Aaron Siebers, 29, of Denver, Colorado, used a small knife to stab himself in the legs, arms, and upper body in November 2009. He then called police and said that he'd been attacked by three men who were either Hispanic . . . or possibly skinheads. Police questioned his story, and Siebers admitted that he'd faked the attack. Why? He didn't want to go to his job at a video store. He was arrested.

America's Money Laundress

The real Mrs. Butterworth wasn't as wholesome as your maple syrup bottle would have you believe.

DESIGNING WOMAN

In the early 1700s, Mary Butterworth was raising seven children and her family desperately needed money. Some women would have taken up sewing—but Mary Butterworth became a counterfeiter. She invented a method of counterfeiting that produced passable bills and left no incriminating evidence.

First, she placed a piece of damp, starched muslin on top of the bill she wanted to copy. Then she ran a hot iron

over the cloth, which caused the material to pick up a light impression of the bill. Then she ironed the muslin to transfer the pattern to a blank piece of paper in order to produce the counterfeit bill. She used a quill pen to touch it up. The incriminating evidence—the used piece of muslin—was then burned.

COLONIAL COUNTERFEIT RING

Her family members helped manufacture the money. Over seven years, the Butterworth gang made over £1,000 worth of bogus bills (roughly equivalent to $130,000 today) without sophisticated technology or detection.

In 1715, the £5 note had to be recalled because there was a flood of phony bills in circulation. At the same time, authorities eyed the newly built Butterworth home with suspicion, but they couldn't prove anything.

EXPOSED

Then in 1723, one of Butterworth's carpenters traveled to Rhode Island to witness the hanging of 26 pirates. At a restaurant there, he tried to pay with the counterfeit bills, but was caught by the innkeeper. After he was arrested, he quickly revealed the details of the counterfeiting operation.

Mary Butterworth was imprisoned, but with no hard evidence, she was released. No one knows whether she gave up counterfeiting after that. She died in 1775, at the age of 89.

I'll See You in Court

THE PLAINTIFF: Rene Joly, 34

THE DEFENDANT: Canadian defense minister Art Eggleton, Citibank, and several drugstore chains

THE LAWSUIT: In 1999 Joly filed suit claiming that the defendants were trying to murder him because he is a Martian.

THE VERDICT: Case dismissed. The judge ruled that since Joly said he isn't human, he "has no status before the court."

THE PLAINTIFF: Gerald Overstreet

THE DEFENDANT: Gibson's Discount Store

THE LAWSUIT: In 1979 Overstreet was shopping at Gibson's. He reached for a jar of jelly . . . and a rattlesnake bit him. He sued for negligence.

THE VERDICT: Overstreet lost. The court ruled "that a store's duty to protect its customers from wild animals does not begin until the store knows the animal is there."

THE PLAINTIFF: Joan Hemmer

THE DEFENDANT: Ronald Winters, owner of a chimpanzee named Mr. Jiggs

THE LAWSUIT: Hemmer was eating at a restaurant in New Jersey when she looked up and saw Mr. Jiggs walk in—dressed in a Boy Scout uniform. She freaked out and bumped into a wall, injuring her shoulder. So she sued. Winters told the jury that Mr. Jiggs was no danger to anyone: he was thoroughly domesticated, lived in a house, could even feed himself . . . and besides, he was actually on his way to a Boy Scout party in the restaurant.

THE VERDICT: The jury sided with Mr. Jiggs.

> "I'm not supposed to say it, but I was not guilty of any crime. I became a target because I was a strong and a rich woman who had been very successful."
>
> **—Martha Stewart**

BEHAVE IN PUBLIC

- In Los Angeles, it's against the law for infants to dance in public halls.

- If you've just eaten garlic in Gary, Indiana, you must wait at least four hours before you can attend a theater or ride on a public streetcar.

- In Rochester, Michigan, anyone swimming in public must have their suit inspected by a police officer.

- In Massachusetts, it is illegal for a mourner at a funeral to eat more than three sandwiches.

- In Xenia, Ohio, it's a crime to spit on a salad bar.

- It's illegal to drive without a steering wheel in Decatur, Illinois.

- By law, all Washington, DC, taxis must carry a broom and a shovel.

- In Louisiana, it is illegal to gargle in public.

- In Winchester, Massachusetts, it is illegal for a woman to dance on a tightrope . . . unless she's in a church.

- In Florida, you may not pass gas in a public place after 6:00 p.m.

CELEBRITIES' DAY IN COURT

THE PLAINTIFF: Singer/composer Tom Waits

THE DEFENDANT: Frito-Lay

THE LAWSUIT: In 1988 Frito-Lay ran commercials featuring a singer with a raspy voice that sounded like Waits. Waits had been approached to do commercials by the same ad agency . . . and refused. So they used an impersonator. Waits sued for "voice misappropriation," claiming using his music to sell Doritos sullied his reputation with his fans.

THE VERDICT: In 1992 Waits collected $2.4 million, the first-ever punitive award involving a celebrity sound-alike.

THE PLAINTIFF: John Hartman, former Doobie Brother

THE DEFENDANT: Petaluma, California, Police Department

THE LAWSUIT: He left the band to join the force, then left the force to rejoin the band. When he wanted to rejoin the force in 1994, the former drummer was turned down. He sued for discrimination, claiming that he should be classified as disabled because he'd done so many drugs in the 1970s.

THE VERDICT: The judge ruled that Hartman hadn't done enough drugs to qualify as disabled.

SIN LIZZIE

When you hear the name Lizzie Borden, you probably think, "the woman who chopped up her parents." But did she really kill them? You be the judge.

THE CRIME: "Physician that I am, and accustomed to all kinds of horrible sights, it sickened me to look upon the dead man's face . . . nearly all the blows were delivered from behind with great rapidity." The dead man was Andy Borden. On August 4, 1892, he and his wife Abbie were brutally ax-murdered in their upscale home in Fall River, Massachusetts. Police arrested their 32-year-old daughter, a Sunday school teacher named Lizzie Borden.

THE TRIAL: Borden pleaded not guilty, claiming that a "wayward tramp" had committed the murders. But the evidence against her seemed damning:

- Her alibi—that she was in the barn collecting sinkers for fishing lines—fell apart after police concluded that no one had entered the barn for days.

- She'd once staged a fake robbery of her father's desk and blamed it on a stranger.

- She said she removed her father's boots before his nap, but in his death photo, the boots are on.

- There was motive: Prosecutors argued that Lizzie was afraid that her stepmother Abbie would inherit Andy's fortune. But if both parents died, the money would go to Lizzie and her sister.

THE VERDICT: Not guilty. The defense was able to show reasonable doubt—a side door had been left open, so someone could have come in. And the defense presented a witness who saw a strange man in the street right after the murders. Plus, key pieces of evidence, such as a recent attempt by Borden to buy poison, were ruled inadmissible. Perhaps most of all, jurors simply had a hard time believing that a rich, churchgoing woman could commit such a brutal act.

THE END: Borden was free—and she did inherit her father's fortune—but the murders, and the uncertainty of her innocence, would follow her to her grave. She lived out her days in Fall River, and died in 1927. No one else was ever charged, and the case remains unsolved.

Famous Felon

STAR: Felicia "Snoop" Pearson, who played Snoop Pearson on HBO's *The Wire*.

BEHIND BARS: In 1994 Pearson, then 14, was convicted of second-degree murder after she shot and killed another girl in a street fight. Pearson served six years and was released in 2000. By 2004 she had slid back into a life of crime, dealing drugs while working at a car wash. Her life changed when Michael K. Williams, who played a gangster named Omar on *The Wire*, spotted her in a Baltimore club. Williams was so captivated by Pearson's thug appearance that he talked *The Wire*'s producers into giving her an audition. They created the character of Snoop Pearson, a killer in a drug gang, for her (and used her name, too). Pearson credits the show with helping her turn her life around, but casting a real-life killer as a killer on TV, and using her real name to boot, has been painful for the family of Okia Toomer, the girl Pearson murdered. They only learned of Pearson's new life when a family member recognized her while watching *The Wire*. "I was devastated. It's like they're glorifying it," Toomer's mother, Carlene Smith, told the *Washington Post*.

Be Careful What You Wish For

The moral of the story: a courtroom is not the best place for sarcasm.

How much does Eric Torpy admire NBA legend Larry Bird? So much that when Torpy was sentenced to 30 years in prison for armed robbery and attempted murder in 2005, he said to the judge, "Why not make it 33?" (That was Bird's jersey number.) Equally bizarre: The judge granted Torpy's request. However, after serving the first few years of his sentence, Torpy wasn't happy with the situation anymore. "Now I wish that I had 30 years instead of 33," he said in 2011. "I've wisened up." Adding insult to injury, the story made the rounds in the press and Torpy was made fun of on *The Tonight Show* . . . which means that Larry Bird himself has most likely heard about it. "He must think I'm an idiot," said Torpy, who will be eligible for parole in 2033.

POLICE

Police & Thank You

A quick overview of crime's archnemesis . . . the police.

- On average, more fast-food workers are murdered on the job than are police officers.

- US police officers are exempt from federal jury duty.

- TV cops shoot their guns regularly, but the average for a real cop is once for every nine years of service.

- New York City's first female police officers— dubbed "police matrons"—went to work in 1891.

- The first US city to use police cars: Akron, Ohio, in 1899. The cars were electric wagons that could go 16 mph and cover 30 miles before they needed to be recharged.

- America's most successful police dog was Trepp, a Florida golden retriever, with more than 100 arrests to his credit.

- Traffic police in South Korea are required by law to report all the bribes they receive.

- 40 percent of Americans believe police shows are "fairly accurate." Only 14 percent of real police officers agree.

Quotes from the Unabomber

Ted Kaczynski: prodigy, professor, survivalist, terrorist, wordsmith. Thanks to interviews and his infamous manifestos, we have a detailed insight into a man who was justified (to himself) setting off several bombs from 1978 to 1995 that killed three people injured 23 (see page 317).

"Never lose hope, be persistent and stubborn and never give up. There are many instances in history where apparent losers suddenly turn out to be winners unexpectedly, so you should never conclude all hope is lost."

"Antidepressants are a means of modifying an individual's internal state in such a way as to enable him to tolerate social conditions that he would otherwise find intolerable."

"Legally there is nothing to prevent us from going to live in the wild like primitive people."

"A chorus of voices exhorts kids to study science. No one stops to ask whether it is inhumane to force adolescents to spend the bulk of their time studying subjects most of them hate."

"I believe in nothing."

SETTLED IN AND OUT OF COURT

The bizarre world of courtrooms.

THE PLAINTIFF: Randall Dale Adams

THE DEFENDANT: Filmmaker Errol Morris

THE LAWSUIT: Adams was convicted of murder in 1977. Ten years later, Morris made a film about the Adams case. The movie, *The Thin Blue Line,* presented the case for Adams's innocence so effectively that he was released from prison. When Adams got out of jail, he sued the filmmaker for $60,000.

THE VERDICT: Settled out of court. Morris agreed that Adams should receive rights to any commercial uses—notably films or books—of his life.

THE PLAINTIFF: Mary Sue Stowe

THE DEFENDANT: Junior Davis, her ex-husband

THE LAWSUIT: When they split up, Mary wanted custody of seven frozen embryos that had been fertilized by Junior.

THE VERDICT: The case went to the US Supreme Court—which sided with Junior. Mary's lawyers said she was "devastated" by the ruling—but would try to "talk one-on-one with her ex-husband" to get him to change his mind.

THE PLAINTIFF: J. R. Costigan

THE DEFENDANT: Bobby Mackey's Music World, a country music bar in Kentucky

THE LAWSUIT: Costigan claimed a ghost "punched and kicked him" while he was using the bar's restroom. He sued the bar for $1,000 in damages and demanded that a sign be put up in the restroom warning of the ghost's presence. The club's lawyer filed a motion to dismiss the case, citing the difficulty of getting the ghost into court to testify for the defense.

THE VERDICT: Case dismissed.

I DIDN'T MEAN THAT . . .

While on his deathbed after suffering a major heart attack in 2009, James Washington, an inmate in a Tennessee prison, told a guard, "I have to get something off my conscience." Washington then confessed to a 1995 murder that had gone unsolved. At the time, he was serving a 15-year sentence for a lesser crime, but shortly after his confession, Washington made what doctors called a "miraculous" recovery. He tried to take his confession back, but it was too late. Arrested and later convicted for the murder, the judge sentenced Washington to life in prison.

Noah's Nark

Ever try to smuggle exotic animals on a plane? It's not easy. Just ask the woman at a Melbourne airport who was caught with 51 live tropical fish inside her skirt. Customs agents became suspicious when they heard "flipping" noises. Also in Melbourne, agents thwarted the plans of a man who thought he could smuggle two pigeons inside his tights. (Yes, his tights.) When a suitcase went unclaimed at a Bangkok airport, agents opened it up and discovered 11 otters inside. Also in Bangkok, agents opened a man's suitcase and a bird of paradise flew out of it. After they apprehended the man, they discovered two pygmy monkeys hidden in his underwear. Not to be outdone, a man with a "mysterious bulge" was discovered with 18 "tiny endangered monkeys" stuffed inside his girdle. (Yes, his girdle.) And finally, there was the story of a mother and daughter who came up with a novel way to get their pet macaque from Thailand to Seattle: They sedated it, and then hid it under the daughter's shirt, making it look like she was pregnant. They actually got away with the crime . . . at first. After bragging about it later, they were arrested.

Blabbermouths

STATUS UPDATE: JESSE GETS 60 YEARS

Jesse Hippolite, 23, went on a bank-robbing spree in Brooklyn, New York, in 2011, handing tellers a note that read "GIVE ME ALL THE MONEY OR ELSE EVERYBODY DIES!!!" (He never actually brandished a weapon.) A partial license plate number from the getaway car led cops to Hippolite and his Facebook page. Hippolite had posted a photo of himself wearing the same sweatshirt he'd worn in the robberies and holding a wad of cash. Two of his posts: "Crime pays my bills" and "What if we all got fed up with this recession and started running inside every f*cking bank to give us the money that belong to us???" Hippolite was arrested.

AIRWAVE AIRHEAD

In June 2011, Susan Cole of Denver, Colorado, was called for jury duty. The 56-year-old beautician didn't want to serve, so she showed up at the courthouse wearing blotchy makeup, curlers, reindeer socks, and mismatched shoes. She then fabricated a sad story to District Judge Anne Mansfield: "I broke out of domestic violence in the military. And I have a lot of repercussions. One is post-traumatic stress disorder." Mansfield immediately dismissed her. A few months later, the topic on a Denver talk radio show was "How to Avoid Jury Duty." Cole was listening that day. She called in and described her ruse in detail. Guess who else tuned in that Day? Judge Mansfield. Cole was charged with first-degree perjury.

"The man who has a conscience suffers whilst acknowledging his sin. That is his punishment."
—**Fyodor Dostoyevsky**, *Crime and Punishment*

THE VIDOCQ SOCIETY: COLD CASES SOLVED

Eugène Vidocq was a pioneering police detective of 1800s France. Part of his legacy is the Vidocq Society—a group of modern-day investigators who follow in his footsteps.

In September 1990, three friends in Pennsylvania— William Fleisher, a former police officer; Richard Walter, a forensic psychologist; and Frank Bender, a forensic artist— founded a crime-solving club. The idea: Invite investigators like themselves to join the group and use their skills to solve cold cases—specifically, long-unsolved cases of murder and disappearance. They founded the new organization in honor of and in the spirit of pioneering detective Eugene Francois Vidocq, calling it the Vidocq Society.

Today the group has more than 150 members from dozens of crime investigation fields, who meet regularly (usually over long lunches) to discuss potential cases. Cases are taken on a first-come, first-served basis and are taken

pro bono, meaning members work for free. Criteria: Cases must be at least two years old, the victims cannot have been involved in criminal activity, and requests must be presented by legitimate law-enforcement agencies at one of the club's Philadelphia luncheons. The Vidocq Society has grown over the years to become a highly respected organization, and its members have helped solve (or resolve) many cases.

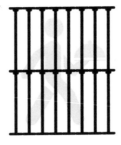

CONVICT DU JOUR

RESTAURANT: Fortezza Medicea Jail Restaurant

LOCATION: Volterra, Italy

DETAILS: There are several jail-themed restaurants in the world, but this is the only one housed in a real, fully operational correctional facility. Members of the staff, from waiters to cooks, are inmates doing time for crimes ranging from racketeering to murder. Under the attentive watch of prison guards, they prepare fancy meals for diners who undergo background checks before they're seated. (Helpful tip: don't complain about the food.)

GUILTY CONSCIENCE

Sometimes, thieves have a change of heart.

STOLEN! In January 2014, a pickup truck was stolen from a parking spot near a home in Bridport, England. The truck belonged to 62-year-old Matt Hart, and most distressingly for him, inside the truck was a red terra-cotta urn holding the ashes of his mother, who had recently died at the age of 98. Hart had left the urn in the truck because he was leaving early the next morning to scatter the ashes in the small town in Scotland where his mother had once lived. RETURNED! News of the theft made headlines all over the UK, and Hart started a Facebook campaign to get the ashes returned . . . and it worked. Two weeks later, one of Hart's neighbors excitedly knocked on his door to tell him the urn had been found on the ground right in the middle of the parking space from which the truck had been stolen. (The identity of the thief is still unknown.)

STOLEN! In 1958 two potted hydrangea flower plants were taken from Centennial Park, in Nashville, Tennessee. RETURNED! In May 2012—54 years later—72-year-old Bill Teitleff showed up at the park with two pots of hydrangeas and confessed to the long-forgotten theft. Teitleff explained that he'd stolen the potted flowers when he was 18 because he didn't have any money and couldn't

afford to buy his mother a Mother's Day present. And in a way, he was actually returning the same flowers he stole more than five decades earlier. The two potted hydrangeas he brought with him had been grown from the root stock of the very flowers Teitleff stole in 1958, which his mother had planted in the family's backyard, and still flourished after all those years. Park officials happily accepted the two hydrangeas and forgave Teitleff for the theft.

STOLEN! One night in October 2014, Aaron Wiener noticed that the Tuscan kale he'd planted in the front yard of his home in Washington, DC, was gone. All that remained of the two-foot-tall vegetable was a small stump and some leaves that had fallen off during the theft. RETURNED! The kale was never recovered . . . but the story doesn't end there. About two weeks after the thief absconded with the kale, Wiener came home to discover a piece of cardboard underneath a flowerpot on his porch. It was a $25 gift card to a local hardware store. Along with it was a note that read,

> **TO:** Wonderful gardener
> **FROM:** A remorseful kale thief
> (I was drunk, and I'm very sorry.)

Wiener used the gift card to purchase another kale plant.

The Case of Steven Truscott

One of the cases that inspired abolition of the death penalty in Canada was that of Steven Truscott. He was 14 years old in 1959, when he gave 12-year-old Lynne Harper, a classmate in Clinton, Ontario, a ride on his bicycle. Two days later, Harper was found raped and strangled in some nearby woods. Because Truscott had been the last person known to see her alive, police zeroed in on him as a suspect almost immediately even though there were no witnesses and no physical evidence linking him to the crime. He was arrested within two days of the body's discovery, and the subsequent trial lasted only two weeks.

Truscott was found guilty and sentenced to death by hanging, making him Canada's youngest death row inmate ever. People all over the world were outraged that a child would be sentenced to death. Weeks before Truscott was scheduled to die, he received a stay of execution. Then his sentence was commuted to life. In 1969, Truscott was paroled. The conviction remained on Truscott's record until 2007, when Ontario's Court of Appeals reviewed the case, decided the original trial had been unfair, and acquitted him of Lynne Harper's murder. The next year, Ontario awarded Truscott $6.5 million in damages. Finally, a victory of sorts—Truscott called the ruling "bittersweet." Lynne Harper's murder has never been solved.

The Wrong Fake ID

*You know, there are a lot of excellent reasons
not to use a fake ID. Here's another!*

Jim was zooming down the road near Lafayette, Indiana,
when he was pulled over by a state trooper for speeding. We
don't know why Jim decided it would be a prudent course
of action to present the state trooper with a fake ID. But if
we had to guess, it was because that way the ticket would be
written to someone else, and Jim could continue his speedy
ways unencumbered by points on his actual license. So up
comes the officer, and out comes the fake ID. It's a good
plan—except for the small detail that the fake ID is from a
real person wanted in Texas for attempted murder, a more
serious charge to have on one's record than speeding. Jim
gets a free trip to jail, and after he presents proof of his
true identity, he is also charged with identity deception and
false informing, the first of which can get you three years
in prison. We also suspect the original speeding violation
was transferred over to Jim's real name. The Indiana State
Police are just helpful that way. The moral of the story is
to show your real ID. Or at the very least, don't show an ID
that has a thicker police file than you do.

HACK ATTACKS!

Computer hacking can be pretty scary.
These hacks, however, are more funny than scary.

TUPAC LIVES!

In 2011, the PBS news show *Frontline* ran a story on Julian Assange, founder of WikiLeaks, the hacking organization that leaked sensitive US government data. A group of hackers called "Lulz Security" didn't like the way Assange was portrayed. So they hacked into the PBS website and posted a fake story about deceased rapper Tupac Shakur, reporting that he "has been found alive and well in New Orleans." PBS took down the story, but Lulz used Twitter to take credit for the attack and send out messages like "F*** Frontline." In 2013 the FBI arrested Hector Monsegur, or "Sabu," one of Lulz's founders. (He turned informant.)

WE'RE JAMMING

In 1990 a Los Angeles radio station held a promotion: the 102nd caller after the station played a certain three songs in a row would win a $50,000 Porsche. On June 1, the station played the songs, and the calls started coming in. The 102nd caller was a man named Michael Peters. He was really a hacker named Kevin Poulsen, who hacked into the station's phone lines the moment he heard the third song play. Jamming all but one of 25 phone lines, Poulsen made himself the 102nd caller and won. The FBI investigated. The story was featured on NBC's *Unsolved Mysteries* . . . whose tip line mysteriously crashed. Poulsen was caught, and he served five years in prison, the longest sentence ever for hacking (at the time).

Stoned Temple Pilot

When a wannabe rock 'n' roll singer named Jason Michael Hurley got arrested in Beverly Hills in July 2014 for shoplifting (razors from a pharmacy) and drug possession (meth), he told the cops that he was Scott Weiland. Hurley actually did look a lot like the 46-year-old former Stone Temple Pilots frontman. The Beverly Hills cops, excited they had a big star in custody, didn't even try to verify Hurley's story. They tossed him in jail and sent a "Celebrity Arrest" press release to TMZ. The gossip site ran the story, and it spread around the globe.

Meanwhile, back at the station, Hurley didn't have enough money to post bail, so he stayed in jail. A few days later, the real Scott Weiland got wind of the story and posted a video from a Los Angeles recording studio: "I just got done reading something quite interesting, a nice piece of fiction from TMZ." He went on to say that he was not in jail, he was recording an album—and that TMZ would be "hearing from my attorneys." So the folks at TMZ alerted the BHPD, but the cops, for some reason, were still insisting they had Weiland. This is after a fingerprint analysis had come back identifying the man as Jason Michael Hurley. It was only after a second fingerprint check also came back as Hurley that the cops realized they'd made a colossal screw-up. As for Hurley, he had another charge added: furnishing false information to the police. To his credit, he managed to fool the police for an entire month.

Family Feud: The Pleasant Valley War

In the 1880s the Tewksburys and Grahams were neighboring cattle ranchers in Arizona's Pleasant Valley. Their quarrels over boundaries and missing livestock escalated when the Tewksburys allowed sheep into the valley. Since the Grahams feared sheep would graze until there was no grass for cattle, the feud became a range war that involved the entire community and eventually killed 20 people. By 1892 each family had only one survivor. When the surviving Graham was murdered, the surviving Tewksbury was suspected, but never convicted. In 1904 the death of the last Tewksbury marked the end of the feud.

Was It Murder . . . or Suicide?

At the 1995 annual awards dinner given by the
American Association for Forensic Science,
AAFS president Don Harper Mills astounded
his audience with the legal complications of a
bizarre death. Here's the story, in Dr. Mill's words:

"On 23rd March, 1994, the medical examiner viewed the body of Ronald Opus and concluded that he died from a shotgun wound to the head. The deceased had jumped from the top of a 10-story building intending to commit suicide. As he fell past the ninth floor, his fall was interrupted by a shotgun blast through a window, which killed him instantly.

Neither the shooter nor the deceased was aware that a safety net had been erected at the eighth-floor level to protect some window washers and that Opus would not have been able to complete his suicide because of this."

A HOMICIDE?

"That Opus was shot on the way to certain death nine stories below probably would not have changed his mode of death from suicide to homicide. But the fact that his suicidal intent would not have been successful caused the medical examiner to feel that he had a homicide on his hands.

The room on the ninth floor (where the shotgun blast came from) was occupied by an elderly man and his wife. They were

arguing and he was threatening her with the shotgun. He was so upset that, when he pulled the trigger, he completely missed his wife and pellets went through the window striking Opus. When one intends to kill subject A but kills subject B in the attempt, one is guilty of the murder of subject B."

AN ACCIDENT?

"When confronted with this charge, the old man said it was his long-standing habit to threaten his wife with the unloaded shotgun. He had no intention of murdering her—the killing of Opus appeared to be an accident.

The investigation turned up a witness who saw the old couple's son loading the shotgun prior to the fatal incident. It transpired that the old lady had cut off her son's financial support, and the son, knowing the propensity of his father to use the shotgun threateningly, had loaded the gun with the expectation that his father would shoot his mother.

The case now becomes one of murder on the part of the son for the death of Ronald Opus."

ALL OF THE ABOVE

"There was an exquisite twist. Further investigation revealed that the son, one Ronald Opus, had become increasingly despondent over the failure of his attempt to engineer his mother's murder. This led him to jump off the 10-story building on March 23rd, only to be killed by a shotgun blast through a ninth-story window. The medical examiner closed the case as a suicide."

The Death of Gerald Bull

Who killed the Canadian "Boy Rocket Scientist" who grew up to design a gun for Saddam Hussein?

Gerald Bull was born in North Bay, Ontario. He graduated from the University of Toronto at the age of 20, got a master's degree at age 21, and a Ph.D. in aeronautical engineering (and a job heading the aerospace division at the Canadian Armament Research Development Establishment) at age 22. Magazines called him "Boy Rocket Scientist." Bull sold his gun-making expertise to anyone in the world market. This included a 1980 sale of 30,000 artillery shells to South Africa, which violated an American arms embargo and led to a six-month prison term. Not long after his release, he was asked to lead Iraq's "Project Babylon." Saddam Hussein is reported to have personally invited Bull to design a Supergun, a howitzer with a 32-inch diameter barrel capable of sending 1,200-pound packages 600 miles into space—meaning Hussein would be able to bomb targets thousands of miles away.

MYSTERIOUS DEATH

On March 22, 1990, in a Brussels suburb, Bull opened his apartment door to find a gunman hiding in the shadows. The killer fired five bullets into the inventor's head. Bull had $20,000 in cash in his pocket when he was shot. The killer didn't take it. In the weeks following his murder, British Customs impounded eight steel "petroleum pipes" bound for

Iraq. The pipes matched Bull's early designs for an enormous gun. Over the next two weeks, five other components were found across Europe. And finally—Project Babylon's chemical-warfare expert, an American named Steven Adams, had discovered Bull's body. Later that day, Adams vanished.

So who assassinated Gerald Bull?

- **Theory #1: The British did it.** A week after Bull's murder, British journalist Jonathan Moyle was found dead in Santiago, Chile, with a pillowcase over his head. He'd been researching a story on British ties to Iraqi weapons buyers.

- **Theory #2: The Iraqis did it.** A week before Bull was killed in Brussels, the Iraqis executed an Iranian-born British journalist named Farzad Bazoft, who was asking questions about Bull and Adams.

- **Theory #3: The CIA did it.** The United States was no friend to Saddam Hussein, and no friend to weapons consultants who helped him.

- **Theory #4: The Israelis did it.** And he's not the only one. Two years after Bull's murder, a British engineer named Christopher Crowley testified before the House of Commons that he and Bull regularly supplied Western intelligence agents with information about the Supergun. In the 1980s, Israel was quick to respond to any threats from Iraq, so Crowley believes Israeli intelligence (the Mossad) had the gun's inventor eliminated.

So who murdered Gerald Bull? The case remains officially unsolved.

FEAR FACT

"Black widow" is a slang term for women
who murder their husbands for money.
Betty Lou Beets of Gun Barrel City,
Texas, killed at least three of her five
husbands and buried them in the
yard outside her mobile home.

MOTIVE: Pensions and life
insurance money.

◆◆◆◆◆◆◆◆◆◆◆◆◆

Witch Hunts

In medieval times, the bar for burden of proof was much lower.

THE DEFENDENT: Walpurga Hausmannin, Germany, 1587
SUSPECTED BECAUSE: She was elderly, and she had gnarled fingers and garlic breath.
ACCUSED OF: The death of at least 40 babies, 2 women, 8 cows, 1 horse, a passel of pigs, and a gaggle of geese.
VERDICT: Guilty. For her crimes, Walpurga was stabbed five times with a red-hot poker, and her right hand was cut off. She was burned at the stake, and—so she couldn't come back from the dead—her ashes were dumped in a raging river.

THE DEFENDANT: Anna Pedersdotter Absalon, Norway, 1590
SUSPECTED BECAUSE: Her husband removed holy images from Catholic churches. (He was a bishop and a man, so she must have made him do it.)
ACCUSED OF: Killing a young boy with a bewitched biscuit, turning a servant into a horse and riding her to a witch's sabbat, and plotting a storm to wreck a bunch of ships and flood the town.
VERDICT: Guilty. Anna was burned to death.

THE DEFENDANT: Neele Ellers, Netherlands, 1550
SUSPECTED BECAUSE: She had scars said to be the "devil's mark." Her mother and grandmother had been accused of flying 100 miles a night (without a plane). Oh, and she owned land a neighboring man wanted.
ACCUSED OF: Bewitching a young girl to faint and puke horse hair, cursing butter so it would not churn, and knocking men into ditches.
VERDICT: Innocent. Neele was released, but 40 years later she was accused again and executed.

THE DEFENDANT: Alison Device, England, 1612
SUSPECTED BECAUSE: Her grandmother was 80 years old, blind, "ugly," spiteful, and outspoken, so . . . Alison was probably a witch, too.
ACCUSED OF: Giving her soul to the devil in return for having whatever she wanted, owning a hellhound, giving blood from under her left arm to a dog spirit named Tib, causing the death of an enemy's daughter, and extracting teeth from skulls
VERDICT: Guilty. Alison was hanged, and her grandmother, Elizabeth, was imprisoned in the dungeon beneath Lancaster Castle, where she died.

THREE FACTS ABOUT WITCH TRIALS

1. Most of the accused were female and poor.
2. An accusation was enough to convict a witch. No proof of guilt was needed.
3. Denial of guilt was seen as . . . further proof of guilt.

IRONIC, ISN'T IT?

There's nothing like a good dose of irony to put the problems of day-to-day life into proper perspective.

He Wrote the Book. In 2009 Bernard Madoff was found guilty of fraud after bilking investors out of billions of dollars. One victim was University of Colorado professor Stephen Greenspan—he lost $250,000 to Madoff. The scandal broke in early 2009, around the same time as the publication of Greenspan's new book: *The Annals of Gullibility: Why We Get Duped and How to Avoid It.*

Who Are You? In 2009 a man named Kevin Mitnick was unable to access his Facebook account. Due to a temporary glitch, the social networking site didn't accept his claims that he was who he said he was. Ironically, Mitnick had previously spent time in jail for impersonating other people in order to access their computers. "I used to be very influential at proving I was someone else," he said. "And now I can't even prove I'm the real Kevin Mitnick."

Right Under Their Noses. In 2006 England's Home Office was embarrassed when five workers—hired to clean their immigration department offices in London—were arrested for being illegal immigrants.

The Great Hamburger Hoax of '15

One of the reasons why there are only a few dozen In-N-Out locations and not hundreds (like other fast food chains) is because the company is owned by a family, not stockholders or a parent company that would encourage rapid expansion. Nobody told that to the investors who were duped out of millions by a California man who sold them fraudulent shares in new In-N-Out locations. In early 2014, a man named Craig Stevens sought out investors to help him open a series of In-N-Outs in the Middle East. About 10 people gave him a $150,000 franchise fee and an additional "royalty payment" of $250,000. All told, Stevens bilked his investors for $4.2 million for restaurants that didn't exist and never would. In November 2015, Stevens was sentenced to two years in prison on fraud charges.

Index of Stories

"E" for Effort, An 161

"Polly Want a Lawyer?" 5

"That Sucker's Coming Off!" 140

America's Money Laundress 375

American Cannibal 36

Angel of Death 294

Anti-hero 220

Are Wii Having Fun Yet? 195

Armed and Dumberous 128

Assault on the Senate Floor 249

At Their Fingertips 226

Baader-Meinhof Gang, The 44

Bad Dr. King, The 146

Bandit Queen, The 178

Bank Robbin' Hood 159

Be Careful What You Wish For 384

Beane's Cannibal Family 322

Becker Scandal, The 269

Behave in Public 379

Behind the (Mob) Hits 199

Belle Gunness: The Terror of
La Porte 344

Benched! 86

Bible John 200

Big Fakers 92

Big Payoffs 210

Bigfoot of Crime, The 98

Blabbermouths 391

Black Panties Bandit Strikes
Again, The 87

Boss of All Bosses, The 209

Busted on Facebook 222

Can't Help Themselves 17

Canadian Gangsters, Eh? 237

Canadian on the Rock 82

Canine Corpse Patrol 38

Capital Punishment 359

Capital(izing) Crime 97

Case for DNA, A 103

Case of Mis-mistaken Identity, A 254

Case of Steven Truscott, The 397

Celebrities' Day in Court 380

Clergy Gone Wild 176

Cleveland Police Scandal, The 46

Close Encounters Make Bad Therapy 259

Code Name: The Milk Man 163

Cold Comforts 251

Cop-Bot 35

Court Transquips 242

Courtroom All-Stars 331

Creativity in the Courtroom 327

Crime Time 364

Crime-Fighting Fake TV 279

Criminal Headlines 112

Criminal Minds 221

Crooked as a Dog's Hind Leg 191

Crooks Love Ozzy 133

Crusaders Against Crime 367

CSI: Contaminating (the) Scene
Investigator 43

Cutthroat World of Texas Cheerleading, The............239

Cyclical Crime....................266

Dad? Is That You?.................273

Dahlia M for Murder.............202

Dam Nation 66

Deadly Year of the Wayne, The......123

Death of Gerald Bull, The.........404

Death of Vicki Morgan, The 18

Did the Punishment Fit the Crime?..213

Disappearance of Judge Crater, The...79

Dismembered Hand Grenade 93

DNA Landmark Cases.............231

Doctor Is in (Your Will), The.......223

Dog, the Bounty Hunter 309

Doin' Time . . . and a Lot of It........94

Don't Leave a Paper Trail...........172

Don't Take It at Face Value 225

Double Whammy.................184

Draken to the Cleaners 238

Dull and Delinquent 145

Dumb Crime.....................114

Dumb Crooks 12

Dumb Crooks of the Old West.......90

Dumb Crooks: Tech Edition 342

Dumb Dognapper 287

Dumb Jock Crimes................262

Early Forensics 361

Easy Busts.......................323

Elephant in the Room, The..........22

Escaping the Rock 181

Evil Twin & the Good Twin, The.....263

Exonerated!.....................284

Facebook Felons 77

Fake McCoy, The...................313

False Alarm......................100

Falsely Accused....................20

Family Feud: The Pleasant Valley War 401

Family Films.....................149

Famous Felon....................383

Famous Phony, A 28

Famous Trials: The Cadaver Synod ..142

FBI Whistle-Blower, The............39

Federal Witness Protection Program, The 186

Feelin' like a Fool 183

Felony Fails 337

Fighting Fire with Fire...............8

First Rule About Fight Club, The 241

Fishy Felony 168

For Sale: A Bridge in Brooklyn 271

Forensic Science—1800s Edition.....74

Freak-Outs.......................23

Gang's Last Stand, The 357

Gentleman and a Scholar . . . and Assailant, A 134

Givin' Him the Fingers 162

Godmothers, The.................167

Gorilla Killer, The.................118

GPS: Great Policing Service 245

Grand Theft Autos 255

Grandma Meth-Head..............125

Great Hamburger Hoax of '15, The ..410

Great Pumpkin Mystery, The 301

Guilty Conscience.................395

Guilty Until Proven Innocent.......206

Hack Attacks! 399

Hairpin Trigger. 201

Half-Baked Schemes 288

Hatfields vs. the McCoys, The. 144

Haunted Crime Scenes 256

Head Case. 111

Hello, 911?. 215

Hey . . . I'm Right Here! 32

Hey, I Recognize That Butt Crack! . . . 212

Hey, That's a Fake 115

Hidden in Strange Sight 360

Holes in the Plan 293

Home Sweat Home 312

Hooligans with a Heart 64

Hot Felon, The 343

Hotel Hell 169

I Didn't Mean That 389

I'll See You in Court. 377

If You Can't Beat It, Eat It 270

In the Big House 305

Instant Justice. 198

Investing in the Future 236

Ironic, Isn't It? 409

Irony in the Court. 81

Is That Spaghetti Sauce on
    Your Shirt?. 84

It's an Open and Shut Case,
    Johnson. 234

It's Not Murder if You Kill a
    Fake Person 349

Jack Ruby's Gun 33

Judges Gone Wild. 121

Judges on the Loose 228

Keep Your Eyes on the Prize,
    Not the Pies 175

Killer Nurse. .151

Killer Quotes. 173

Kinky Killer Colonel, The 150

Know Your Technology 152

Kooky Crooks 326

Law Sure Did Ketchup with
    Her, The. 352

Lawyers on Lawyers 56

Leech of Your Worries, The. 73

Legal Landmarks for Forensic
    Science. 246

Legally Speaking. 282

Legislating Irony. 261

Let's Dig Up Jimmy
    Hoffa . . . Again. 335

Lewis Keseberg: Donner
    Party Desperado 365

Life After Death 363

Life Imitates Art. 47

Lindbergh Baby: Part I, The 130

Lindow Man, The. 338

Lizzie and O. J. 154

Long and Lonely Road, A. 211

Loony Laws 347

Lord High Executioner 194

Ludicrous Lawbreakers 368

Madoff Madness. 332

Making a Monster 317

Making Faces 370

Marijuana Mishaps 138

Meaty Case, A 320

Medieval Due Process 275

Mediocre Masterminds 15

Mega Trials 291

Metalhead 356

Miami Vice 319

Milkshake Murder, The 229

Mob Accountant, The 13

Money to Burn 106

Monkey See, Monkey Do. 29

More Lawyers on Lawyers 105

Munchausen by Proxy 324

Murder of Chico Mendes, The 333

Murder of Dian Fossey, The 372

Murder of Harvey Milk, The 156

Murder of Julien Latouche, The 310

Murder, He Wrote 267

Murderous Eyes of Logtown, The. 76

My Precious President. 62

New Bedford Highway Killer 283

Night Guard Whistle-Blower, The . . . 307

Night Stalkee, Part I, The. 30

Night Stalkee, Part II, The. 171

No Body, No Crime. 53

Noah's Nark 390

Noasis 340

Nobody Helped. 60

Not So High Horse. 129

Not Too Bright. 101

Not Your Average Nuclear Family. 71

Nudes and Prudes 188

Oldest Trick in the Book, The 51

One-Man Band. 274

Pants on Fire. 374

Pentagon Paper
     Whistle-Blowers, The 354

Phoning It In 57

Playing to Stereotypes 49

Police & Thank You 385

Police Blotter: Cheeseburger
     Edition 88

Police Blotters. 346

Poorly Executed 185

Power of the Pen, The 314

Prison Buddies .353

Public Enemy No. 1 69

Put Your Phone Where I Can See It. . 373

Queen of the Jail. 299

Quotes from the Unabomber 386

Rampart Scandal, The 83

Real Fugitive, The. 252

Real Jekyll & Hyde, The. 264

Real Scruff McGruff, The 120

Real Soprano on The Sopranos, The . . 42

Role Models Are People Too 174

Royal Toast, A .40

Sane Clown Posse, The 336

Sarajevo Pistol, The 153

Seeing Double 25

Settled in and out of Court 387

She's a Liar! (Whew!) 248

Sin Lizzie. 381

Singing Detective, The. 281

Sniper in the Tower, The 136

Snowballistics. 258

So Sue Me Then 78

Social Media Mayhem 308

Sold!. 96

Son of Sam 250

Speedy Justice. 141

Spy Who Wasn't, The. 139

Stars Behind Bars. 232

Stoned Temple Pilot 400

Stoneman, The .11

Stoner Report, The 304

Stop, Drop, and Roll 72

Stop, Robot! Thief! 158

Strange Crime Quotes 189

Strange Crime? 147

Strange Lawsuits 233

Suin' for a Tattooin' 166

Summerdale Scandal, The 63

Swift Hand of Justice, The 7

Tale from the Mounties, A 278

That's Awkward 298

Think It Through 24

Throwback Case of Affluenza, A 9

'Til Life Do You Part 50

Tip for Stupid Criminals, A 280

To Tell the Truth 196

Toilet Seat Whistle-Blower, The 124

Toronto's First (Botched) Hanging . . . 295

Tough Pills to Swallow 316

Tragic End for a Comic Star, A 329

Trial of the Century, The 276

True Crime or Tall Tale? 34

Truth Is in There, The 334

Unauthorized Vehicles Only 132

Underwear That's Not So
    Fun to Wear 16

Unsolved Case of the Rainbow
    Maniac, The 102

Urban Legend: Crime Edition 204

Video Games vs. Reality 157

Vidocq Society: Cold Cases
    Solved, The 393

Vigilante Justice 27

Wannabe Dexter 108

Was It . . . Murder? 54

Was It Murder . . . or Suicide? 402

Wasn't Expecting That 297

Watergate Whistle-Blower, The 366

Weird Crime News 119

Westfield's Murder Mystery 109

What a Clown .351

What, Is That a Crime? 205

When Celebrities Attack 126

When the Bullet Hits the Bone 286

Who Wants to Sue a Billionaire?
    (Everyone) .244

Who Was D. B. Cooper? 216

Whodunit? 302

Whoops, Wrong Skull 190

Why the Juice Wasn't Loose 116

Wild Wild West 68

Witch Hunts .407

World's Second-Dumbest
    Outlaws, The 58

Written in the Pen 180

Wrong Fake ID, The 398

Ye Olde Crime and Punishment 207

You Are Feeling Verrry Generous 107

You Don't Know Jack 218

You'd Think She'd Know Better 193

Zero Tolerance for Zero Tolerance . . . 164